Agénor Étienne Gasparin

America Before Europe

Principles and interests

Agénor Étienne Gasparin

America Before Europe
Principles and interests

ISBN/EAN: 9783337312817

Printed in Europe, USA, Canada, Australia, Japan

Cover: Foto ©Suzi / pixelio.de

More available books at **www.hansebooks.com**

PRINCIPLES AND INTERESTS.

BY

COUNT AGÉNOR DE GASPARIN.

TRANSLATED FROM ADVANCE SHEETS, BY

MARY L. BOOTH.

THIRD EDITION.

NEW YORK:
CHARLES SCRIBNER, 124 GRAND STREET.
1862.

PREFACE.

My first work on the United States awaited its completion; what I had affirmed before events, it was important to establish afterward; the demonstration *à posteriori* was to finish what had been begun by the argument *à priori.*

Few books have passed through such an ordeal as has been endured by my *Uprising of a Great People.* Whether it has stood the test well or ill, is not for me to say. Has the crisis which we are witnessing the character of an uprising? The reader will judge.

The encouragement which has come to me from America, and for which I can never show myself sufficiently grateful, has had something to do with my resolution to write this new volume.* It seems to me, as to those who have addressed me so many kind invitations,

* I owe thanks to those persons from whom I have been continually in the receipt of information of all kinds. I have been particularly gratified with the collection of official documents which the Secretary of State, Mr. Seward, has had the kindness to send me.

that the time has come to treat the question in the European point of view. It is at the moment when the issue of the conflict is still uncertain that it is important to set forth the principles which it involves; later, whether successful or disastrous, the fact alone will appear, the right will be forgotten.

Thank God! the truth of the study which I publish does not depend on events; it does not place me under the necessity of being right in case of success, and wrong in case of disaster. Through changing things, I seek that which will endure. My theories will subsist, whatever may be the result of the campaign in Virginia and Tennessee.

Woe to us when we make up our mind to suit the calculation of probabilities, when we ask, "Which will prevail?" instead of asking, "Which is right?" It does not depend on us to succeed, but to obey. "Do what thou ought," is the true maxim; I know none more luminous, either in politics or elsewhere. And mark that obedience to duty is the highway to success; our principles, in fine, are the best guardians of our interests.

I have always liked the method which, in the entangled affairs of earth, puts aside what is accidental to cling to what is substantial and durable, which evolves nothing but what is true in itself, and must remain true, whatever may be said, may be done, or may happen.

When, to-day, after a long and suffering year,* I cast

* To-day, the 4th of March, as I finish this volume and put it to press, a year has just been completed since Mr. Lincoln took possession of the Presidency.

my eyes backward, I see the soil strewn with prophecies; those foretelling easy triumphs have fallen by the side of those foretelling irreparable defeats. Able men have not ceased to tell us, "All is lost," until the precise moment when with the same assurance (and the same infallibility) they have begun to say to us, "All is saved!" I wrote my first pages to the sound of death warrants pronounced universally against the United States; I have just written the last to the sound of the acclamations of those who think that the United States will soon be out of the affair, and that there will be nothing difficult left for them to accomplish.

Convinced that the troubled sea is not calmed in an hour; knowing, too, that external triumph is of no value if it be not also triumphant in the region of ideas, I have not hesitated to continue my work. For ourselves, as well as for America, it is important to dissipate certain errors which have too long prevailed in Europe, and which, we may say, still prevail there. Let no one deceive himself; the thought of meddling in the American quarrel is by no means so fully abandoned as it seems; if decisive successes be long in coming, if the sufferings of our manufactures become aggravated, if the Mexican expedition produce irritation, the peril will be grave anew. There are more men in Europe than are imagined who at heart desire the weakening and parcelling out of the United States, and who would not fear, should opportunity offer, to encourage the resistance of the South, and contribute to the prolongation of the civil war by manifesting the conviction that the separation (that is, the Southern programme) must necessarily prevail. How combat these always persistent and menacing errors? By enlightening minds, by treating of questions little understood, by recalling imperfectly known facts. Public opinion is our force; it has sufficed, it will suffice.

We have vast interests in America; the American crisis has aspects which have not been sufficiently remarked; it affects us everywhere, through the United States and through Mexico, through present and future complications. The question is not only to sound there those destinies of democracy which have fixed the attention of our political philosophers since De Tocqueville; other problems no less grave are implicated in the discussion. I have endeavored to examine them on the way.

Whether the United States prevail decidedly, or suffer new reverses, whether Europe repudiate irrevocably the tendencies which had so nearly won her over, or again experience in a few months the temptation to intervene, it will be by no means useless for us to take account of the faults of the past, which may be, let us beware! the dangers of the future.

I have twice undertaken this work. On learning of the *Trent* affair, I threw my MS. in the fire; I have since recommenced it with firmer assurance. Have we not seen with our own eyes the power that is at our disposal? At the first cry of alarm uttered by the public conscience, have not evil passions and lying interests recoiled? Courage! they will again recoil. In proportion as the character of the American struggle is better manifested, the sympathies of the Old World will be better called forth.

I think with Seneca that "it is not the storm but the nausea that wearies us." What wearied us in America was the spectacle of ignoble discussions, the progressive debasement of a people tossing about without advancing. But since it has advanced, even in the midst of the hurricane, our moral lassitude has ceased.

America will escape the storms which have assailed it. It has been granted me to encourage it at the dark hour of peril and abandonment; should it be granted me now to win its welcome to counsels offered by a sincere friend, I should consider this second privilege still more precious than the first.

AU RIVAGE, March 4, 1862.

CONTENTS.

PART FIRST.

EUROPE AND THE AMERICAN CRISIS—A CONSCIENTIOUS EXAMINATION.

PART SECOND.

ENGLAND.

PART THIRD.

ERRORS CREDITED IN EUROPE.

PART FOURTH.

THE INTERESTS OF EUROPE IN AMERICA.

PART FIFTH.

TO AMERICANS.

PART SIXTH.

TO CHRISTIANS.

DOCUMENTARY EVIDENCE.

AMERICA IN THE SIGHT OF EUROPE.

PART FIRST.

EUROPE AND THE AMERICAN CRISIS.

CHAPTER I.

THE ATTITUDE OF EUROPE.

WHEN, last March, I pointed out without hesitation to the sympathies of men of heart, the uprising of a great people, I was not yielding to the absurd fancy of propounding a paradox, but obeying the need of proclaiming a great and serious truth; of proclaiming it at the very hour when it was about to be almost universally misunderstood. The lovers of paradoxes seldom seek after negro emancipation; to maintain that slavery has its good sides, to take in hand the cause of the South, to chafe at the common places of philanthropists and Christians, makes a fine show—all the piquant theories are found on this side.

When, later, I published the second edition of my book, the time seemed ill-chosen to persevere in my optimism. There had ceased to be but one opinion on the desperate condition of the United States. Their armies had been defeated, their capital was menaced; we heard of nothing but the lack of discipline of the troops, the incapacity of the Government, and the waste of the public funds; riots were predicted in the large cities; the question of slavery seemed ready to shatter in a thousand pieces the momentary unanimity of the North; lastly, winter was approaching, we were about to enter upon those terrible six months, from December to June, which had always been designated as destined to bring some sort of a European intervention in favor of the South. I had then to ask myself whether my first thought had not been an illusion, and whether events had not given me the lie. It was the time to beat a prudent retreat, or at least to confess that the unexpected turn of the crisis had weakened my hopes. But the fact was that my hopes were not weakened; aside from Europe, where the manufacturing interest was beginning to clamor loudly, and a storm was visibly forming, no legitimate cause of discouragement presented itself to my mind. I have the weakness to believe in the final success of good causes, in spite of their passing decay. I know of something here below that is stronger than armies. I know of Some One on high whose blessing signifies more than the sympathies of great powers. Such was the reason of my obstinacy, which was inscribed in most unequivocal terms in the preface to the new edition. After proving that Europe had become the only serious danger to America, I concluded in this wise: "For the present, I have only sought to repeat with a strengthened conviction, what I said a few months ago; then I believed in the uprising of a great people, now I am sure of it."

If I refer to these precedents, it is not because I take delight in speaking of myself; on the contrary, I abhor it, and hope never to revert to the subject; neither is it because I pretend to set myself up as a prophet, but because of the importance of establishing the fundamental theory which I advocate as a deliberate opinion, adopted after mature reflection, and maintained before and after the occurrence of events.

Of the two great crises which the uprising of the United States had to encounter in the beginning, one, the American crisis, is already left behind; its greatest difficulties are surmounted, as I shall have no trouble to prove. The other, the European crisis, is not yet at an end; far from it, although the incidents of the *Trent*, which was near destroying every thing, may have furnished the means of safety by casting a sudden and beneficent light upon the dangerous complicated positions caused by misunderstandings.

It is, therefore, most of all in Europe, and for Europe, that the American question should be studied to-day. Europe has just made a sad campaign. We had thought ourselves justified in saying, without exaggerating its chivalrous sentiments, that the cause of the South would excite in it a hearty indignation; that this rebellion in favor of slavery would meet naught but anathemas among us; that the nineteenth century would not suffer this single occasion to be lost of seconding otherwise than by words the most glorious work of modern times. We were mistaken; the narrow policy too often prevails over the broad. Instead of entering frankly into the path of large sympathies, instead of encouraging, instead of believing in good, which is one of the surest means of doing it, Europe has chosen rather to be suspicious, to find fault, to recall old grievances, to gather up new complaints, to treat, in fine, as an enemy or a suspected power, this youthful Government, sprung from a generous reaction against injustice, and charged with pursuing its redressal. It was first necessary to love it, in order to counsel it, and to aid it to become better. Supported by us, it would have proceeded without hindrance to its end; not to immediate abolition, as has been pretended, but to certain abolition, through the growing preponderance of the North, through the abrogation of odious laws, through the inevitable and progressive suppression of slavery, confined within a continually narrowing circle. On the day that it was decided that it should no longer increase, slavery would have begun to die, yet it would not have died a death of violence—gently, tranquilly, by pacific and Christian means, the redoubtable problem would have been resolved, for the common safety of the North and the South, the whites and the blacks.

We did not desire this. To desire it would have been to quit the beaten track and depart from the precepts of false policy. A most impolitic policy in any case; for, to speak only of our material interests, it has endowed us with the civil war which is desolating America, ruining the cotton production, and calling forth sufferings in our Old World which will go on increasing. If the South had known in advance that it could not count on us, it is not probable that it would have attempted an insurrection. At all events, this would not have been of long duration. It deludes itself less than people imagine; it knows the strength of the national Government, and is not ignorant that resources will ere long be lacking to the insurrectional government at Richmond. Even its victories have never given it the audacity to take a single step in advance—its plan is to secure time for Europe to intervene. Europe needs its cotton, Europe is at its mercy, Europe is about to aid and recognize it, Europe will seize on the first pretext that offers; she will break the blockade and impose peace. Take away these convictions from the South and you will cause the weapons to fall from their hands. Suppose Europe, for a moment, not to exist, and America to be a duelling ground in which no one can interfere, and you can no longer imagine possible a continuance of the struggle.

Four months will suffice for the reduction of the South, from the day that it shall have ceased to count on Europe. It is said that Mr. Seward has more than once expressed this conviction. I believe it to be well founded, as well founded as that noble complaint in the last message of Mr. Lincoln: "Every nation distracted by civil war must expect to be treated without consideration by foreign powers."

What is it, then, that has gone wrong among us? Simply that we have been lacking in youth of heart. Instead of asking on which side were justice and liberty, we have hastened to ask on which side were our interests, then too on which side were the best chances of success. It seemed to us that this rebellion without a pretext was not without a future. From this we had not to go far to find in it some appearance of right. And thus it is that, after having protested for the acquittal of our conscience against the "crime of slavery," after having declared (the thing is granted) that slavery is detested by those who, moroever, never fail to serve it, we have refused to the generous impulse of the North that spontaneous, cordial, and, as it were, naïve support which would have decided all questions on the spot.

I have long been acquainted with those declamations against slavery which never end in any manly action, and I know them for what they are worth. The orators who labored to maintain slavery in our colonies, all commenced by an almost abolition profession of faith; and later still, at the time of the importation of free negroes from the coast of Africa, which was finally ended by the letter of the emperor, the writers who advocated the measure scarcely ever failed to begin by stigmatizing the slave trade. Was this hypocrisy? No. The absence of strong convictions suffices for its explanation. Men would be glad for slavery to disappear; they hope that it will disappear; it will do so by itself if no one meddles with it. It is by such reasoning that interests constantly gain the victory over principles.

Now, interests always stand in the way of principles; the question is to override them. God wishes progress to cost us something. It is true that it will some day bring back much more than it has cost; but in the mean time it has its costs, and we are forced to begin with the sacrifice. Were it otherwise, duty would be too easy.

Here, the sacrifice to be made is more apparent than real. No matter, the appearance is enough, as the movements of our manufacturing towns have proved for some months past. In France, as in England, have there not been moments when they have taken the rebellion of the South under their protection? Have they not urged the recognition of the South? Have they not demanded the suppression of the blockade?

In France, as in England, public opinion has bent more or less to the same side. There have been noble exceptions, I know, and they are becoming less rare; nevertheless, taking facts as a whole, we are forced to admit that the government of Mr. Lincoln has not met the sympathetic support among us on which it seemed to have a right to count.

I must seek with care for the causes of this coldness. By the side of interests imperfectly understood, we find errors systematically propagated, which have succeeded in gaining acceptance in Europe, and which it is high time to refute. Have we not been persuaded, or very nearly so, that slavery had nothing to do with the quarrel of the North and South? Have we not been made to believe that the South, in seceding, availed itself of its right? Has not the impossibility of conquering the South been raised to the rank of an axiom? Has not that been determined on the spot in the name of Europe, which America alone is in the position to decide; namely, that the South, even though conquered, cannot be brought back to the Union?

I do not misunderstand, as will be presently seen, the complex character of this last question. Neither do I misunderstand the importance of the interests which rest upon the policy of governments. Do those who speak in ironical terms of calico and cotton forget that behind cotton are men, women, and children—miseries already great, and which will go on increasing? Do they comprehend the significance of the words—deficiency of raw material, restriction of markets, stoppage of manufactories, discharge of workmen, diminution of wages? As for me, I hope that the feeling of the rights of the negro will never make me close my eyes to the sufferings of the white man. These sufferings, I may say, have not ceased to weigh for a year past upon my saddened imagination, and not the least evil, in my eyes, of the attitude adopted by Europe, is that of having prolonged the manufacturing and commercial crisis by avoiding to discourage the rebellion.

One would have said that Europe leaped with joy at the thought of rending the United States in twain. From the first moment, she seemed to cling to this idea and to be unwilling to renounce it. That the scheme may perhaps be realized, I have no wish to deny. Men who fear a republic of a hundred million men may be tranquil; whatever is too large must necessarily fall apart. Those who fear that a portion of the country may be maintained in the Union by force alone may reassure themselves; a territory representing in surface one-half of the United States will not be kept garrisoned; if the Southern people really wish to separate, their wishes, expressed in a legitimate manner, will not fail to prevail, and this for the excellent reason that no person in the world would succeed in opposing them. But these are not the questions which the present crisis has put to us Europeans. When a friendly government, attacked against all right, attacked in the name of an odious principle, fulfils the simplest of its duties in suppressing the revolt, the only question raised is this: "Shall right prevail over injustice, and liberty over slavery?" Later, I repeat, after the suppression of the reign of terror which rules in a portion of the South, it will be time for free America to examine whether the tendencies which prevail in some of the States do not constitute, in default of a right, a sort of political necessity to which political wisdom should know how to submit.

For my part, I have no opinion to give; although I have followed the progress of ideas and facts, in the South as in the North, with all the attention of which I am capable, I cannot say in what measure the wish to set itself apart will subsist in the future, when the South shall have laid down its arms; when it shall know that Europe detests its flag; when it shall have learned to comprehend that the ruin of its cultures, begun by war, will be completed by isolation; when it shall have likewise learned to comprehend that its slavery cannot long survive in any case; when it shall have again beheld the ancient national colors, the Stars and Stripes; when it shall have found itself again in contact with brothers in country, religion, and blood; when it shall have been called to resume its place and part in those institutions which are an instrument of union because they are an instrument of equality, in those institutions which neither recognize nor create any but citizens, and which know no subjects, so that the vanquished of yesterday finds himself the equal of his victor.

As things stand now, to settle the question of separation as has been done, needs either a clairvoyance which I do not possess, a rare indifference with respect to slavery, or a hatred of America which seizes on the first occasion to sâtisfy its longings. There are some minds, enlightened in all else, upon which America produces the effect of a nightmare; they ask to be rid of it at any price; what wounds them in it is not only the real and serious evil which appears therein under various forms, but also, and perhaps chiefly, the good, the brilliant, the superior sides of the United States—that energetic Christianity, those self-sustaining churches, that absence of administrative tutelage and centralization, that individual liberty, those small armies and small expenditures (I speak of the American ideal, changed for the moment, but which will, I hope, soon return) which are the astonishment and sometimes the scandal of the Old World.

The fact is that from the first instant we *decided* instinctively, and in some sort authoritatively, that the separation was definitive, that the South would attain its end, and that there must be henceforth two rival republics. This decree rendered in Europe, can alone explain the constant misunderstanding which has existed during a whole year between us and America. On taking it into account, every thing becomes clear—our obstinate refusal

1*

to believe in the moral character of the struggle, our haste to admit the superiority of the South, our incredulity with respect to the success or the resources of the North, our impatience at a war which we deemed useless, our injustice toward Mr. Lincoln's government, our disposition to see belligerents where there were only rebels, to transform our position as friendly into that of neutral powers, and to seek occasion in an incident like that of the Trent, or in the practical difficulties of the blockade, to end the crisis and officially recognize the new Confederacy. In the face of such a tendency, (and on looking at the general outlines of our conduct in America I do not see how it can be contested,) no one can be surprised either at the claims or complaints with which the diplomatic correspondence of the cabinet at Washington is filled, or at what is called *the spleen of Mr. Seward.* One might-be sad for less cause. To meet in its path a decision of this kind at the very moment when it counted on the warmest sympathies, when it was putting its hand to one of the most difficult and most glorious works that it was possible for a people to undertake, the reaction against the democratic party and the extension of slavery, to see its friends transformed at once into neutrals, and the rebellion of a day pass at a bound into the rank of governments *de facto*—we must admit that this was sufficient to sadden a nation.

Europe commenced by discouraging Mr. Lincoln when, after the attack on Fort Sumter, he took the resolution to suppress the rebellion. One might have said that he was almost wanting in his duty in replying with bullets to the bullets fired at the national flag.

Then, the war once begun, we predicted the rapid and decisive success of the insurrection. The ministers of Mr. Buchanan had arranged matters so well that the national government had neither army nor money, whilst the government at Montgomery lacked for nothing. The capital was exposed, Baltimore was in insurrection, Virginia and Maryland were ready to facilitate the progress of the rebels. It was foretold that the affair would be ended in a few days. The master of Washington, Jefferson Davis would be in a position to dictate terms, which would be no other than the final separation of the North and South. Proposed in this wise, it would be accepted by Mr. Lincoln, and ratified by Europe—happy to recognize the new Confederacy and prevent a crisis direful to the whole world.

Nevertheless, affairs changed face. In spite of our prophecies, Jefferson Davis did not take possession of the capital. The patriotism of the North silenced its divisions; unanimous, energetic, it recoiled before no sacrifice; in a few days it improvised its first volunteer regiments; each family gave a child; astonished Maryland saw herself invaded by the North instead of the South; Baltimore endeavored vainly to block up the way; the capital was saved, and the champions of slavery lost one of their chances of success—that given it by the surprise of the beginning, the momentary superiority of the South, and the extreme embarrassment of a government which combined treasons in advance had delivered disarmed into the hands of its enemies. Since then, the South has lost other chances, but this was assuredly the best of all. It was an hour for victory which will never again be found; it seemed to re-appear after the battle of Bull Run, but was turned to no better account; it is improbable that it will ever return.

The question was to maintain the confidence of the rebels. Daring no longer to affirm their approaching triumph, they confined themselves to affirming their invincibility. They renounced the pretension of dictating terms to the North, but defied the North to dictate terms to them. It was to be, as it were, an endless game of chess, without either winners or losers. Now, as such games cannot be played without injury to the whole world, why should not Europe determine to put an end to it, both for its own interest and for that of America? Thenceforth, the idea of European intervention gained credit, and gave certainty to the ringleaders at Montgomery that, sooner or later, provided they succeeded in maintaining themselves, they would see decisive aid come to them from across the seas. Mediation was talked of, recognition was talked of, indignation was excited against Mr. Lincoln's government for rabidly attempting impossibilities.

How often has it been demonstrated to us that the South could never be conquered, much less subjugated and brought back into the Union! The South was unanimous, the North was divided! The South was ruled by men of genius, the destinies of the North were confided to incapable hands! The slave labor was secure, riots of workmen thrown out of employment were about to break out in New York and Philadelphia! The army of Beauregard was admirable; on the other side of the Potomac, there was nothing but lack of discipline, cowardice, and impotence, and enlistments would soon become impracticable! And the constant conclusion of this veracious information was this: The inaction of Europe is about to cease, France and England will accomplish the duty imposed on them by the necessities of their manufactures and commerce, and will break the blockade, while awaiting the fitting time to proclaim recognition.

I do not accuse European governments of having held

or authorized this language; many projects are doubtless attributed to them of which they are innocent. I accuse ourselves, the people of the Old World, who, for lack of enthusiasm, have failed to impose silence on evil designs. In the face of the unanimous manifestation of our sympathies for the North, the tendencies which I point out would not have dared show themselves, or at all events would not have acquired the extended influence which they now possess; there would not have been so many voices to say to the champions of slavery: "Stand firm, we are about to come to your aid. Stand firm, give us time to triumph over a few old prejudices by which we are still hampered. Stand firm, we will elude the blockade. Stand firm, we will demand cotton. Stand firm, we will impose our mediation. Stand firm, we will not let you be crushed; we will not suffer you to be brought back into the Union; if any favorable incident offers, we will avail ourselves of it to interfere in your affairs, to recognize your independence, and to impose peace on your enemies."

This is not the language of a few men, a few intriguers in the pay of the South; it is, I confess with grief and humiliation, a sort of public opinion that has taken form among us, if not in favor of the South, (I do not wish to exaggerate,) at least in favor of the success of its plans. There are many honorable men who second the movement without measuring its scope; the question with them is only to put an end in one way or another to a bloody and ruinous war. Perhaps they have arrived at the conviction, which may seem indeed tenable, that the separation is at present a fact to be accepted by wisdom and political moderation, after having shown that it is by no means admitted as a right. They do not see that such questions should be resolved in America and nowhere else; that to impose the separation in the name of Europe is to sanction it on the score of right, to cast aside principles, to say to interests, "Reign alone!" This rebellion has not even the merit of being a successful one, since it has won no decisive victory, and the real struggle has scarcely commenced. This rebellion has no other claim to favor, than the audacity with which, in the midst of the nineteenth century, it has inscribed the motto of slavery upon its banner. This rebellion has boasted that it would force us to an adjustment, and compel us, willing or unwilling, to range ourselves on the side of the cotton merchants and slave dealers. Now, what it proposed, it executes, and what it hoped for, it obtains. Docile Europe comes to its aid at the proper time; we demonstrate to ourselves that it is right, and not content with believing so ourselves, find it quite natural to ask Mr. Lincoln to think so likewise. Is not this, step by step, what is passing before our eyes?

I hope that we shall not continue to the end. I hope this above all, let me repeat again, since the affair of the *Trent*, which, in bringing us to the brink of the abyss, forced us to measure its depth. On seeing herself so near to drawing the sword for slavery, Europe could not help shrinking back in consternation. She comprehended that terrible wars might lurk behind this great love of peace, and that, in attempting to put an end to the quarrels of the United States, we run the risk of kindling in the present, or laying up for the future, unnatural quarrels between the United States and ourselves. Slumbering sympathies began finally to awaken, Christians and Abolitionists saw the path into which they were to be forced without their knowledge. It may be, therefore, that after having had victory almost within reach on the day of the arrest of Mason and Slidell, the partisans of Southern recognition will henceforth find themselves thrown far back from the end which they are seeking to attain.

Let us beware, notwithstanding; they still have great influence, of which I ask no other proof than the astonishment, I might say scandal, excited among us, on hearing the Southerners called *rebels*. We, Frenchmen and Englishmen, who have never hesitated to qualify an insurrection in Ireland or La Vendée, much more in Algeria or India, as a rebellion, suddenly change our principles when Americans are in question.

We have invented for their use a complete political theory, the first article of which is liberty of dismemberment. At the very moment when this friendly people, in the plenitude of its right, declared that it would admit of no separation, we almost decided that it was at once legitimate in itself, necessary to Europe, and beyond the possibility of suppression. To foresee events, is in part to create them; and nothing has better aided the South, than the prediction of its final triumph.

In other terms, we have until recently conceded every thing to the South—fact and right. This is what we have called taking sides with no one! If I belonged to the South, I should ask nothing more, well knowing recognition and intervention to be the inevitable conclusion of these premises, which we must necessarily soon reach, if we go on in the same way. Who would have believed, on the day when the banner of Charleston was unfurled for slavery, and when the indignation of the Old World burst forth on every side—who would have said, that at the end of a few months we would come to admit all the theses of the South, without excepting a single one—the legality of its secession, its immediate transformation from a rebel into a belligerent, our moral neutrality between the United States and the insurgents, the forgetfulness of the infamous cause defended by the latter, the conviction of their final success, the condemnation of the repressive measures directed against them, beginning with the blockade intended for their reduction? From the moment that we began to wish for the separation, we aided it—that is certain. Shall our assistance become effective and direct? Shall we leap over the interval which still separates us from official recognition and intervention? This depends on the movement of public opinion which the affair of the *Trent* has just called forth. If it acquire the proportions of a true moral awakening, if the opposition which Lord Palmerston and the *Morning Post* have just encountered in their path spread more and more, if the party in sympathy with the United States and liberty complete its uprising, the old traditions of hatred inherited from George III. and Chatham, must resign themselves to return to the shades.

However this may be, it is evident that the real centre of the American question is to be found now in Europe: it is at Paris and London, not at Washington and Richmond, that the essential resolutions are taken on which depend the future of the United States. This is a serious reason that we should watch over ourselves, for our responsibility here is immense. I shudder when I think with what lightness we amuse ourselves by carving up America. There will be two Confederacies, or rather three—that of the North, the South, and the West! Such are the speeches that we carelessly throw out! How do we know that our witticisms may not become weapons in the hands of the champions of slavery—in the hands of the enemies of all the causes that we hold most dear!

It will be found at a given time that, to discourage good and encourage evil, a great political crime will be attempted; the idea of an impious war with the United

States, a war made to add to their generous sufferings, a war in which Europe risks appearing supported by the friends of slavery, will gain acceptance. The first energetic act of the Old World, its first message to the New, will be an ultimatum. Such is the support which we will lend it at the darkest, the most glorious hour of its history, and Europe will be the sender of this message.

Europe. My readers will understand why I have adopted this collective term. There has been a European policy in opposition to that of America. Despite the differences which have sometimes succeeded in gaining ground between our policy, for instance, and that of England, unity has always triumphed, and the two governments have continued to go on together. As to the other powers, if we except Russia, which has adopted an independent and sympathetic course toward the United States, they have hitherto appeared to consider England and France as their natural representatives in this crisis. England, upon the whole, has had the chief part and the chief responsibility; through the ties of every kind which unite her to America, through the importance of her navy, through her enormous consumption of American cotton, and still more, perhaps, through the special competency conferred upon her by the services which she has rendered to the emancipation of the negroes, she was evidently more deeply interested and implicated in the conflict of the North and South than any other nation. Her resolutions should have and have had a preponderating influence. It will be proper, consequently, to examine them more closely, and to this duty I devote the second part of my work.

Meanwhile, I take a more general standpoint, which is also true. In speaking of Europe, without particularizing France and England, I gain the advantage of warding off many complicated and actually insoluble questions. I need no longer ask whether it has been England or France that has sought to ènsure the triumph of a system having the recognition of the South for its end, and the inefficiency of the blockade for its means. We accuse the English, the English accuse us in turn. In default of official documents, it is impossible to decide with certainty which is right. I prefer to believe, till proofs are furnished to the contrary, that neither is right. It seems to me more probable that public opinion has had a great share in the evil with which governments are unjustly charged. The real criminals, once again, are ourselves, the whole world, European ideas, which, instead of openly taking the part of the North, have let themselves be persuaded to adopt the theories of Charleston, and to proclaim the secession of the Slave States as lawful, beneficial, and final.

CHAPTER II.

WHAT OUGHT TO HAVE BEEN THE ATTITUDE OF EUROPE.

"IT is well to distrust first impulses." This motto of Prince Talleyrand seems to have been our watchword during the past year. The first impulse of Europe was warmly in favor of the North; its right, at least, was doubted by no one. We could not comprehend the new greatness which was promised it, but thought rather of the sufferings of the crisis in which the uprising must end; but that the cause of the North was just, that the election of Mr. Lincoln was a great national act, that the human conscience was relieved of a weight that had oppressed it, that iniquity was struck with death, we did not then dream of contesting. Since that time, we have distrusted ourselves; able men have taken it upon themselves to instruct us; our convictions have become modified by degrees, and we have repented of our first innocence.

I have retained my first impressions, I admit, during the past year. When efforts have been made to move my feelings toward the South, the so-called weak engaged in a struggle with the strong, I have remembered other weaker beings, its slaves, and my compassion has refused to change place. It has seemed to me that a free country, which, by the mere energy of its institutions, opposes insuperable barriers to the extension of slavery, and boldly undertakes the solution of a problem before which so many others have recoiled, is a country deserving some esteem and respect. These men of the dollar who unhesitatingly provoke a foretold and certain crisis which may swallow up their fortunes, who accept without a murmur the immediate loss of debts to the value of a million of dollars in the South—these men, these *merchants* if you will, do not appear to me altogether destitute of nobility.

Let us now see, the study is worth the pains, whether the frank policy dictated by our first impulse would not have been as good as the would-be able policy of which the world is beginning to reap the fruits.

Europe would have simply manifested its sympathies. The American Union, a friendly power, would have become still more friendly at the instant of its courageous reaction against the crime which has sullied its history and debased its institutions. Far from seeking a quarrel with it or treating it with coldness, we would have encouraged it by all means. We would not have invented in behalf of the champions of slavery, a theory which in some sort from the beginning elevated the rebels to the character of belligerents. Without interfering effectively in the struggle, we would not have gone out of our way to seek for ourselves the false, strange, and complicated position of neutrals when we had naturally that of allies. As to the questions which might present themselves in the future, supposing that, by a series of decisive victories, the South should succeed in conquering a place among the governments *de facto*, we should have experienced no need of providing for such an hypothesis in advance, but would have contented ourselves with declaring that a republic officially founded on "the corner-stone of slavery," was sure at all events of obtaining no favor.

How would Europe have offended against international laws if her governments had expressed themselves in the following manner?

—"We know no president but the one regularly elected. There is to us but a single rightful government in America, that which has its seat at Washington. As to the South, we await the final issue of its armed struggle, and the consolidation of its government *de facto*."

Certainly, by holding such language, the insurrection would have been weakened and many misfortunes prevented, without in any wise lessening the significance of the internal impulse of the United States. To meet important questions face to face is at once loyal, sympathetic, and generous, and best fitted to resolve them. What would Jefferson Davis and his friends have done, had they known, known beyond the possibility of mistake, that they could not count on Europe? Would they not have renounced their designs? Would they have long pursued them? No war at all, or a very short one—such is the result that would have been at once obtained by simply abstaining from granting the South an exceptional favor which seemed to promise it many others.

At the same time, the North would have been strengthened in the noble cause which it had just entered; a current of warm sympathy would have been established between it and us; the combat against slavery would have preserved the character of a pacific and Christian struggle, instead of assuming perhaps in the end, that of a warlike act and violent proceeding; slowly, doubtless, but surely, the progress marked by the election of Mr.

Lincoln would have been completed by legal ways: to-day, the non-extension of slavery; to-morrow, its abolition, with indemnity, in those States best prepared for freedom; by-and-by, complete measures, rendered constitutionally possible by the increasing majority of the adversaries of the "institution."

Those who have taken into account the nameless calamities which negro insurrections may comprise, will not hesitate to prefer the less rapid method which would have prevailed, according to all appearances, if Europe had not encouraged the South. There would have been calamities of another kind, proposed compoundings, attempts at compromise; but the power of principles is great, and the impulse which produced the election of Mr. Lincoln is not of those that move backward. The death of slavery is written therein in shining characters which deceive no one, either in the South or the North, America or Europe. Suppose that Mr. Lincoln had shown himself weak, and that the compromises had been shameful, it is none the less certain, that, before the end of his four years of administration, the question would have made decisive progress. No more territories abandoned to slavery, no more conquests for slavery, no more new States affiliated with the party of slavery; by the force of events, by the action of public opinion, the good cause would have marched onward, sweeping before it all the impotent barriers which had been placed in its path.

Instead of this, we have had a civil war which will become a war of emancipation, (there are moments when certain causes rule so absolutely that every thing serves them, war as well as peace, defeats as well as victories, obstacles as well as means,) a civil war which is in danger of precipitating the progress of the reformatory movement beyond measure, of affranchising more speedily and more harmfully those slaves whose definitive affranchisement was no longer in question, This civil war, in being prolonged, runs the risk of ruining both South and North, and Europe into the bargain; perhaps it will substitute servile insurrection for the transformation prudently effected by legislative means; perhaps it will substitute the remediless destruction of the cotton culture for the pacific introduction of free labor. In any case, when ended, it will leave behind it a sad inheritance of bitter and hostile memories, arising between America and Europe, and unceasingly threatening to engender foreign wars in the sequel of intestinal conflicts. May God preserve us from such a misfortune! The shudder which ran through the whole world, but the other day, when a messenger of Queen Victoria crossed the ocean bearing a despatch for Lord Lyons, will not soon be forgotten. We had taken the wrong road; will we have energy enough now to adopt a better course? Will we form a public opinion in Europe capable of enforcing its commands? The answer to this question does not alone include the future of America, it also contains our own; according as we shall have aided or disserved the great American people in the dark hour of its distress, we shall have in it a friend or an adversary when it shall have accomplished, either with us or despite us, the work of its uprising.

It is now, it is during this decisive year, which will never more return, that it is necessary to give the United States pledges of our affection for them, and our warm adhesion to the cause which they defend. There are services rendered at certain moments which are never effaced from the memory of nations; what France did for the foundation of the United States in the eighteenth century, Europe may do, for their second foundation, in the nineteenth. She may cast into the soil of both worlds imperishable seeds of peace and amity.

How many mistakes would have been spared us if we had sooner adopted this resolution! It will suffice for me to recall a single one. When Mr. Lincoln offered to sign the great international agreement of 1848, and consequently to proclaim with us and like us those laws for the protection of the rights of neutrals, of the importance of which we have been just reminded by the *Trent* affair, we imposed one condition on him which very rightly changed his determination. And why did we do this? Because we had invented the position of belligerents for the benefit of the South, because we ourselves had assumed the position of neutrals, officially proclaimed as such, because we had departed from truth and simplicity, because we found ourselves thenceforth charged with watching over the threatened legitimacy of the privateers of Jefferson Davis. If we had remained in our natural position, if, in conformity with our sympathies and the right of nations, we had seen in America only a friendly nation struggling with rebels, we would not have had in some sort to refuse its signature. Our ports would have been closed of course to the armed vessels of the South; it does not seem to me that this would have subjected us to great inconvenience. And as to the Southern privateers, supposing them to have been also called in question, nothing would have prevented us from announcing that, in the interest of humanity, we had decided not to treat them as pirates. The government at Washington would have comprehended—I say more, imitated us.

To sum up the whole, our counsels would have had more weight if we had remained friendly powers, having no relations (save the local necessity of consulships) with any except the single government whose ministers were regularly accredited to us. As friendly allies, we would have obtained a hearing. I even affirm that, in case it might be some day advisable for the American Government to resign itself to the separation of a few States, the influence of a friendly Europe would give more chances for the acceptance of such a sacrifice than all the mediation offered by our official neutrality.

CHAPTER III.

HOW TO EXPLAIN THE ATTITUDE OF EUROPE.

It is not enough to describe and deplore our attitude; the most important thing of all is to explain it. By going back to causes, we may chance to fall in with remedies. Whence comes the fact, so strange at first sight, that, so long as the United States were governed by slavery and for slavery, they were let alone; as soon as they begun to react against slavery, and against the whole system of violence, conquests, and attempts on humanity or the rights of nations therein involved, the hitherto unknown theory of belligerent insurgents was forged for their use?

The explanation is not difficult. From the first moment, Europe arrogated to herself a sort of benevolent patronage over divided America; she saw in it minors, infants I should say, whom it was the duty of reasonable men to direct. Toward this republic, toward this imperilled confederacy, we did not feel ourselves bound to obey the laws applicable between States on a footing of equality. We never once thought of saying, "Whatever may be our opinion of the future chances of the rebellion, it belongs to the American Government alone to determine the course of conduct which it deems proper to follow; if it be wrong in opposing the separation, this concerns only itself, and we know of no other American Government." Far from this, we have taken it for granted, without premeditation, and as if by instinct, under the impulse, doubtless, of the interest that we bear America, as well as of the European interests involved in it, that this affair is our own, and that we have the right to interfere in it.

This principle once admitted, (and every one remembers that if it were not so in formal terms, its influence made itself no less promptly felt among us,) the consequences could not be long in coming. An immense country demanded separation; the republic thus broken was nothing but a simple confederacy, in which the sovereignty of the individual States seemed at first sight to authorize the pretensions of the secessionists; the North was disunited, disarmed, unmilitary, and appeared incapable of reducing the rebellion; in a prolonged struggle, the prosperity of America might perish, and that of Europe also be exposed to serious dangers. Why then should not the patronage of the Old World come to aid the inexperience of the New? Why not indicate by a decisive act that the rupture was held to be final?

This established, the conduct of Europe is no longer obscure. The struggle had scarcely commenced when we proclaimed, by an act the signification of which deceived no one, the impotence of the Government at Washington—it could not reduce the South, the South was certain to make itself recognized by-and-by; in the mean time we treated the latter almost as a government *de facto*, and conferred upon it the quality of belligerent. Between belligerents, England declared herself neutral, then awaited events. To see the eagerness with which the incident of the *Trent* was at first seized upon by England, justified us in believing that Lord Palmerston saw in it, beyond the violation of neutral rights, the pretext for an American intervention. To recognize the South, to sanction the definitive separation, to reëstablish peace, and thus to transact the business of the whole world, by force of arms, if need were—such was the programme.

And a proof in the minds of many that our mediation is only postponed, is, that the arrangement of the incident of the *Trent* was near ending in nothing. Messrs. Mason and Slidell had not yet reëmbarked when new difficulties came under discussion. Europe censured the measure taken to close the harbor of Charleston; Europe was disposed to contest the efficiency of the blockade. In other words, Europe, which had decided for the good of young America that it should not be suffered to carry the folly too far which it had taken into its head, seemed determined to arrive sooner or later to its end, the recognition of the Southern Confederacy.

I like to look at things as they are. There are fewer accidents in the life of peoples and the relations of States than is supposed; almost always, on going back a little way, we meet a directing principle which gives the key to all the rest. It is necessary to ascend from secondary to ruling questions; thus only will light break forth.

If Europe had not believed herself called to lord over America, she would have remained faithful to her natural rôle. Whatever might have been her theoretical previsions concerning the issue of the crisis, she would have known no government but that of the United States. She would have seen nothing in this civil war but a struggle between the regular government and rebels, a struggle between the adversaries and champions of the extension of slavery. The sympathies of European opinion would have been then displayed in their full truth, instead of being hampered and perverted, as they have not ceased to be during the past year. Had it not been for this gross falsehood of a question decided in advance, we should have held our true convictions, and not those impersonal and involuntary ones which are accepted from the hand of necessity. We should have wished success with all our hearts to the great people of the United States, which is destined to so noble a mission on earth. We should have execrated as it deserves this rebellion, unique in history, which seems a challenge hurled at the gospel and civilization. In our journals, our books, our meetings, at the tribunals of our deliberative assemblies, we would have made the avowed champions of slavery understand clearly the kind of welcome that awaited them among us. We would not have distrusted our best sentiments, we would not have taken counsel of prudence, policy, the foresight of things which might or might not happen; we would have admitted at the outset that justice is a power, and that by this sign do men conquer. At the sight of the ringleaders of the South, who, for the sole reason that they have been defeated in an election, call their fellow-citizens to arms, fire on the flag of their country, attack the free government to which they had sworn allegiance, and hasten to supplicate in Europe assistance from foreign powers, we would not have restrained our repugnance, but would have told them what we thought of the twofold crime—the attempt to destroy the United States, and to found a new State on the corner-stone of slavery. The reprobation of Europe, thus signified to the Southerners, might have facilitated the accomplishment of what we have delighted in calling impossible, and have caused the monstrous edifice, whose completion we have so coldly demonstrated as certain, to totter from the very first day upon its base. To deny things is sometimes to prevent them; to affirm them, is sometimes to render them sure.

Shrewd men find no better way to encourage evil than by prophesying its success and thus summoning upon earth by subtlety of reasoning, calamities which frankness of moral sentiment would have conjured down. But the time soon comes when moral sentiment, baffled for an instant, regains its sway. It becomes necessary then to act in accordance with it, and to prove that, by supporting the evil cause, the triumph of the good one has been but the better ensured. Such is the manœuvre which has been attempted among us during two or three months past. Not only is it more than ever affirmed that slavery has nothing to do with the insurrection of the South, (we will presently see the value of this incomparable paradox,) but it is said that the triumph of the North would strengthen slavery, and that the South, on obtaining the recognition of Europe, would pledge itself to emancipation.

What are we to think of this double assertion?

There was a moment, as I have always admitted, when the reëntrance of the South into the Union might have been purchased by lamentable concessions. In the beginning of the war, and even for some time after, the fears which were expressed were not destitute of foundation. Doubtless, such compromises would not have ensured long life to the patriarchal institution which had received its death-blow in the election of Mr. Lincoln. Nevertheless, there would have been fearful struggles, the public conscience would have had to suffer anew, our brows would have blushed at the news of numerous acts designed to conciliate the South, even though vanquished, and to heap up constitutional guarantees about an expiring iniquity.

The error here does not consist in supposing that such a policy might have been possible, but that it may still be so. Whoever has closely studied the Northern States, knows that an important change has been wrought there by the very fact of the prolongation and aggravation of the civil war. By degrees, a true and simple idea has broken loose from the clouds of prejudice by which it had been surrounded—the great enemy is slavery; the great conspirator is slavery; the great rebel is slavery; the great enemy of peace and Union is slavery! Since the entire North has comprehended this, it has taken an immovable resolution not to end the war without also ending the cause of the war. The conviction on this point has become so general, that at the present time, neither a President nor Secretary of State could be found, willing to take it upon himself to propose, whatever might be its immediate advantages, a measure designed to perpetuate slavery. Supposing, contrary to all appearances, such a measure to be proposed and passed by Congress, it would encounter so violent an opposition in the nation, and even the army would oppose it so strongly, that there would be no means of securing its execution; then, at the next presidential elections, the measure and its authors would be voted down by a burst of wrath which would sweep away all compromises, and bow beneath its violence all servile institutions from the banks of the Potomac to the distant shores of Texas.

It is a marvellous fact, and one which, as far as I am concerned, I admit without regret, that, in case the South should return to the Union before the Federal army shall have broken down all its opposition and passed in triumph through its entire territory, slavery will subsist there in the position of an accursed institution, condemned to perish, abolished definitively in principle, but tolerated for a given time in order to smooth the way of transition and prepare for a peaceful emancipation. Such a slavery would possess neither influence nor future; hemmed in on all sides by victorious liberty, despoiled of the prejudices and prestige which lately surrounded it, having no longer power either to demand fugitive slaves or to acquire new territory, it would tranquilly but surely vanish.

Such an abolition, I admit, seems to me preferable to that wrought by a servile war. It is no less sure, and is better for the blacks as well as the whites.

As to the abolition which is promised us on condition of Southern recognition, I have this to say:

I am glad, in the first place, that the awakening of public opinion caused by the affair of the *Trent*, has brought the advocates of the South to the necessity of thus amending their programme. Hitherto, they had not taken this trouble, but had contented themselves with declaring in general terms that separation would result more favorably than union to that *great humanitarian cause*, the triumph of which, as all knew, was ardently desired by the whole world. Now, they have taken a great step in advance; they have the semblance of announcing in the name of Jefferson Davis that he is ready to accord a promise of affranchisement in exchange for recognition.

Jefferson Davis, I am convinced, will never haggle for the conditions of recognition. To be recognized is the essential point. After that, we will see.

Moreover, is it not certain that henceforth every thing, without exception, must end in abolition? Has any man of sense doubted it since the election of Mr. Lincoln?

Mr. Davis has intellect enough to comprehend with us what the South in general does not yet comprehend, that the battle for slavery is lost—lost if the South return to the Union, lost if the South be recognized as an independent Confederacy.

If this point only be accorded, we have no need of his concession. A power superior to his, the force of circumstances, guarantees to us that, whatever may be done, slavery will finally disappear. What the balloting of 1860 decided, neither victories nor defeats, neither Europe nor America, will succeed in setting aside.

But, it is said, Jefferson Davis makes more definite promises. Well, let us examine these promises. He will pledge himself not to reclaim slaves who have taken refuge in the North! I can easily believe it; such a demand would not meet a very hearty welcome. He will pledge himself to admit the competition of free labor! I am likewise convinced of it; in the first place, because this competition exists already in some measure; next, because it is the only means of furnishing a substitute for expiring slavery, of infusing fresh life into Southern cultures, and of drawing European emigration into the new Confederacy.

He will pledge himself to procure the passage of a decree of progressive emancipation, in consideration of certain delays justified by the difficulties of the position! Here, my doubts begin. What will this progressive emancipation be? May it not consist in the suppression of a few abominable practices, sanctioned at present by the laws of the South, and which too deeply offend the conscience of the Old World? "No," is the exclamation. "Jefferson Davis promises to procure the freedom of all children born from this time!" I must see this before believing it. However rapid may be the progress of providential retribution in some cases, I do not imagine that the South, after rebelling in the name of slavery, is already reduced to bow its head to the dust, to disavow the principles laid down so lately in its name, to undertake humbly the task of destroying the holy institution, to the support of which it had devoted itself with so much ardor and eclat. To revolt in 1861 because the extension of slavery was menaced, and to promise in 1862 to destroy slavery with its own hands, would be to show itself too eager to arrive at the forced disavowal of its dearest principles.

It is true that to make promises and keep them are two different things. If the question were only that of obtaining, by an apparently important concession, this recognition, without which its ruin must be accomplished, the South would perhaps consent to the *diplomatic* abolition of slavery; this depends on the degree of distress which it may have reached, and its powerlessness to maintain its rebellion without that moral support from Europe which must necessarily bring material support in its train.

Suppose, in consequence, that Jefferson Davis promises to obtain abolition. What is this *promise to obtain abolition*, in reality? A promise to present to the Congress at Richmond a bill overthrowing the social constitution of the South from its very foundation. The bill will be then discussed by the Senate and Representatives. Will they not find good reasons to maintain that such a change cannot be improvised in this wise, that the people are not prepared for it, that they cannot brave their colossal displeasure, that they cannot destroy the Southern Confederacy on the morrow of its foundation?

Those who retail among us the nonsensical tale of abolition promised in exchange for recognition, must suppose that we have short memories. It is not long since the Constitution of the South was adopted, and the two essential articles which distinguished it from the ancient Constitution were, on the one hand, the sanctioning of slavery, and on the other, the sanctioning of the sovereignty of each State. These two articles, closely allied together, as the whole history of the United States proves, are designed for each other's protection. Let slavery be menaced by the negotiations of the President or the provisions of Congress, and directly the local sovereignty rises in its might. Each State demands by what right you have decided in its name what it alone had power to decide. In fact, it will be impossible to stop short of this reasoning. So long as Jefferson Davis does not bring us laws decreeing the freedom of unborn children, passed by each of the Southern States and ratified if need be by State conventions, his *promise to obtain them* means absolutely nothing.

It means nothing, it is true, but it effects something, nevertheless. It is producing a great effect upon that portion of the European public who would ask nothing better than to intervene with honor, to ensure the existence of the South, to put an end to the crisis, to raise the blockade, and to obtain the transmission of cotton. This part of the public, as I have seen with my own eyes, is delighted to learn that all this can be done without too strongly opposing the question of emancipation; it may be, while serving it. It believes you on your word, without caring to scrutinize it very closely. The rumor is already becoming widely diffused; it has crept into all the journals; we hear it argued in every discussion: "If we recognize the South, it is understood that it will emancipate all children unborn."

If we recognize the South, it will find full recognition, even though it should afterward inform us that the liberation of unborn children was met by unforeseen difficulties which could not be surmounted on the spot; that time was needed, but the end would be pursued and, doubtless, finally attained. A recognition is not as easily recalled as a promise. Once accomplished, the recognition will produce its effects: the strengthening of the administration at Richmond, the exasperation of the administration at Washington, a probable war between the latter and Europe. In a word, the position of affairs will become changed in a day; the South will henceforth have all it desires, and no one will think, in the midst of these conflicts, of asking about the fulfilment given to its promises; no one except, perhaps, a few European abolitionists, whose tardy anxiety will excite but little interest. We will have something else to do when the rupture has taken place between the United States and ourselves, when our journals are filled with their misdeeds, when angry passions are stirred up, and when the national honor is at stake. Our whole attention will then be given to the unrecognized virtues of the South, and perhaps, for we are sure of nothing, to the felicity of its slaves.

One does not need to be a prophet to predict all this; a very little study of history and the human heart will suffice. Note, moreover, that in causing the emancipation of unborn children to be talked of among us, the agents of Jefferson Davis attain an important result, supposing even that they do not succeed in gaining this would-be conditional recognition. They have made it seem possible, they have mirrored it before the eyes of the community, they have restored some consistency to the great hope on which the South built its chances, and the absolute loss of which would destroy all its energy.

But I refrain from discussion. It seems to me that I have sufficiently demonstrated the vanity of the pledges and conditions held forth; for serious inquirers I have already said enough; for men whose minds are made up, who are determined to believe in whatever they are determined to do, I should never say enough. I wish only, before closing this chapter, to dwell upon the moral aspect of the projects extolled among us during the past year—projects which have been unceasingly embellished, ameliorated, and arranged to suit our taste, and the uniform conclusion as also the sole end of which has been the recognition of the Southern Confederacy.

Their common characteristic, although they talk much of peace, is a war in the background. It is true that this is not a war of the North against the South, but of the United States against Europe. I do not inquire whether this new war will be less ruinous than the old, whether it will not at once stamp the present struggle with a character of atrocity and devastation, whether it will not be the beginning of general conflicts before which the mind recoils with horror. We will set aside considerations of this sort, however important they may be in themselves. I speak of another kind of destruction—the destruction of the friendly feelings which exist between America and ourselves.

According to some, this would be but a trifling loss. I think differently. The day will be a fearful one, in my opinion, when, by sowing injustice, we shall prepare for ourselves and our children after us a harvest of long-lived and inextinguishable enmities, always ready to embroil the New World and the Old.

The United States will not be destroyed; thank God! it is given to no one to strike from the list of great nations this people, now passing through a crisis as grievous as salutary, and which will emerge from it stronger because it will be better. The point in question is not simply that of irritating this people by a measure which will wound them in the most sensitive part, but of introducing a measure which will produce a state of perpetual antagonism.

The policy recommended by the friends of the South is nothing less, let us not forget, than the rule of Europe in America, by which I do not mean any mingling of Europe in American discussions. No, I am not one of those who believe that the Monroe doctrine should remain intact amidst the conflicts of the nineteenth century. I believe in the frequent intervention of Europe in America and of America in Europe; I believe in the future entrance of the United States into the concert of great powers; I believe, in fine, that electricity and steam have overthrown many artificial distinctions, and that it will daily become more difficult to live in isolation. But I believe at the same time—and this question will be discussed with all the care it deserves in another part of my work —I believe that there should be neither European supremacy in America nor American supremacy in Europe. Nations are no longer in a state of pupilage, and pretensions of preponderance will soon cease to be tolerated anywhere.

It is certain, as we have seen, that such pretensions lie at the bottom of the policy which we are urged to practise. "The separation ought to prevail! We have decided that you are not in a condition to terminate it! You shall fight no longer! At least you shall only fight in such or such a manner!" Such is the language which is dictated for our use; and as men are laboring to secure, by artificial means, the foundation of a State which could not live of itself, and which will always stand in need of the protection without which it would not have been born, it thence follows that European influence, and almost domination, will gain footing in the very heart of the Southern States, at the gates of Washington.

Friends of peace, ye who are so eager to arrest the present conflict, who at need would draw the Popilian circle around President Lincoln by forbidding him to maintain the blockade and pursue its advantages; have you reflected on the endless wars which you are laying up for the future; have you caught a glimpse of the consequences of your enterprise; do you imagine, by chance, that you will kill the United States; and if you do not kill them, do you suppose that they will live in peace, having you some day on both sides of their empire in Virginia and Canada, and feeling you at Quebec and New Orleans, the mouths of their two great rivers?

But we will leave this point also; we will go directly to "the" true question, that of morality, and look the theory in the face which covers the future recognition of the South.

This may be summed up in a sentence: the true way to emancipate the slaves is to ensure the triumph of the partisans of slavery. I have little faith, I confess, in the good results of injustice, nor do I forget how the Apostle Paul branded the maxim, "Do evil that good may come." We always have excellent reasons for favoring the triumph of bad causes. And what happens next? The human conscience becomes troubled and perverted, as it were, by this double spectacle of our complaisance toward both evil and the good which appear to result from it.

Ah! if evil gave birth to nothing but evil, evident evil, immediate destruction, the recoil of civilization, if the consequence always followed directly after the principle, like the child after the mother, the danger would be less. But the logic of history, true and pitiless as it is at the bottom, does not present this incontestable sequence upon the surface; it often happens, and the American crisis offers an example, that certain progressive events make their way in spite of every thing, and that the agents of Jefferson Davis end by obeying, in spite of themselves, the impulse commenced by the election of Mr. Lincoln. Emancipation will take place, as I have said, through war or peace, under favorable or adverse influences, with union or separation. If, therefore, the separation should be consolidated through our mediation, we will say at some future day: "Since the separation did not prevent affranchisement, it effected it."

Is it nothing, I ask, to weaken the few moral ideas which subsist among us in the midst of triumphant materialism? Indignation against slavery was one of these ideas; but on the day that we shall be seen to strike hands with the South, to propound theories in favor of its rebellion, and to demonstrate that it has been of service in its way to the cause of liberty, the human soul will pass through a fearful crisis, and the light of conscience will wax dim.

Occasions to show the importance of a principle are rare. What a valuable lesson would it have been to our whole generation, to have seen Europe, in spite of the temptations of policy and the demands of interest, determined not to compound either intimately or remotely with those who had dared adopt as the motto of their flag, "the sanctity and perpetuity of slavery!" By this single act, we should have elevated the standard of morality. Such a victory is not without its value.

This, I know, is not *shrewd policy;* but to us weak minds, who think that man does not live by bread alone, and that communities also die of hunger when we forget to satisfy their highest needs, to us, the success of Europe in America would have been complete if it had manifested there its natural sympathy for good and its natural antipathy to evil. The rebellion, proclaimed in the name of slavery, would have known on what to rely; it would have had to examine by itself whether it could by its own strength conquer that independence in fact, which should precede and not follow its official recognition. It is probable that, reduced to these terms, the question would have been ere long resolved, and that the civil war would have been of short duration. In any case, the South would have had no right to say: "I hold Europe through cotton; she must walk straight. I predicted that I would conquer her repugnance, and I have done so; I said that I would force her to take my part, and I have succeeded."

In other words, there is neither good nor evil, but interest alone: rest your claims on your interests, and you will succeed; and it will be even demonstrated, through the refinement of modern times, that in immolating principles, you have rendered them good service. May God preserve us from receiving such a lesson! We should profit by it but too well. Believe me, there are moral defeats which tell on the destiny of nations.

CHAPTER IV.

BELLIGERENTS AND NEUTRALITY.

If I enter unembarrassed on the examination of our American policy, if my criticism bear with equal freedom upon the propositions which are made to us, and the resolves that we have already taken, it is not only because the chief initiative has belonged to England, or because the collective responsibility, the European responsibility, covers every thing, so that I have much less to blame in the faults of a government than in the low state of public opinion and the moral languor of the whole world; but also because I love my country, and because it is a real duty in my sight to warn it when it seems to me in danger of straying from the right path. That this duty is a right, no one will certainly think of doubting.

I shall therefore proceed, sure of my sincerity and respect for good intentions, sure of mingling no hidden thought of any nature whatsoever in the loyal study of our relations with the United States. Let us go back at once to the measure which contains the germ of all the rest. In the quality of belligerents, granted so speedily to the insurgents of the South, is found comprised, as we may say, the entire series of acts which, commencing with official neutrality, has recognition for its extreme term. Would you refute a sophism? Examine the major proposition—the snare is there. Would you study a political tendency which disquiets you? Examine its earliest manifestation.

To confer on the insurgents of the South the title of belligerents, and to claim for ourselves the position of neutrals, seems quite in conformity with that circumspect and unchivalrous wisdom which is sure of obtaining general approbation. What is better to be done, in the presence of such a crisis, than to stand aloof, to wait a little, to entertain neither opinions nor preferences? This is the first view of things, at which it is usual to stop. It is only by scrutinizing more closely that we discover that the neutrality thus proclaimed is as little neutral as can be imagined; it settles the constitutional question discussed in the United States, and decides that the United States are a league, not a nation; it grants to the South all that it demands; it bears so slight a resemblance to non-interference that not one of the first-class European powers would for an hour endure the application to its own affairs of the theory which they apply to the government at Washington.

The latter government, too, has unceasingly protested against it. It may be said that it protested in advance, for the despatches of Mr. Seward to Mr. Dayton foresaw the possibility that Europe might entertain the thought of treating the Southern rebels as belligerents. The fears of Mr. Seward being speedily realized, he has never wearied, as all will remember, of demonstrating in his diplomatic correspondence that the character of belligerents belongs to independent powers, to established governments struggling with each other; that it cannot belong, that it has never belonged in fact, to a self-styled State, founded by a rebellion not yet victorious and out of danger.

The importance of the principle is such that the resistance upon this point has never staggered for a single moment. The United States have maintained—and why should it astonish us?—that they are still the United States; that a sovereignty attacked is not a sovereignty destroyed; that the pretensions of the South do not constitute a right; that no one is authorized to hold them as conquered before they are so, before the war has even commenced in good earnest. They have maintained their principle, that is, their right, with an energy full of sadness and dignity; adding moreover that, so long as Europe shall not join positively hostile acts to an insulting doctrine, they will content themselves with expressing their sorrow, and will continue to count on the friendly sentiments of the powers.

Let us be just toward all! The attitude of the cabinet at Washington in the presence of so grave a difficulty, has been of a nature to conciliate universal esteem. Grieved, without being violent; energetic, without being aggressive; refusing to listen to despatches wherein the rebels were styled belligerents, yet not hesitating to acknowledge the amicable proceedings by which Europe has more than once redeemed the harshness of her official language, it has understood how to preserve its position on a great question of principle, and at the same time to avoid exaggerating it so far as to compromise the practical interests of the day.

Europe, in fact—I recall it to her honor—after having taken the enormous stride of declaring the South belligerent and herself neutral, felt the need of proving that she by no means intended to carry out her theories to the end, and that her declarations did not comprise all that men fancied they saw in them. In closing her ports and those of her colonies to vessels with prizes, she struck a death-blow to the privateers of the South; which, moreover, have made more noise than they have done harm, and which have never been able to exert an appreciable influence on the issue of the conflict. But this, on the part of Europe, was simply the regular accomplishment of the duties imposed by the blockade; she did more, she did not treat the blockade of the South by the Federal fleet with rigor. If this is now effective, it has not been always so, and nothing would have then been easier than to have given a fatal blow to the North; it would have only been necessary to make a rigorous application thereto of the rules of international law. France and England have been unwilling to do this; it has been repugnant to them thus to lend an avowed support to the champions of slavery. This mark of good feeling, for which the cabinet at Washington has shown itself grateful, has established an important difference between the real conduct of the European governments and the policy attributed to them by plotting intriguers.

That this policy has been hesitating, I am convinced; that it committed a great fault in the beginning by proclaiming the insurgents to be belligerents, I have just said, and am about to demonstrate; but that it acted in this manner deliberately, with the fixed design of proceeding thence to recognition, cost what it might; that it had in clear view the attainment of an end, and not an unavowed tendency or temptation, I deny: a Europe determined to cut the United States in twain, would not have hesitated to contest last year's blockade. I have therefore great hopes. Provided that public opinion be fully aroused, all will go well; we have already crossed over more than one dangerous defile, we will pass safely through others. Between the rumors which the patrons of the South have an interest in propagating, and facts as they really happen, the difference is great, God be praised! Under favor of this remark, I resume the examination which I have undertaken.

You remember the shudder that ran through our veins—ours, the declared friends of the United States—when the English journals brought us the speech of Lord John Russell, in which the word belligerent was uttered for the first time. Mr. Seward had no need to teach us the scope of such a word; we understood it on the spot, and were struck with consternation. It seemed to us that a tongue so liberal as that of Lord John Russell was not framed to give such encouragement to the South. It seemed to us that England, which had not shown herself really prepared in the Crimea until ten or twelve months had elapsed, was ill placed to proclaim at the end of a few weeks the military powerlessness of the United States. Their ministers had not yet reached the shores of Europe when this powerlessness was already admitted to the rank of proven facts; whence it followed that the insurrectional government, sure of existence, deserved to be considered as belligerent. When we remember that the despatch in which Mr. Seward announces his refusal to receive correspondence containing this term is dated on the 17th of June, we are brought to acknowledge that the resolution of Europe was taken from the beginning of the civil war. The South had a chance of success unique in history; its first gun passed for a victory; its rebellion was immediately transformed into a revolution; it had no childhood, but was born full-grown. The rebellion of a day, behold it a government in fact, while waiting till it should make itself acknowledged as a government by right! *

It is not usually thus; before perceiving two States where there was lately but a single one, before placing on a footing of equality a regular government and those who are attacking it, we ordinarily wait until the latter have been victorious, have maintained their existence, and have shown some other sign of vitality than a first success, secured by treason!

To judge the value of the favor thus accorded to the South, we have only to ask ourselves what we should have thought of the United States if they had consented to concede to it this belligerent character? Would there have been hisses enough found for them in all Europe? What would not have been said of a country which did not even know enough to respect itself and to fall with dignity? What! to strike its flag at the first summons; to admit with a good grace that its existence as a great nation had ceased, that every rebellion against it was invincible, that every rupture founded a government within its borders, that its sovereignty had fallen on the south of the Potomac, that it might make war there, but only such war as takes place between States, the war of belligerents!

What America could not honorably accept, could Europe legitimately establish? History will reply.

When Ireland, a distinct kingdom notwithstanding, rose in insurrection against England in 1796, who among friendly powers thought of conferring on the Irish the

* If the question were only that of constituting a government and securing the working of a partially regular administration, every fraction of a country in revolt against the nation of which it formed a part, could, without delay, procure this title to the position of belligerent. To constitute a regular government!—but this has now become the first letter of the alphabet: every rebellion begins in this wise.

title of belligerents? It would not have been a very safe proceeding, I think, to have declared by official means that they were any thing else than insurgents.

When, at the time of our religious wars, (I take the epoch when the present centralization was not in existence,) a few of our French provinces were in arms against the Valois, what answer would have been given to the ambassador of an allied country sent to say that the south of France would be henceforth held as belligerent, and that neutrality would be observed between this belligerent power and the king?

Let us take more modern examples. Look at Hungary. She is a kingdom apart, having her own constitution and her local sovereignty. In her insurrection against Austria, she certainly gained more battles and kept the field longer than the men of Charleston had done when it was deemed proper to transform their civil war into a foreign one. Hungary had given itself a government as well as Montgomery. This government even could not be destroyed until Russia came to aid in its suppression. Yet notwithstanding, did the thought ever occur to us to speak of it as a belligerent?

Neither did we talk of belligerents when Poland, a distinct kingdom also, and guaranteed by treaties, fought against Nicholas in 1830. During this heroic and several times successful war of the Chlopicki, the Czartoryski, and the Skrzynecki, I am not aware that the theory of belligerents made its appearance anywhere; the Russians would have seen in it a mortal insult.

Let us ask ourselves, for I will end where I began, how we should have welcomed the title of belligerent bestowed on Abd-el-Kader? Our neighbors across the Channel would have also protested, I imagine, and in a somewhat haughty tone, if, during the revolt in India, any power had bethought of proclaiming its neutrality, by recognizing in this great people, risen in behalf of its nationality, the quality of belligerent.

I need not go out of America, moreover, to demonstrate that the theory which recognizes belligerents at the end of a few weeks, was never invented and put in application before the Southern insurrection. The insurrection of the colonies in the last century, which was about to create the United States, was no slight thing, I fancy; it was truly a national, energetic, sustained movement. Nevertheless, even the enemies of Great Britain would have thought themselves setting at naught the most elementary principles of the right of nations, if they had hastened beyond measure to treat the Americans as belligerents.

This time, our haste is explained by arguing the importance of the movement—it is the half of the United States that has seceded!

A figure is often thrown in to support this summary assertion—twelve millions, fifteen millions of inhabitants.

Does the separation become more lawful, when those who decree it are more numerous? I will dispense with investigating this question, for the importance of the seceding States has been strangely exaggerated. We forget, in the first place, to strike out the Border States that remain faithful to the Union. We forget next to strike out the slaves, who have not voted for separation, that I am aware. The truth is, that, supposing even the white population to be unanimous, (and we have many reasons to doubt this,) scarcely six millions are in question, six millions out of twenty-eight. And mark that these six millions of whites are charged with guarding three million three hundred thousand slaves.

The insurgent South comprises vast territories, almost destitute of inhabitants; beautiful countries rendered sterile by slavery. The States most numerously populated are elsewhere—New York, Ohio, and Pennsylvania, known as the Keystone State. Manifest destiny, too, is elsewhere; the West seems fated, ere long, to govern the United States.

But I am careful not to stop at such considerations; there must be a rule, a principle in the matter, and it is this principle that I wish to discover. So long as we have not reached it, we are treading on unstable ground.

I hear a great deal said about modern law—the law of nationalities. We are asked why we refuse to the Southern Confederacy, organized, armed, supplied with a constitution and a president, the benefit of a doctrine which has been practised elsewhere. Is not this also a government *de facto?*

I am willing that every successful rebellion should be metamorphosed into a government; I add, even, that I think it just, although I am no lover of rebellions. There is no other way, in fact, of averting the interference of foreign powers; and if foreign powers are not to interfere, it is clear that governments must be founded by success.

But this success is indispensable. In the nineteenth century as in those preceding, in modern as in ancient law, a rebellion remains a rebellion so long as it be not victorious. Here is an armed conflict, whose first successes, which it was easy to foresee, have not been followed by any serious result; it is less triumphant than on the first day, for the national armies have gained a footing everywhere on its soil, whilst it has not taken a step in advance; the struggle, moreover, has not commenced in earnest. I see here neither a government *de facto*, nor a belligerent; modern, no more than ancient law, commands me to see any thing else than insurgents.

Modern law is something less absurd and less arbitrary than those who extol it on every occasion, but who seem to understand but little of it, would make us believe. Laying aside high-sounding words, modern law is simply justice, for it is non-intervention; nothing more, nothing less. Let each people settle its own affairs and determine its own destinies; we outsiders are at liberty to approve or blame its acts, but not to meddle with them. This theory is not without nobleness; the point in question is not to worship power or success, but to respect the independence of nations. A nation is independent only on condition of being free to commit follies within itself, if it please without fear of punishment from any.

This admitted, if the South had rendered evident the powerlessness of the North for its reduction, if its independence had ceased to be contested by arms, at least, in a serious manner, if, in fine, it had surmounted the chief difficulties in its way, we might be authorized in saying, "The South is not insurgent, but belligerent; it has acquired the consistency of a new State, which by and by will receive recognition, and which contends with the Washington Government meanwhile on a footing of veritable equality." But the position of the South is that of a rebellion which is weaker to-day than it was a year ago, and which will succumb the moment that it is left alone to face the United States. To invoke modern law, the right of nationalities in its behalf, is out of the question.

The first right of nationalities is that of subsisting, of suppressing anarchical movements, and of maintaining the action of the laws. The theory of the right of rebellion is a new one, that we would do well to scrutinize closely. "We have the *determined will* to overthrow the established government! We are *resolved* to separate!" Will this henceforth suffice? Is every portion of a territory that chooses to detach itself from the whole, to be transformed at once into a sort of new, semi-recognized State, whose defenders will be soldiers instead of insurgents, and whose flag will take rank among national banners?

Let us beware! It seems to me that rebellions stand in no need of encouragement, as times go. Nothing can be better than to let them run their course, to recognize those which are victorious, to admit as belligerent a new State detached from an old one as soon as it has decidedly made a place for itself on earth; I go thus far, for it is impossible to stop short of it without desiring foreign intervention. But to invent a special category of rebellions which, without being victorious, may some day become so, and to which shall be accorded before trial the benefit of possible success, would be to establish foreign intervention under another form, the most dangerous of all.

Imagine a foreign power weighing from a distance the obscure chances of an intestine conflict, and judging in its wisdom (that is, according to its caprice, preference, or interest) that this insurrection is hopeless, while the other will succeed; that this separation is ephemeral, while the other will be perpetual! Before every serious struggle, before the separatists shall have shown their strength or weakness, they are either to be discouraged by the verdict of the great powers which leaves them confounded among the vulgar class of insurgents, or encouraged, on the contrary, by the title of belligerents. This is not a trifle; such a moral support very nearly promises a material support, and takes the place of it at need.

It must not be concealed, in fact, that there is already in the title of belligerent a beginning of recognition. It is the proclamation of an intermediate, equivocal position, unknown to us hitherto, and which we shall do well to renounce after the unhappy trial that we have just made of it. Formerly, there were insurrectional and regular governments. The moment that an insurrectional government had gained its cause, it was recognized; and from that day forward, if it made war, it was in the capacity of belligerent. The idea had not yet been conceived of belligerents without recognition; that is, imperfect and in some sort probational States, having the right to raise an army and display a flag, without having the right to demand admission into the family of nations.

That Europe should have invented this theory on the occasion and for the benefit of the Southern rebellion, cannot sufficiently astonish me. Of all rebellions, this one seems least deserving of advances and favors. "You have had the misfortune to rend asunder a free country, and, not having been able quite to destroy it, have dared unfurl a banner sacred to the perpetuity and sanctity of slavery! We will make a strict application in your case of the rules established by the law of nations; ask us for nothing more. When you are conquerors, if you ever become such, when your independence can be no longer seriously contested, we will see in you a government *de facto;* and as we have no choice, as the principle of non-intervention exacts that all shall be admitted, the evil and the good, those which shock the human conscience and those which embody social progress, we will recognize you then, and not an hour before."

Such language I would have understood. I am well aware that the moment of official recognition is rarely marked by signs so striking that it can be by no means mistaken. The application of the principle by virtue of which governments in fact become governments by right, is almost always somewhat discretionary, I will not say arbitrary. The recognition may be to some extent hastened or retarded; whence it comes that all powers do not proclaim it on the same day.

This is quite explicable; all do not sympathize alike with the cause that has just triumphed; some adopt, others detest it. It is natural that they should not acquire the conviction at the same moment that victory is won beyond recall.

For my part, I like this slight share left to moral preferences in the interpretation of modern law; it proves that the doctrine of governments *de facto* is more spiritual than has been pretended; it takes causes into account.

To take account of causes is important, be sure, in order that certain enormities may meet with chastisement on their way, and that success may not stand for every thing. Yes; whatever may happen, in virtue of a superior law, we shall always feel authorized to keep such or such a victor waiting. If an insurrectional government should be anywhere created, announcing its intention of trafficking in men and women, selling families at retail, and virtually suppressing marriage, I do not think that we should show ourselves eager to recognize it, or to confer on it, meanwhile, the character of a belligerent.

Alas! what I have just presented as a hypothesis is a reality; the South has revolted and seceded, announcing to the whole world that, without this act, she would have been in danger of being hampered in the sale of men and women, in the retailing of families, in the virtual suppression of marriage. And her rebellion has seemed worthy of special favor! We have not been contented to treat it as a plebeian rebellion, but have invented for its pleasure this probationary position of unrecognized belligerents!

To encourage rebellion when it is only rebellion, when it does not even put forward an honorable pretext, and has nothing in its favor but its fair face, is certainly very imprudent; to encourage it when it hurls defiance at our sentiments of humanity, sure that the material advantages which it has at its disposal will gain pardon for every thing, is more than imprudent, it is sad.

And as the fault comes from us, from our moral torpor, from the lethargy of our public opinion, I hope that the remedy will come from us also; public opinion, awakened, will undertake to teach the South that it need hope for no more favors, and that it must return to the domain of the common law. There are causes which may conquer the official admission of the governments which represent them to the rank of recognized powers before the precise moment; that a king of Italy, who has become such in order to shut out foreign troops from the Italian frontier,* and to constitute a great nation, may be eagerly welcomed, we can readily conceive; but that a Southern Confederacy, which proposes to break up a great, free nation, and to compensate the human race by presenting to it an ideal State based on slavery—that this Confederacy, whose sole hope is in foreign powers, shall be recognized when it has not yet been victorious, is a

* I ought not to treat of the Italian question here, in passing. I belong to those who love the independence of Italy, and are not alarmed by its unity, but who do not think that such a work gains any thing by being accomplished in a few days. By giving it more time and good conduct, liberal Piedmont might have given a liberal meaning to the too much decried adage: *Italia fara da se.*

pretension which Europe owes it to herself to repulse with indignation.

It was, it is said, for the interest of the United States themselves, that the character of belligerent was attributed to the insurgent South. How, otherwise, could they have regularly exercised all the rights of war? How, otherwise, for instance, could they have maintained the blockade, and instituted a search for contraband of war on board foreign vessels? Can you conceive of a blockade, can you conceive of a right of search, where there are no belligerents?

We can easily conceive of them, and the writers who are authorities in respect to the right of nations have always conceived of them, likewise. Grotius speaks at length of wars which he calls "mixed;" that is, of those which take place between a legitimate government and a considerable party in insurrection against it. Wheaton remarks, and no one that I know of has contradicted him, that civil war gives to the two contending parties all the rights of war with respect to each other, and with respect to neutral nations.*

Of what use is it, moreover, to consult heavy books, when simple good sense suffices to settle the question? Who ever dreamed of a state deprived of the right of employing against attacks from within, the means of war that it would employ against enemies from without? What! are we not at liberty to blockade an insurgent port? What! are we not at liberty regularly to maintain this blockade, except on condition of first according to the insurgent government, the position of a government *de facto*, independent and distinct from our own? At the

* *Eléments du droit international*, tom. I., Part I., Chap. ii., §§ 7–10, and Part IV., § 7.

time of the insurrection of the American colonies in the last century, England did not think for a moment of seeing belligerents in them; yet, notwithstanding, she showed little hesitation in exercising the right of search, and would have showed no more in establishing a blockade, had it been necessary to aid her military operations. I add that she would have been right.

Here is a new scruple, no less wonderful than the first —if Europe had not transformed the Southern rebels into belligerents, she would have been forced to hang their privateersmen, who would have simply been pirates! I do not see that we are ever forced to hang men when we do not wish to. Would it have been so difficult then to declare that, through motives of humanity, the vessels armed as privateers by the South should not be treated as pirates; that even, in case of distress, an asylum should be granted them in our ports? In acting thus, in welcoming and protecting their refugees, Europe would have been only fulfilling a duty and conforming her conduct to the prevailing sentiments of our times. No one would have opposed it, and Mr. Lincoln's government has proved by deeds that it would not have hesitated to imitate our example. Do we not already see this government, which refused to recognize the South in the character of a belligerent, rejecting the *soi-disant* logical doctrine, by virtue of which its prisoners of war should be punished as traitors? Does it apply the penal law to them? Does it not negotiate exchanges of prisoners? Has it itself hung any privateersmen?

It is not so difficult as some pretend to avoid excessive rigor while maintaining the truth of positions. We have seen, it seems to me, revolutions and civil wars enough to know how to escape from embarrassment. If rebels remain rebels, purely and simply, it does not thence follow that foreign powers are bound to trample under foot the commonest principles of humanity. If we had not created belligerents in America, we should have renounced but two rights: the right of permitting arms and ammunition to be sold among us to the Southerners; and the right of limiting the sojourn of United States men-of-war in our ports. I cannot think this particularly vexatious.

Is it true that, by acting in this manner, we should have taken sides? This is another very simple question, which has been studiously rendered intricate. We will attempt its disentanglement.

It appears strange, at first sight, that to maintain things as they are, to see a regular government where there is a regular government, to see a rebellion where there is a rebellion, is to take sides. Without declaring one's self neutral toward a friendly power, neutral between it and the insurgents, it is certainly justifiable to refrain from interference in the conflict. This kind of neutrality, known as non-intervention, will not of course be contested by us. France and England would have failed in their first duty if they had not been thus far neutral; if they had brought any aid whatever to the Federal Government.

Two very different things have been confounded here: the neutrality in fact, which every one desires in this, as in all other civil wars; the neutrality founded on that act of veritable intervention which transforms insurgents into belligerents. We might be neutral, and perfectly neutral, without recognizing belligerents; we might interfere in nothing and give no support to any one, without beginning by a forced modification of accustomed positions. When I hear it said that, if there had been no belligerents, there would have been no neutrality, I seem to be dreaming. The contrary is true; in order that the neutrality should remain real, it was important that the prodigious moral and social advantage should not have been accorded to the South which was conferred on it from the first.

We excel in being satisfied with words. Is not recognizing belligerents, maintaining equality? Is not maintaining equality, giving proof of impartiality and absolute neutrality? No; to establish equality where it does not exist, is to serve the one and to injure the other; to place a belligerent where there was a rebel, is to show one's self as far from neutral as is possible to imagine.

Let us be neutral, let us hold aloof, let us leave to Americans the care of regulating the affairs of America, let neither side have any thing to fear or to hope from us, let them have before them a loyal struggle, *fair play*, as they say in England—the friends of the United States have never demanded any thing more.

I am mistaken—they have also demanded what harmonizes marvellously with official neutrality; namely, the partiality of sympathies. Sympathies neither know nor should know neutrality. And here again I encounter one of those audacious sophisms raised up within the past year to hinder us from doing our duty. We have been almost persuaded that political neutrality involved moral neutrality in its train!

What is this? because I am neutral, am I bound to be indifferent? Because I abstain from every act which might nearly or remotely contribute to the success of either, am I bound to repress within myself my most cherished sentiments, to manifest no preference between rebels exclaiming, "Long live slavery!" and a government representing right, justice, and humanity? The day that the neutrality of Europe shall be indifferent in the face of such conflicts, that day Europe will have committed a crime, and signed an abdication.

Thank God! nothing of the sort is yet true; and everywhere else than in America, the great powers have no fear of compromising the reality of their non-interference through the expression of their sympathies. Italy, with regard to which the policy of non-intervention is expressly proclaimed, has oftentimes received encouraging communications. In any case, if cabinets believe it their duty to be silent, nothing prevents parliaments from making their voice heard. When they keep silence, I no longer call it neutrality; a different word must be found, for a different thing is in question.

Nothing has been so grievous as the silence observed by the English parliaments. These parliaments, usually so noisy, and which are so fully conscious that they have not only to cast votes, but also to diffuse ideas, to propagate sympathies, to approve and to blame, have seemed to measure their most trifling speeches as if each of these speeches were a diplomatic note. And the meetings have been no less prudent: it was necessary to be neutral, or in other words indifferent!

We shall hear no more, I hope, of a neutrality understood in this wise. It has had its time, it is dying out; meetings are re-appearing, addresses are being signed, members of parliament are speaking out, liberal and Christian England is returning to life. This is well. This is the right way to be neutral in point of justice and charity. It will not prevent governments from maintaining their attitude of effective impartiality.

What is done is done; there are, thanks to us, belligerents in the South. It now remains to know how to set to work to avoid aggravating this fault, committed perhaps in the inconsiderateness of the first moment. Neither France nor England has aggravated it hitherto; their neutrality has been sincere. Is there nothing to do besides?

The word "belligerent" will not be withdrawn. May it not be interpreted by the conduct and language of Europe? We have been unwilling to say that the South is not in rebellion. We have been unwilling to say that the South has become a government in fact, an independent State. We have been unwilling to say that the South has obtained our moral support, and is entitled to count on it in the future. This granted, the scope of the term will become narrowed more and more, until it finally remains a word almost void of meaning. A word is something, but it is no great thing. Once informed that the point in question is only to forbear hanging privateersmen, and to give a salient form to the principle of neutrality approved by all, the United States will disregard an expression, untoward, it is true, but become well-nigh inoffensive.

It has done harm, it will do no more. It has encouraged the South, which has taken it in earnest, and fancied it a promise; it has irritated the cabinet at Washington, which has likewise taken it in earnest, and thought it a negation of its right. It was mistaken. Well, so much the better! If we must suffer yet for some time from the consequences of such an error; if the war be prolonged; if the manufacturing distress be increased by reason of the hopes conceived by Jefferson Davis; if Europe have the vexation of seeing a Southern privateer burn merchant vessels in the very waters of England

and Spain, and then enter laden with prisoners into those ports which would have been closed to the flag of a rebel, but which are open to the flag of a belligerent, it is a misfortune for which we shall soon find consolation provided that Europe, comprehending that she has taken the wrong road, henceforth adopts, resolutely and publicly, the principles of true neutrality.

CHAPTER V.

BLOCKADES.

The good side, hitherto, of the course held by Europe, is that she has given proof of real kindness to the United States in forbearing to elude the blockade. The cabinet at Washington has never ceased to acknowledge this, especially in the celebrated despatch addressed by Mr. Seward to Mr. Adams, on the 21st of last July.

The value of this friendly conduct cannot be denied; for the blockade is the principal weapon of the United States; it is the most humane and in some respects the surest means of reducing the rebellion. Can it be true that, since the pacific conclusion of the *Trent* affair, there has been serious question of modifying the attitude of the great powers upon this point? A great deal has been said on the subject, and this one and that one accused. In England, the Tory journals, and also those reputed to represent the ideas of Lord Palmerston, have demanded for some time that the Southern ports should be opened, if necessary, by force. Several French sheets have appeared to sustain the same theory, perseveringly urging the suppression of the blockade and the recognition of the South.

I refuse to believe, so far as it concerns me, that the governments will ever suffer themselves to be drawn into such a policy. As times go, we should suspect the reports which are constantly circulated among us by the champions of the South. The most amicable movements are transformed into menaces, the most inoffensive observations are to lead to a rupture, while the violation of the blockade and the recognition of the South are always found at the bottom of every thing.

Let us wait for official acts, nor lightly admit that Europe, scarcely delivered from the visions of war which the incident of the *Trent* had conjured up before her, can be persuaded to seize upon, we may say, to seek a new subject of quarrel. There are those in England, I am well aware, who urge extreme measures, who were little rejoiced at the liberation of the commissioners, and who are in quest of pretexts to intervene by force of arms to impose peace on the combatants, to obtain a fresh supply of cotton, and to reëstablish commercial relations. But without going out of England, these men will find listeners, and I do not know why we should afford them pleasure by taking their hopes for realities.

Nothing is so long-lived as certain hopes. Although Lord Russell, by his despatch dated February 15, has officially recognized the American blockade as regular, they have not lost courage. In my opinion, we should remain on our guard; the serious study of the question is far from having become useless. I will therefore say a few words concerning it.

The blockade is more effective now than it has ever yet been; it would be consequently at least strange if any power should think of attacking to-day what it did not attack some months ago. The fixed purpose of arriving at an end marked out in advance, would thus be clearly manifested.

I repeat that I believe nothing of the sort; but if, by any possibility, I am mistaken, if Europe should come to contest the American blockade, would she, by strict right, be authorized to act in this wise? Let us examine.

The first argument of the adversaries of the blockade consists in saying that, the United States not having recognized the South in the capacity of belligerent, it thence follows that the Southern ports are their own; and, they add, no one can blockade his own harbors.

And why not, if you please? Where have you discovered this interdiction, so favorable to the rebellion? What! here is an insurgent town; we can blockade it by land and besiege it according to rule, (I do not suppose that this too will be forbidden us,) and we cannot blockade it by sea? To do this, must we first make the *amende honorable*, declaring that the rebellion is not a rebellion, and that our insurgents have become belligerents?

I do not care to dwell on the point. Let us pass on speedily to the true problem: is the blockade, legitimate in itself, sustained by sufficient force—is it effective? Effective! This is a word which is in every one's mouth, but of which no one can give the definition. A few treaties have determined the number of vessels and guns which must be stationed before a port in order that it may be effectively blockaded; but this minimum figure (which, let me say in passing, has been constantly exceeded by the American cruisers) has not been reproduced in the most general conventions which establish the right of nations. There is here again an important matter to be regulated, as in the navigation of mail packets—the precise determination of despatches which are contraband of war, and the circumscriptions beyond which neutrals shall not be visited. The phrases, effective blockades and neutral rights, are so many words behind which must be put tangible, precise things that will leave no more room for controversy. It remains to know whether, while waiting till this shall be regulated, we are at liberty to settle the question which meanwhile arises; whether it be just to apply retroactively to America the probable decisions of a future Congress.

On consulting the principal treaties and comparing their terms, we arrive at the conclusion that an effective blockade is that of ports *which there is evident danger in entering.* No one has ever dreamed of saying that, in order to be effective, the blockade must render the entrance *impossible.*

The expression which I have just employed is precisely that which we read in the famous declaration published in 1780, by Catherine II., to guarantee the right of neutrals. Article 4 is couched as follows: "To determine what characterizes a blockaded port, this denomination shall be accorded to those only which, through the disposition by the assailing power of stationary vessels, placed sufficiently near each other, there is evident danger in entering."

The second armed neutrality holds the same language as the first. I cite article 3: "A port can be regarded as blockaded only if its entrance be evidently dangerous in consequence of the dispositions made by one of the belligerent powers, by means of vessels placed in its proximity."

Let us leap over that long interval of violence when the rights of neutrals and the freedom of the seas were immolated without ceasing, when paper blockades were established, when England declared the whole coast of the Continent blockaded, while the decrees of Milan and Turin proclaimed all the shores of the British Isles in a state of blockade; let us arrive at the epoch when true principles were proclaimed anew by France and England. What do we find in the concerted instructions given by both governments to their navies at the breaking out of the Crimean war? I open those emanating from M. Duclos. Article 7 reads: "Every blockade to be respected must be effective, that is, maintained by sufficient force that there may be imminent danger in penetrating into the ports invested."

The "evident" danger has become "imminent" danger. I cannot perceive any great difference between the two epithets. At the same moment, moreover, the neutral powers themselves also publish instructions in which the word "evident" again appears. Those of Sweden are thus expressed: "By a blockaded port, is understood one so far closed by hostile men-of-war, sufficiently near together, that no one can enter it without evident danger."

The treaty of Paris, concluded at the end of the war, contents itself with a vague expression, the scope of which it would be impossible to determine. "Blockades," it says, "to be obligatory, must be effective; that is, maintained by sufficient force really to forbid the enemy access to the coast." As force sufficient really to interdict access to the coast would be insufficient to stop all attempts without exception, it always becomes necessary to return to evident or imminent danger; which was done last year by M. Rouher, in an admirable circular, in which he asked our chambers of commerce to respect the Southern blockade. "An effective blockade," he writes, "is that of places which cannot be approached without exposure to evident danger."

The most credited writers, Klüber, for instance, (*Droit des Gens Moderne*, § 297,) holds exactly the same language. It will be difficult to go beyond these generalities, so long as the number of vessels shall not be determined which must be stationed before each port. This was attempted in the commercial treaty concluded in 1742, by France and Denmark; its Article 20 exacts that, for a port to be considered blockaded, its entrance must be closed by at least two vessels. This condition is found stated again, in identical terms, in the treaty of 1818, between Denmark and Prussia.

Let us now see whether the United States have conformed to the rules which I have just repeated. What Southern port is there before which they have not stationed at least two vessels? These vessels are stationary; they are sufficiently near together; lastly, there is everywhere evident or imminent danger in entering. The access, therefore, is really intercepted, at least in the measure which has seemed to result hitherto from national conventions.

It is easy to exclaim before a Lancashire meeting, "The blockade is not effective!" It would be more difficult, perhaps, to demonstrate it. I sigh to see a man like Mr. Massey exciting the passions of his voters by making these poor workmen believe that between them and the cotton which is to give them support, there is only an American falsehood; and that in treading this falsehood under foot, and opening the Southern ports, they would not be committing a reprehensible act, but exercising a right, and even rendering a service to the United States.

The blockade does not cease to be effective solely because a number of vessels have succeeded in running it. The American cruisers are forced to contend with a terrible enemy—English commerce. Night and day, in the hundred openings of a coast pierced in every direction by natural inlets, behind innumerable islands formed from the alluvion of rivers, lie a whole army of small craft, ready to profit by darkness or foul weather. Never had cruisers such a task ; and, far from finding cause for blame, there may be, perhaps, good reason to praise this blockading navy, improvised and without doubt insufficient in the beginning, but which has become inured to war, increased, and strengthened in every respect, and which to-day places in "evident" danger all that seek to escape it.

If the special formation of the coast (which can be seen by every one who possesses a good map of America) cannot furnish a valid excuse; if it belong to the blockading government to take into consideration the exceptional difficulties of a blockade, it is certain, at all events, that the accidents of the sea, which render the surveillance powerless at times, do not permit us to conclude therefrom the inefficacy of the blockade. During a storm which prevents the action of the cruisers, small vessels can easily dart through the narrow passages for which their draught of water is sufficient. Sir William Scott, whom the English do not challenge, while recognizing that the blockade ceases to be valid when not constantly maintained by a proper force, admits the restriction nevertheless: "As far as the weather will permit."

Let us add, that the intervention of steam has modified the conditions of the struggle, and tended to render the action of the cruisers less efficacious. It is extremely difficult, even with a cruiser of considerable size, to arrest the sure and rapid progress of a vessel hastening forward under full steam in a dark night, at the risk of two or three bullets that have small chance of reaching her.

It may be that, during the past year, on an extent of

coast exceeding three thousand miles, a considerable number of vessels have succeeded in evading the blockade; but there are hundreds also that have been captured. Much fewer have escaped than have not escaped, and the blockading squadron, which was composed at first of fifteen vessels, is to-day not far from numbering two hundred and fifty.

The fact is, English commerce must know that there is evident danger in running the blockade, for the list of its vessels seized and confiscated is not small. The ports into which vessels of heavy draught can enter are all sufficiently guarded; which does not mean, I repeat, that one will ever be sure of preventing a steamboat like the *Bermuda* or *Nashville* from piercing the line of cruisers.

It seems to me, on the whole, that the blockade is *effective* enough which results in interrupting communication and almost entirely suppressing the import and export trade. It would not occasion so much complaint if it were not effective. Consult those interested; interrogate, for instance, a witness beyond suspicion, the *New Orleans Crescent.* I quote from a number of last November:

"We hear a great deal said about what is called *running the blockade.* Reports, and it will be found that they are nothing but reports, pretend that five hundred and sixteen vessels have run the blockade since the 16th of May. This estimate is open to much dispute, even though it may be supported by official documents in the ministerial departments at Richmond. The blockade was established at the mouth of the Mississippi on the 25th of May, when forty vessels were found freighted for foreign ports, and were allowed to depart. The blockade was commenced almost at the same moment at Mobile and Pensacola; vessels were at liberty to quit these ports until the 6th of June. As far as New Orleans is concerned, the last arrivals through the Balize took place the 29th of May. There have been a few arrivals and departures of schooners in the lower inlets of the gulf. A small number of coasting vessels have run the blockade on the Carolina coasts, but all of these together do not amount to five hundred and sixteen. On the other hand, the steamer *South Carolina* has taken seventy schooners attempting to run the blockade between New Orleans and the Texan ports. There have been but three or four European vessels, among which was the *Bermuda*, that have succeeded in running the blockade. A few West India vessels have also reached the Carolina coast. But *it is deceiving the European governments to maintain that it is easy to escape the blockade, when not a vessel has entered the harbor of New Orleans by the river for the last five months, and when but a single foreign ship has arrived by the way of the Lakes.*"

Such is the truth taken from facts in a moment of frankness. This number of the *Crescent*, published at a time when the blockade was far from being as complete as it has since become, permits us to estimate at their true value, those lists of five or six hundred vessels which have made so much noise in Europe. We know now that nine-tenths of them are mere barks, accustomed to threading the inlets of the coast. We know that real commerce is *most effectively* suppressed. If necessary, the grass growing in the streets of New Orleans will testify to this. No more vessels in the harbor, no more bustle on the piers, no more business, no more life; the descriptions contained in the very journals of the country put us in a position to admire the effects produced in America by "the paper blockade."

This does not signify that the United States Government should not take all necessary measures that its cruisers may be still more efficient, and that the spirit of cavilling may find nothing in them to blame. But, meanwhile, we will do well to measure our words in Europe. The orators who gain popularity in the industrial centres by declaiming against the blockade, should inform themselves beforehand of the sufferings caused by this blockade in jest. To violate it, moreover, would be to declare war against the United States. Now, aside from the higher considerations which may be pleaded against an impious war, this war would have the bad effect of reducing the wages of operatives far below the rate to which it has now fallen. The security of the production so indispensable to England, depends on the success of the North. To endanger this success would be to call in the use of revolutionary measures, which would be to ensure the ruin of the South and the prolonged distress of Lancashire.

The United States thought for a moment of joining to the blockade a measure which, in their opinion, would have finally rendered this blockade perfect in the eyes of foreign powers—to close the Southern ports by an act of the legislature. I am rejoiced that they did not persevere; we have already subjects enough of controversy, without going in quest of another. If, on one side, every nation be free to close its own ports, (and the Southern ports belong to the United States,) if it be a question of municipal regulation to determine what places shall serve as ports of entry, it has been maintained, on the other hand, that this right ceases to exist in the event of civil war. The legal counsellors of the crown, when consulted in England concerning a similar act of the government of New Granada, replied that it was impossible thus to close, by a single act, ports which were *de facto* in the hands of insurgents; in which case, international law exacted that there should be an efficient blockade.

Mr. Lincoln has acted wisely, therefore, in taking into account the objections of England, and leaving the bill authorizing him to close the Southern ports to slumber among the state parchments.

Another idea seemed to make its way: in the lively desire of harmonizing the necessities of the war as nearly as possible with the satisfaction of the industrial needs of Europe, America might have substituted for the blockade, the collection of duties effected on board her cruisers; in this manner, cotton could have gone out and European merchandise have come in. This project proved abortive, both on account of the determination of the insurgents, who would not export their cotton, but clung to the idea of subduing—such was the word—the hesitation of Europe, and also and most of all because, in organizing this new service, (supposing the thing practicable,) it would have been necessary to relinquish the powerful action of the blockade in suppressing the rebellion.

The blockade will be maintained, therefore, purely and simply. To theoretical objections, the United States will continue to reply by facts. Doubtless, the enterprise is gigantic, and we might have doubted, with some reason, at the first moment, that it could be conducted in good faith. I can comprehend the surprise, akin to incredulity, which was manifested by Lord Lyons in May when Mr. Seward made the bold declaration, "The government intends to blockade the whole coast, from Chesapeake Bay to the mouth of the Rio Grande." Lord Lyons observed to him that this coast measured about three thousand miles in length, and that the United States would not probably have sufficient force to establish an efficient blockade of such an extent. "The whole coast will be blockaded, and efficiently blockaded," was Mr. Seward's reply. He has kept his word.

A few days after, the same question was debated in the Upper House; and if Lord Derby, always hostile to the United States, hastened to maintain the impossibility of an effective blockade the whole length of the South, Lord Brougham did not hesitate to support the contrary opinion. "It is not necessary," said he, with reason, "that the blockade should be established in such a manner that ingress or egress shall be actually impossible."

Do what we may, we will be forced to persist in this. Wherever the ports are guarded by a number of vessels, wherever there is "evident danger," in entering or going out, the efficiency of the blockade cannot be contested.

Other pretexts have been also sought. The obstruction of Charleston harbor has just furnished an admirable one; and the *Morning Post* has not delayed to denounce this measure, "in conformity with the barbarous policy of a government which fills Europe with indignation."

I am very glad that there is still indignation among us; those who see no cause to be indignant at a treason plotted and a rebellion proclaimed in the name of slavery, those who forget to be indignant on learning that the first act of the insurgent people of Charleston was to set at liberty the captain of a slaver, will be at least indignant at the thought of the vessels laden with stone which close the harbor of this city. A city which has so far signalized itself by its passion for slavery really deserves better than any other to excite our feelings of humanity.

Let me be understood rightly; neither do I myself approve the measure employed against Charleston; but as to this noisy and pharisaical compassion, as to these tears at command, as to this virtuous indignation which has but one end—that of arriving at European intervention and the recognition of the South—I take the liberty of esteeming them for what they are worth; I reserve my pity for other woes, which may be found without seeking very far, within the very walls of Charleston.

An act, moreover, may give cause for regret, without opening the way to the mediation of strangers. It is pitiable to see what arguments are used as a basis to demonstrate that Europe is right in opposing its veto, and employing force at need. Nature creates a port, and man steps in to suppress its use; he suppresses it even for generations to come; he deprives vessels in distress of a needful refuge: this is contrary to international relations; the preservation of commercial ports, like the free navigation of rivers, interests all nations; therefore, the people that takes it upon itself to change the primitive configuration of a coast to the detriment of the rest, deserves to be punished by the entire world.

There is but one misfortune; this new, revised, and considerably corrected edition of the rights of nations, has been published expressly for the sake of America, and, I suspect, for its exclusive use. We heard of the "stone fleet" a full month at least before it put to sea; who at that time experienced this lively emotion? There was no effort to display it until the *Trent* affair had been arranged, and it was necessary to seek elsewhere for a means of intervention. Great crimes do not permit the human conscience thus to waver. Now, with the exception of the English cabinet, which took its precautions, and presented its observations to Mr. Seward, not a person in Europe, not even a single editor of the *Morning Post*, exclaimed against this scandalous proceeding, this criminal attempt, this violation of the rights of humanity. If we had been seeking a quarrel with the United States, we would not have acted differently. It would indeed have been a shorter, and, above all, a franker way, to have declared once for all that it is their pretension to bring back the South into the Union which constitutes the violation of international law. Its barriers close the harbors! Yes, but bombardments destroy them; will we also argue the illegality of bombardments? It would be somewhat difficult, provided we still held our own wars in remembrance.

War, alas! is always more or less destructive to the works of God, and dangerous to the use of the good things which He has placed at our disposal. It is easy for one to reason thereupon with his feet on the fender; it is somewhat less easy, perhaps, when he feels himself struggling with that double peril—a formidable insurrection, and a continually threatened foreign intervention. At such a time, between the ruin of a city and the ruin of a nation, one may choose the first without therefore being barbarous.

I do not pretend to maintain that the somewhat unfriendly policy of Europe has been the sole cause of the measure taken against Charleston; I affirm, notwithstanding, that if America had had a greater feeling of security, if she had not trembled for her blockade, if she had not seen herself under the formidable obligation of triumphing in some sort within a given time, she would not have sent stone ships to the South. Let those who judge her place themselves for a moment in her place. No one destroys his own cities for mere pleasure.

But, it is exclaimed, the question concerns a commercial city and not a fortified town; fortified towns alone can be bombarded and destroyed! This distinction—who would believe it?—has been borrowed by the English journals from the celebrated Berlin decree. Eager to discover grievances against England, the Emperor accused it of extending to unfortified commercial harbors "the right of blockade which, in accordance with reason and the usages of polished peoples, is applicable only to fortified places."

This distinction has been long rejected by all authors, the French with the rest. War may render the blockade of a commercial harbor as indispensable as that of a harbor of men-of-war; and not only its blockade, but its siege. No means of attack is excluded.

If when, at the time of the Crimean campaign, the allies bombarded Sevastopol and spared Odessa, they did perfectly right, not because Odessa was a commercial harbor, but because the destruction of Odessa was not of the least importance to the success of their operations. Was the destruction of Charleston harbor essential to the military success of the operations of the United States? I will not decide the question, disposed though I should be to determine it against them; I say that the question concerns them alone. Having the right to decide, they have the right to act. I was astounded, I acknowledge, to see the note presented by Lord Lyons regard the obstruction of Charleston harbor as a proof of the discouragement of the United States; they despaired of reëstablishing the Union, otherwise they would have never thought of destroying a city which rightfully belonged to them.

When they fire upon a Southern fortress, they are destroying a fortress which rightfully belongs to them. When they attack a Southern privateer, they are endeavoring to sink a vessel which rightfully belongs to them. The first and inevitable condition of war is the unceasing destruction by the national government of things that rightfully belong to it. "Since you make war on the

South, since you injure the South, it is a proof that you despair of reducing the South and reëstablishing the Union." Such would be the natural conclusion of the English note.

I hope that in writing this note, despite the ill feeling which prevailed at that time, there was no design of making it mean all this; I hope that it was dictated chiefly by the desire of giving friendly counsel to the Americans, and persuading them from objectionable measures; I hope it, because I read at the bottom the name of Lord Russell. The truly liberal statesman who signed this document was the same who has just recognized officially the regularity of the blockade. He certainly is not among those who have espoused the cause of the South, and are watching for an occasion to intervene in order to secure its independence.

We see that, even though a real obstruction were in question, it would fall within the rights of war, and that Charleston, a peaceful commercial harbor (with its two fortresses, its population in arms, and its batteries pointed a year ago at the Federal flag)—that Charleston would have only been subjected to the existing laws of warfare, which permit bombardments and the closing of harbors. But the real obstruction of its port has been neither effected nor attempted; the National navy has only sought to close a few of the channels which connect its harbor with the ocean. In fact, since the sinking of the stone ships, vessels have succeeded in entering and going out of the harbor. If it has been entered, there is an entrance, and the partisans of the South will do well to set about seeking some other pretext of complaint. Mr. Seward has taken the liberty of making the same remark to Lord Lyons,* in terms which, though strictly diplomatic, are none the less clear and pointed.

I pause at this unhappy quarrel, precisely because it seems ended, and because it offers us a most instructive subject of study. If we had taken the trouble to read the New York journals, we should have spared ourselves so vexatious a misunderstanding. As early as November, these journals, in announcing the departure of the stone fleet, declared in explicit terms that it was not designed to obstruct channels of use to commerce. The harbor, they said, will remain open, and after the rebellion has been suppressed, all nations can visit it as before.

The English journals, which, for a moment, flung themselves with so much eagerness on this subject of quarrel, and which, in default of a better, endeavored to discover in the obstruction a *casus belli*, not only forgot to gain some information about it before complaining, but never gave a thought to the numerous examples which, in case of need, might have justified the extreme measures which the United States *did not take.*

And here I do not mean to speak of the Russians burning Moscow (their own city), or obstructing the pass of Sevastopol (their own city) in order to repulse the enemy from a territory which they certainly did not renounce on this account; neither do I mean to speak of the advice given by these same journals, so compassionate today, who wished to destroy Delhi "so that one stone should not be left upon another," which would seem to

* He adds that the obstructions will be removed after the submission of the South. On the demand of England, a vessel which had been sunk in the harbor of Savannah, was raised in 1815 by the Americans, after peace had been signed at Ghent. The English Admiral Sartorius himself acknowledges, in a letter published in the London papers, that the obstruction of harbors is among the rights of war, and that this obstruction may be removed on making peace.

indicate, according to the reasoning of Lord Russell, that they despaired of India, and had no longer any thought of preserving it! No; I will simply recall the acts of war and plans of operations which history has mentioned hitherto without the least indignation. Anvers, a commercial harbor, and more important, I think, than Charleston, was destroyed by the closure of its channels. The project of filling in the entrance to the harbor of Boulogne will be doubtless found on the minutes of the Admiralty, and that this was not pursued was by no means on account of scruples founded on the fact that Boulogne was not a fortified town.

It has been said again and again that none but Yankees could be capable of conceiving the abominable idea of sinking ships in the entrance to a harbor; but Lord Dundonald was not a Yankee, yet notwithstanding, a letter, written by him on board the *Imperious*, April 3, 1809 —a letter of which he is by no means ashamed, since he quotes it literally in his memoirs, contains the following passage: "Vessels laden with stone would forever destroy the anchorage of Aix; and a few old ships of the line, deeply laden, would be excellent for the purpose."

This was addressed to Lord Mulgrave, the first lord of the Admiralty, who forgot to address to his correspondent "remonstrances" similar to those which Lord Lyons addressed to Mr. Seward. But here is what is still better—the South Carolinians themselves, in January, 1861, wishing to deprive the United States of the means of revictualling the Federal forts situated on the waters of Charleston, sunk five schooners in the principal channel of their harbor. The rebels of Georgia, on their side, have endeavored to render Savannah inaccessible by water; and have obstructed the channel by old vessels.*

* They have just extinguished nearly all the lights on the Southern

These acts of the South were recounted at the time, and Europe was not moved by them—it is true that it was the South! As to the North, let it beware! Its movements are watched; its conduct must be irreproachable; we shall excuse nothing.

I am of those, I repeat, who would have preferred that no ships should have been sunk; but between a regret and a grievance, the distance is great. Alas! it is but too true that by heaping up unsound grievances, we end by exciting hostile passions. To-day, we denounce "the barbarity" of the Federal Government, which closes harbors, changes the configuration of coasts, and forever destroys the advantages which God had assured to commerce. To-morrow, we will complain of "the sufferings inflicted on manufacturers by a pitiless blockade," as if the Federal Government itself did not take care to open harbors by the side of those which it had closed, Beaufort by the side of Charleston; and as if it depended on the North to force the South into no longer systematically holding back its cotton in order to conquer the lingering repugnance of Europe. The other day, on the contrary, we cried out against the "paper blockade," and deplored the lists of six or seven hundred vessels which had escaped the cruisers, confounding time as well as tonnage; we did not say that the greater part of these vessels had run the blockade while it was still incomplete, neither did we say that most of them were mere barks, and that large vessels, with the exception of steamers, encountered, in entering Southern harbors, the "evident peril" which constitutes effective blockades.

coasts, numbering one hundred and twenty-seven. This is rather more troublesome to navigation than the obstruction of one or two passes at Charleston.

CHAPTER VI.

CONCLUSION OF THE FIRST PART.

I SHOULD be wanting in frankness were I to conclude this first part without briefly expressing the thought that has weighed on me while writing. In studying what the attitude of Europe has been for nearly a year, I have been forced more than once to ask myself what it may become.

Yes, Europe, under certain given circumstances, may resume her policy and carry it through to the end, instead of stopping half way; a decisive resolution may be taken; some disaster to the North may give the signal for extreme resolutions; some unforeseen incident may furnish the pretext which was vainly demanded for a moment from the blockade or the obstruction of Charleston harbor; the distress of the manufacturing districts may increase to such a degree as to force the powers, as it were, to action; the first blast, the precursor of a storm, which came to us the other day from Salford, and which was afterward appeased, may be followed by a fearful tempest; the debates in Parliament may bring forth later manifestations of a nature to precipitate events.

All this is possible, possible, though far from probable, to my mind. Already, I admit, leading men have taken sides in favor of intervention, and have signalled out the "paper blockade" to the indignation of the working classes. The idea of "opening a road for cotton" has been recommended to those who live by cotton, and who have hitherto so honorably withheld these scruples which have just been so lavishly displayed. They were afraid of becoming allies of slavery—but slavery is not in question! They were afraid of violating the rights of the United States—but the United States have no rights, and their blockade is not a blockade! They were afraid of kindling war—but there will be war only to secure peace!

Thus the cause of the South—who would have believed it?—may become almost popular. Did not journals important through their ministerial relations, the *Observer* and the *Morning Post*, issue to the people, before the recent awakening of public opinion, news designed to maintain the chances and the hopes of the South? They announced from time to time that European mediation was resolved upon, and was about to be imposed on the people of the United States.

That this was a falsehood, I know. The Emperor, on opening the Assembly, has declared formally in the name of France, that so long as the rights of neutrals are respected, we will not meddle with the quarrels of the United States. The Queen's address and the speeches of the ministers have announced the maintenance of a neutral policy. Notwithstanding, there exists a current of opinions, or rather interests, which still threatens to draw in Europe some day, if we do not succeed in mastering its power.

That we will master it, I have confidence; but it is necessary for this that we all do our best; it is necessary for this that, without hesitation, without miserable calculations of prudence, we expose the worthlessness of false theories and erroneous assertions. Never was more important mission confided to men of heart. Already, the glorious reaction which is appearing in England, has come to prove that we are not mistaken in defending principles and counting upon them.

Let us give our attention to principles, nor be anxious about events. Be events what they may, they will work no change in principles. If Europe should ever throw her sword into the balance and recognize the South, the act will become none the better by reason of its accomplishment. We will not have, therefore, in any case, to repent of our resistance.

To recognize the South! I cannot comprehend how such a measure can be recommended, even in the point of view of material interests. When the conflict shall have been thus exasperated, when war to the death shall have commenced, when revolutionary measures shall have been employed, nothing will be left but to bow the head and yield to ruin.

I hope that we may succeed in avoiding this extremity; nevertheless, the fact remains that the right will have been violated, and that violated right is always avenged. On the day when Europe shall say to America, "I intervene, because it is of importance that my commerce be reëstablished, because I cannot indefinitely endure your dissensions, because the delay fixed by me has expired;" on that day, an act of injustice will have been done. No one is ignorant of the condition of regular recognition. We recognize governments *de facto*, who have secured their independence. Even when the destruction of an enemy has been in question, France has never consented to proclaim a premature recognition. Without going out of America, as I have already said, we find a decisive proof of this. The insurrection of the English colonies took place in 1773; the battle of Bunker Hill was won in 1775; 1777 saw the victory at Saratoga and the surrender of Burgoyne; yet, notwithstanding, the French government waited till the following year to recognize the United States. Six years of war and of decisive advantages, with the acquired certainty that the independence could be no longer seriously menaced, were necessary at that time to legitimatize recognition. Why is less necessary to-day? Why would our century, so justly in favor of non-intervention, admit this form of intervention in a struggle which is not ended?

We have been told again and again that we can recognize the South, and yet remain neutral! As we could not recognize it to-day and suffer it to be invaded to-morrow, it is certain that the recognition would lead to an armed intervention. This would be, therefore, a rupture with the United States. That it might not be followed by immediate war, I willingly admit, for the Union would doubtless give way before a hopeless struggle. But what a peace would this be! What a fund of hatred reserved for the future! And what a crisis for our manufactures!

I doubt whether France will then congratulate herself for having destroyed her work of the last century, and whether England will be greatly proud of having struck hands with the champions of slavery.

This is the chance which I have been obliged to force myself to look in the face. I have pointed it out; I will not wrong Europe by dwelling on it. A word only, addressed to the Americans.

They know now on what to rely. It is generally believed among us that they are not making war in earnest, that they will end by drowning themselves in preparations, that their expenses of two million dollars a day will exhaust their last remaining resources, that their war will soon be brought to an end by the force of circumstances.

It is for them to demonstrate by facts that these are so many calumnies. Their armies are ready, their fleets are built, the season favorable to operations in the South has arrived; the question is to go forward with energy, and inaugurate an era of brilliant successes. At the price which their war is unfortunately costing them, it is necessary that it be short, under pain of becoming impossible. Their paper currency disquiets their best friends.

They have a few months of real security before them —a few months, no more. Let there be no illusion on this point! If, in a few months, the superiority of the North be not established, if the issue of the conflict remain in the least doubtful, seditious interests will perhaps intervene in favor of the South.

To act to-day, therefore, to act quickly, to act energetically—such is the first article of their programme.

And this is now the second:

In case that, contrary to all appearances, the campaign which is about to open should not result in the brilliant triumph of the North; in case that, contrary once more to all appearances, the decisive successes of the North and the measures taken by it for the progressive abolition of slavery in the conquered South should not bring forth the manifestation of the Union sentiments now suppressed, it would then be necessary to take one of those difficult resolutions which a great people should know how to adopt at need. To take necessities into account, to see things as they are, to be resigned to what cannot be helped, is also to serve one's country.

He who is resigned too soon, is cowardly; he who is resigned too late, is in danger of entering into conflict with the very designs of God. Perhaps God has willed precisely the course that grieves us most; perhaps, according to his sovereign plans, emancipation must be wrought by separation; perhaps the South must be chastised by its victory; perhaps the uprising must be accomplished through great sorrows.

If this should be unhappily true, it would be wisdom to recognize and become openly resigned to it. After an unfortunate or inefficient campaign, when the mediation of Europe should be offered, (and it would be in this case, without doubt,) when the question should be to order new Treasury bonds, to brave ruin, to hasten to bankruptcy, to defy the great allied powers, to undertake a new war, a colossal war, a hopeless war, good citizens would be those who should counsel peace.

It costs me an effort to write this; but I should fail in my duty if I did not say all that I think. I love America too well not to prefer the danger of displeasing to that of disserving it. I hope for its success; I count on it; for I know that it is fighting for justice, and there is victory in the word. It may be, however, that we are mistaken; the victories which God has in store for the North may be of a nature which we have not foreseen; they will consist, perhaps, in the first place, of completing the work of emancipating the slaves and rehabilitating the free negroes within its own borders; then in effecting the same work, by its example, in the States which have seceded from it; then, it may be, in bringing them back some day, when isolation shall have borne its bitter fruits, and when the great cause of discord shall have disappeared.

However this may be, if we have the unexpected pain of witnessing the unsuccessfulness of the Federal arms and the combined mediation of the European powers, we will offer up ardent prayers that the United States may resolutely accept all the consequences of such a position. There is no glory to be lost, but a great deal to be gained in simply accepting what cannot be prevented.

We must foresee every thing, even what is improbable. It would be no trifling thing, moreover, to reduce the army and expenditures, to bring back the former prosperity, to recall European immigration, to withdraw the paper currency, to pay debts, to reëstablish liberties a moment suspended, to strengthen institutions. The present war has its perils; all the friends of America are troubled at seeing it forced to repudiate for a time some of its glorious traditions; its six hundred thousand soldiers please them but little, any more than their expenditure of two or three millions per day. They cannot help fearing that, the war ended, the free America of former times will not again be found. If any thing could console them for a peace favorable to the independence of the South, it would be the thought that this would also seal the independence of the North. Delivered at length from the yoke which had weighed on its institutions and policy, it would recover the liberty of becoming again itself. The difficulties of a partial separation—difficulties, doubtless, most real, and which the makers of projects do not take sufficiently into account, are not to be compared, considerable as they may be, with the difficulties of another nature which the least plan of conquest and armed occupation would involve in its train.

To tell the truth, the North would be itself for the first time, for hitherto the baleful influences of the South have corrupted every thing. The South, with its slavery, with its unsound and illiberal democracy, with its spirit of conquest and strife, with its contempt for the right of nations, with its hatred of Europe, with its break-neck policy, with its repudiations of debts, with its laws for fugitive slaves, with its pretensions and violence, unceasingly lowered the moral and social level of the United States. Every thing was going, beginning with self-respect. A few years more of this rude prosperity, and all would have been over with the United States.

Now, the United States have reappeared. Whether they triumph over the rebellion, as I count upon their doing, or are forced to accept manfully the consequences of a reverse and European mediation, they are about to know the greatness of liberty and justice, while awaiting what the future has in store for them.

ENGLAND.

PART SECOND.

CHAPTER I.

TWO NATIONS IN ENGLAND.

OUR work would be of no value, if, confining ourselves to estimating the general attitude of Europe, we neglected to study more closely the conduct of Englishmen. It is among them that the true, the vital, and practical questions are propounded; it is among them that we are to seek their solutions. With respect to the United States and the crisis through which they are passing, England has the chief authority.

This is not due only to the ties of blood which unite her to America, to the importance of her commercial relations with it, to the solidarity established between her manufactures and American cotton, of which she alone absorbs two-thirds; a nobler motive imposes on her a special responsibility—as slavery is in question, all Europe has instinctively recognized the competence of the nation which has been honored by its great act of emancipation.

Nowhere else, moreover, not even in France, as we must modestly acknowledge, could the events in America alarm so many interests, and nowhere else, it seems to me, should they attract so many sympathies. The English opposition to the cause of the North would naturally be violent; the English adhesion to the cause of the North would naturally be enthusiastic.

If the first of these previsions alone has been realized during many months, this proceeds from causes which it is important to examine with care in order to find a remedy. Whatever may be done, indeed, it is probable that the chief initiative in all that concerns the United States will continue to belong to England. Faithful to an alliance, the maintenance of which is of importance to the whole world, France, without abdicating her free will, will nevertheless as far as possible avoid separating her action from that of England. I have no hesitation, therefore, in turning to the latter, and calling her to account for an attitude which has disappointed so many hopes. Why has England been so cold? Why has England had so long for Mr. Lincoln's government neither encouragement nor equity?

England, I am happy to say, is beginning to question herself upon this point; the land of Wilberforce is awakening and becoming itself again. Would that, in recalling what it has done or suffered to be done during the past year, I might second its generous return to good!

A first reflection strikes me—the same which presented itself when I examined the attitude of Europe, the same which has besieged me from one end to the other of this work—how much evil might have been avoided by simply maintaining the action of principles! And here I do not speak only of the sympathy due to those who have risen to prevent, by means of great personal sacrifices, the extension of slavery; I speak also of the respect due to the right. Suppose for a moment that England, without even giving way to her abolition sympathies, had taken the side of the right, her conduct would have no longer encountered either difficulties or embarrassments.—Here is justice and there injustice; here is a president regularly elected, and there are men in insurrection against the free constitution of their country, their flag, and their oaths; well, we are on the side of justice, which is also that of liberty. Without intervening, without meddling with that which does not concern us, we will maintain our natural relations with the Government of the United States; and as to the Southerners, we owe them nothing, we are determined to see in them only what they are, rebels against the law, rebels in favor of slavery.

It has been a source of pleasure to me, in pursuing this work, to discover everywhere the confirmation of one of my oldest and most cherished convictions—the immense value of principles. There is no right against right—to practise justice, such is the only simple, luminous, effective, and truly useful policy.

Suppose for a moment that England had had no other policy than this, what would have happened? Civil war would have been prevented or abridged; a painful misunderstanding would not have weighed upon the relations of two great peoples; grievances and chances of war would not have been infinitely multiplied; there would have been much less suffering; cordial relations would have been strengthened in the Old World as in the New.

There are hours of struggle and peril when the least encouragement, the slightest grasp of a friendly hand, leaves ineffaceable memories. They are seeds of love and friendship, sown in ready prepared soil. What we sow to-day, we shall reap hereafter.

In sketching this picture, I have described in advance and by way of contrast, the sad effects of a policy in which principles are treated as follies—a policy which, fearing before every thing to appear sentimental, seems to take pleasure in doing the opposite on all points to what the instinct of justice would prescribe. To establish no difference between right and rebellion, to take delight in displaying an impartiality little in conformity with the rights of nations, to abound in suspicions and scruples with respect to those who are defending the cause of law and liberty, to invent favorable interpretations and privileged positions in behalf of those who are treading under foot the national constitution at the same time with humanity, to discover that the separation might be useful before asking whether it be just, to impose silence on indignation and sympathy, not even to be disquieted about the balefulness and immorality that must at all events arise from the triumph of iniquity, to refuse the glorious rôle which offers itself to England, to let go the occasion of proving once more to the world that she sets something above her interests, and that the Bible can beat back cotton in case of need, to turn her back upon the only chance of conciliating at once the friendship of America and the esteem of Europe without entering, moreover, in any manner into the quarrel of the North and South—such are the advantages which have been procured by force of distrusting the candid application of principles. It would have been too malignant, indeed, to have admitted with the first comer that slavery was at the bottom of the difference, that the adversaries of slavery should be preferred before its partisans, that, in any case, the result of an election should be respected, that right was right, that the national Government was the national Government, and that the insurrection was an insurrection.

What, therefore, has occurred? The American people, which expected much of England, has experienced with respect to it a disappointment full of bitterness. Friendship has been wounded and confidence mistaken—great evil has been wrought. It counted on the relationship, the natural alliance of free peoples; it counted, before all, on the cordial support of the nation which had expended a million of dollars and overcome the resistance of interests to emancipate the slaves of its colonies. They beheld meetings in advance, they fancied that they already heard the pleadings of orators; parliament was about to resound with encouragement and friendly exhortation to America; the churches were about to rise in turn; the Christian public, the living bond of the two countries, was about to learn the meaning of the glorious mission in store for it; Americans were about to hear the cry from all sides: "We are with you; we entreat you not to fall back or stagger in your enterprise. It is a difficult one—to arrest the growth of slavery and then ensure its gradual suppression, is to accomplish the greatest social revolution which a people has ever been permitted to pursue on earth. Courage! You will set a noble example, you will do more than we ourselves have done for the cause of abolition. You will devote to it more efforts, more sacrifices, more money, and more blood; but you will succeed, and your success will ensure the final triumph of emancipation in the whole world."

This is what was hoped of England. It was hoped with the more confidence, that the Prince of Wales had scarcely quitted the American soil, where an enthusiastic welcome had appeared to seal the lasting forgetfulness of old quarrels. This confidence was such that, deceived at the first moment, it was nevertheless persevered in with touching obstinacy. Men could not resign themselves to hearing no word of affection from beyond the seas. The day of peril had come, it was impossible that friends, kindred, and brothers should not take their part in this honorable distress, accepted for the service of humanity. They waited long; they long repeated to themselves that there was some mistake, that the nature of the conflict was not yet comprehended by England. At length it was necessary to yield to evidence—the evil, a mysterious evil, had done more harm than had been believed. With icy sang-froid, the English nation signified to America, that its struggle was of interest to no one, that the flag of slavery displayed by the South was revolting to no one, that the success of the South dismayed no one, that the dismemberment of the United States saddened no one.

No one! I go too far in saying this, and honorable exceptions should be signalled out; but these exceptions have been so rare, expressions of sympathy have been so nearly lacking, the leading organs of public opinion have treated America with so much rudeness, that indifference has been the incontestable attitude of the nation.

I say these things without circumspection, because I say them without hatred. My affection has also suffered decline—a decline resembling the grief which we experience when a friend disappoints, by some action, the esteem in which we have held him. And where is the friend of liberty that would not be a friend of England? Far from wishing it harm, we consider its good as much as that of America itself, when we deplore the culpable coldness of which it has just given proof. We feel that impartiality has its penalties; one suffers on both sides.

At no price would I wish to join in the mad declamations which are hurled against "perfidious Albion." I will not say, for I do not think that her policy is always unscrupulous, that she never yields to a generous impulse. When she arms her volunteers, when she increases a navy whose superiority is the very condition of its existence, I am neither astonished nor irritated thereby. Petty jealousies with respect to it have never touched my heart, and if the punishment of its conduct toward America should rebound on its head, I would be the first to be grieved by it.

It is precisely for this reason that my remarks may be of use. An accusation would be wounding; the expression of the grief of a friend, the organ of many others, may find its way to the conscience.

There are two nations in England. Whoever does not begin by admitting this, must renounce all hope of understanding the history of this strange country.

There are two nations, I say it to the glory of England. How many peoples are there, among whom energetic reactions toward good are unknown! How many countries are there, whose rivers flow smoothly down an even slope, where no block of granite ever falls to turn aside the current! Blocks of granite have fallen into the current of England.

Oftenest, doubtless, the river turns aside, then descends tranquilly to the sea, while nothing announces that an obstacle has disturbed the flow of the waters. These are the epochs of inertia, languor, and forgetfulness of principles; a policy then prevails, not more selfish, perhaps, than the policy of other governments, but less attached to forms, and more offensive, by reason of unceremoniousness and bad taste. But suddenly a reaction is wrought; a great moral truth comes to light, agitation becomes diffused, a superior force arises in opposition to the power of habits and interests. Humanity then wins one of its victories. To-day, it is the abolishment of the slave trade; to-morrow, it will be the abolition of slavery; the day after, Catholic emancipation; then, the reform of Parliament; then, the protective system. There will be extended investigations, there will be persevering efforts to obtain religious liberty everywhere, there will be powerful sympathies in favor of the independence of peoples. When Christian and liberal England rises, when its journals and meetings begin to protest against a great social iniquity, we feel that this will not be a passing and feeble desire, a well-meaning caprice, such as we have witnessed too often, but a fixed design which will be pursued to the end with that manly energy which delays discourage no more than reverses.

Before the reactions of which I speak, the common traditions of the British administration always yield in the end. We know in what manner the crimes of the Indian government were openly denounced in Parliament. We know what voices were raised, even during the American war to obtain the independence of the United States. If, some day, the opium trade should succumb, upon which I count, it will fall, be sure, beneath the blows of a moral reaction aroused in England.

This is how it happens that English history contains so many contrasts, so much good, and so much evil. He who sees nothing but the evil, is in the wrong; he who sees nothing but the good, is likewise in the wrong. There are two nations, I repeat. When unprincipled England grieves us, let us turn with confidence toward liberal and Christian England! Thank God! the latter is constantly gaining ground. For fifty years, it has not ceased, as it were, to give battle. For a moment in torpor, it was not long in awaking. It is at hand, it is advancing; a little late, doubtless, but nevertheless in time; it is about to reform with its generous hand the policy pursued with respect to the United States.

We must be patient; English reactions are always somewhat slow. This proceeds, it is just to remark, from a sentiment of patriotism. Before openly attacking the conduct of their country, especially outside itself, the English usually begin by associating themselves with it. Their instinct urges them to form one body, to see nothing at first but the British flag. Independence of opinion is lacking them at the first moment, and their ministers of foreign affairs are almost sure to be followed. But, by degrees, they reflect, they become enlightened, they discuss, they redeem by great noise and energy the docility of the beginning.

How could it be otherwise, among a people reared for so many years in the school of free discussion? For six or seven centuries, England has possessed her *Magna Charta*, her *Habeas Corpus*, her Parliament, and her jury; for more than two centuries, these institutions, mere forms under the Tudors, have been the sovereign and indestructible law of the land. England had her freemen when we had only courtiers; she had her great parliamentary struggles at the epoch of our *petits abbés*. Brilliant on other sides, and needing to envy no one in point of glory, it would ill become us to despise the country of Russell, Sydney, and Defoe, the nation which escaped by force of vigor from the fearful peril of the Stuarts pensioned by Louis XIV., and charged with disciplining England according to the French method of the time. If we resemble it too little to fully comprehend it, it seems to me that nothing hinders us from rendering it justice.

It is a strange spectacle, which certainly has its greatness—a people which now suffers itself to be dragged down almost to degradation by those who govern it, and which then rises up with incomparable energy, confessing its faults, attacking the wrong, its own crimes, beginning and pursuing one of those searching investigations which end in reform; a people in which the moral sense speaks loudly; a people among whom uprisings against injustice are something else than the caprice or fashion of a moment. How many generous voices have been raised since that of Burke! How many liberties have been laboriously won, by speech, by perseverance, without shedding blood or overthrowing the Constitution—the liberty of slaves, religious liberty, political liberty, commercial liberty, colonial liberty! This powerful England, where designs endure and are carried into action, where the reclamations, I should say, the outbursts of the human conscience redeem the sometimes odious acts of an unscrupulous policy—this England, which makes itself hated by good right, and which makes itself loved by better right still—are we justified in judging it by the evil which it was near doing, without remembering the good which it has accomplished?

It is the most liberal, yet least revolutionary of all peoples. A loyal nation, loving its Queen, plunged entire into mourning by the death of Prince Albert, it has never confounded progress with levelling, it has never believed that respect for the law could be contrary to the passion for liberty. Faithful to its ancient traditions, conservative without being stagnant, it looks in the face its three mortal enemies—the spirit of absolutism, the spirit of conquest, and the spirit of revolution.

A heroic nation, our equal on the battle field, England has escaped from the mania of uniforms and plumes; by her instincts, by her interests, by the influence of the Gospel, she loves peace.

I have spoken of the Gospel; therein—why shall it not be said?—therein is found the source of those great moral reactions which, becoming more and more frequent since the religious awakening has strengthened its empire, will end, ere long, by transforming English policy. Formerly, English policy was in bad repute, and, frankly speaking, it deserved to be. More cynical than Machiavellian, placarding, exaggerating its selfishness as if designedly, little pharisaical, but very gross, it seemed to have taken upon itself the task of provoking and defying hatred.

To-day, all this has changed. If a few antiquated spirits still repeat the *civis sum Romanus* of British pride, if the cry of war against America has been repeated for a moment by the crowd, if the disposition rudely to break down all resistance is still manifested here and there, a better disposition is also making its appearance, another people is rising.

This other people is that which gives its gold to spread through the world the word of God, which courageously undertakes the mission at home and the healing of the gaping wounds of pauperism, which believes, which prays, which consecrates itself, which endows its country (a strange fact, which we cannot enough admire) with a literature decidedly moral, which accosts Christianity on the side of holiness and duty, which links together with jealous care the chain of faith and of good works. This is the people whose persevering sympathies for all that is generous has forced policy to bow before justice.

CHAPTER II.

CONDUCT OF ENGLAND.

There was need of writing the preceding pages; they will explain and corroborate those which are about to follow. If it be our duty to resist evil, it is also our duty to believe in good.

This duty, we rarely fulfil; for want of not fulfilling it, our criticism resembles hatred.

Hatred never served a good cause. I know neither men here below who are all of a piece, nor nations who are wholly devoted to perverse designs. The South itself, I have taken care to say, contains many more sincere men and noble hearts than we should suppose if we judged it by its institutions or passions, forgetting to take into account the influence of surroundings.

I will remain an optimist with respect to England as I have been, it is said, with respect to the United States. To be an optimist is usually to be right. Our grumbling age, which willingly fastens on the dark side of things, would fall into misanthropy and discouragement if no one showed it the bright side.

I wish to define in a few words, without either enlarging or extenuating, the grave fault with which I have to reproach England.

To pretend that she has taken part with the South, or even that she has deliberately wished for the separation of the South, would be to go beyond the truth. Her crime is that of having been indifferent. Her moral neutrality is what has dismayed and grieved to the soul all those who remember her true claims to glory.

On the 1st of August, 1834, when eight hundred thousand human beings passed from slavery to liberty, England contracted a solemn engagement, for which the public opinion of the whole world should hold her to account. Since that day, there has not been an enemy of slavery who has not looked toward her shores, there has not been a poor negro whose heart has not beat at her name, there has not been a slave trader who has not dreaded, before every thing, the appearance of the British flag. If Portugal and Brazil have renounced the slave trade, it has been through the urgent demands of England; if Spain feels her odious practices in Cuba menaced, it is because there is an England to reproach her with them publicly. Let her seize upon Whydah and Lagos, and all will applaud; even those whose jealousy is most alarmed by her aggrandizements, know that Lagos would be an advanced post from which she would watch over, and ere long put down the infamous King of Dahomey.

The greatness of England is in the principle which she represents. Even though she should lose Gibraltar and Corfu, and I believe that she will lose them some day, even though she should lose Canada itself and her Indian empire, she will suffer no diminution, provided she remain the land of political liberty, of religious liberty, and of negro liberty.

Ah, well! we who do not wish the decline of England, we who do not talk of its "corrupt institutions" have suffered from its attitude during the past year beyond what I can express.

For a year, its leading journals have had little else than mockeries or insults for America striving to uprise. The fall of the Southern supremacy, which had debased and was on the point of destroying every thing, has been applauded by no one. The English government has accorded the title of belligerents at the outset to the Southern rebels. As to the American nation, the only one which it should have known officially, it has not given it the moral support of a word of sympathy.

I need not go further to become indignant. Violated right has not moved these champions of right; liberty at stake has not moved these champions of liberty. Their impartiality in such a matter has been one of the scandals of our times.

Let no one mistake my thought! England had to intervene in nothing; even though she had not elevated the insurgents to the rank of belligerents, she would have been bound not to act. Woe to the country whose civil wars witness the unfurling of a foreign flag! It was necessary therefore to be impartial, but not in the manner that has been seen. We shall have fallen very low on the day when, under the pretext of remaining neutral, great nations shall affect to distinguish no longer between good and evil. I strive to be moderate, in order to remain just. To the crime of indifference, I will not join that of complicity with the South. All sorts of rumors have been spread abroad, which I refrain from accepting. The early recognition of the South was nearly fixed upon several times! The separation of the South and North was considered as an advantage to be preserved by all means! The incident of the *Trent* furnished a pretext to the policy of the cabinet! In default of this pretext, others would have been sought, if public opinion had not been at length aroused!

That this may have been true of some members of the cabinet, it seems to me difficult to doubt; but that Earl Russell, Mr. Gladstone and still others would have accepted such a programme, who could believe? Many things are said as times go, and the evil desires that flash at moments across the imagination of statesmen are easily transformed into systems.

I adhere, for my part, to the public acts of the English Government. It has addressed serious warnings to the shipowners who have announced their design of trafficking with Southern ports; it has refused to inquire into the efficiency of the blockade at a time when the blockade was not as efficient as it is to-day; it has repulsed, in fine, the overtures which have been certainly made to it by the agents of Jefferson Davis, commissioned to promise every thing—every thing, even to the liberty of unborn children, in exchange for recognition. It is evident that, in concert with France, it insures some months of security to the military operations of the North.

This is little; it cannot be said that it is nothing. If the English Government has made a show of a lamentable indifference, if it has encouraged the rebellion by avoiding to say from the beginning what would have discouraged it, it has given proof of some merit, notwithstanding, in restraining the impatience of the manufacturing population. In other times and among other peoples, an interest as colossal as that of the cotton manufacture would not have been long in dictating the law. It is honorable to the age in which we live, that such a victory of matter over mind has been hitherto impossible, and that, in the presence of a country which has not permitted it, we have a right to censure more than praise. It ought to do still better. We esteem it too much to judge its conduct to have been worthy of it.

I maintain this judgment, although I regret moreover the accusations of different kinds which have been directed against the English government. If it suffered the *Nashville*, which had just burned an American merchant ship, to enter the harbor of Southampton, it only conformed in this to the rules of neutrality; the *Sumter* has also been able to take shelter successively at Martinique, Cadiz, and Gibraltar, without authority having been given by the law of nations to the French, Spanish, or English governments, to give her up to the American ships in pursuit of her.

Even with respect to the export of arms and ammunition to the rebellious South, the English government may maintain that it has strictly fulfilled its international obligation. I say "strictly," for it is certain that with a little good will, and by the terms of the Queen's proclamation, which forbade exportations of this nature, it might have succeeded in preventing whole fleets, under its eyes, in the midst of the Thames, and in sight of Downing street, from being loaded with arms, addressed to Charleston. In Canada, shipments of this sort have not ceased to take place. Would nothing have been obtained by repeated warnings, by the energetic manifestation of the blame that would be incurred by such operations? In any case, patience has been carried somewhat far.

This has also been true in other circumstances. When the outbreak of the rebellion took place in the South, impolitic men were found there who were not afraid of showing the horror inspired in them by abolition England. An English captain of a merchant vessel was tarred and feathered. Usually, the English government is most prompt, for which I praise it, in avenging such insults; it must have a public, striking reparation. What happened this time? The affair was brought by Mr. Duncombe before the House of Commons, which found the thing amusing, since it burst into laughter. The ministry talked of inquiry; and the whole was doubtless ended by some trifling indemnity, accorded under the rose to the tarred and feathered captain.

In the same manner, English subjects were enrolled by force in the Southern army, and English property was confiscated. Was reclamation made? I know not. One thing is certain; noise was avoided. Impartiality, as it was then understood, exacted this caution.

But when the point in question is to estimate rightly the conduct of a country like England, we are not to rely upon considering the acts of government, but to read journals, to hear speeches, and to interrogate parties. The policy of the nation is formed there much more than in the council chamber of the ministry.

The importance and influence of the *Times* are well known. The *Times* has given the tone, we may say, to English opinion with respect to America, and this from the beginning. From the first moment, it maintained, with that capricious abruptness for which it is distinguished, that slavery had nothing to do with the separation of the North and South, that the disruption was final, that it was desirable and right, that the Washington cabinet was at once insane and criminal in fighting against the Richmond government, that abolition would speedily find its account in Southern independence, that the insurgents had been raised by good right to the character of belligerents.

Since opinion in England has shaken off its torpor, and

the prospect of an alliance with Jefferson Davis has aroused the public conscience, the *Times* has modified its bearing. We have seen it, now recommending a sort of relative moderation in the *Trent* affair; then returning to its former violence, and exploiting, with passionate injustice, the stone blockade of Charleston. Nevertheless, upon the whole, it has become marvellously calm; it does not recommend the violation of the blockade, it has even published strong and noble words to demonstrate to the English that to cease now to recognize the blockade would be to degrade the national policy. Its theory, until further orders, is absolute neutrality.

It has even had a few satirical strokes here and there for the slave States; and no one has forgotten the article in which, recommending that no ovation should be prepared for Messrs. Mason and Slidell, it signified to them in fitting terms that England esteemed neither their cause nor their person, and that she would have done for "two negroes" precisely what she had done for them.

The *Times* is impartial in its way, for it spares no one. It is also impartial in a more honorable manner, inasmuch as it admits full liberty to its correspondents, who repair, in some degree, the harm produced by the leading editorship.

This is essential; for the *Times* correspondents are often men of the greatest merit, and through them are pursued investigations full of energy, perseverance, and clearsightedness. Important services were thus rendered by the *Times* in the Crimean campaign, and even those who were angered by its articles were forced to admit that, without it, the reform of the military administration would not have taken place.

Mr. Russell, the *Times* correspondent in America, has followed and recounted the march of events with little goodwill, doubtless, but with a sincerity and talent which cannot be denied. His letters, nearly all of which have been copied by the American journals, have not been useless to Mr. Lincoln's government. The admonitions therein are sometimes severe, but often salutary. Without rendering—far from it—full justice to the North, Mr. Russell is not at least among those who are mistaken in the true causes of the war or the chances of success. He has the merit of cordially detesting the South and saying so.

I have been anxious to signalize this spirit of serious inquiry, this search into facts which characterizes the organ of the city, even at the times when it wanders most astray. It would be impossible for me to pay the same compliment to the journal which passes for expressing the ideas of Lord Palmerston. The *Morning Post* has not extenuated, by the impartiality of its correspondence, the violence of its leading articles. To deny the successes of the North, to exaggerate with enthusiasm those of the South, to be irritated at every thing that could increase the chances of the Washington Government, to be indignant when the Orleans princes generously placed their swords at the service of the United States, frequently to announce recognition as almost certain, if not immediate, to deny the legality of the blockade, to discover in the obstruction of Charleston harbor a veritable cause of war, to renounce as tardily as possible the occasion furnished by the *Trent*, and to seek directly for another to take its place, to give out the impression, in fine, that the patience of England is well-nigh exhausted; such are the principal features of a line of argument which has profoundly alarmed the friends of America, and no less profoundly grieved the friends of England. At times, it is true, the *Morning Post* has seemed to change tactics; we have seen it once offer resistance to those in too much haste, and the recent progress of public opinion has wrought a transformation in its editorship. Nevertheless, it has done immense harm, through the sole fact that men have thought that they saw in this editorship the more or less faithful reflection of the prime minister's ideas. This, perhaps, will be now denied; I had rather, I confess, it had been denied a little sooner.

As to the journals of the Tory party, their opinions cannot be doubtful—England must procure cotton, "by fair means or foul;" such has been the profession of faith, brief and clear, of the *Morning Herald.* Toward the end of January, moreover, it demanded that ships-of-war should be stationed before all the Southern ports to insure freedom of trade to neutral merchant vessels!

Has there been, then, no journal in England which has defended the right cause, and been faithful to the liberal traditions of the country? Let us forbear to believe it. The *Daily News*, which is regarded as the habitual organ of Earl Russell, the *Star*, the *Globe*, the *Scotsman*, the *London Quarterly Review*, and several others have opposed the *Times*, the *Morning Post*, and the *Morning Herald.* The cheap press, whose importance cannot be mistaken, has also declared itself, since the *Trent* affair, in favor of a less provoking and more courteous course of conduct. Decidedly, a reaction is becoming wrought, and principles are being arrayed in battle against interests, while waiting till men shall have learned fully to comprehend that interests have no better allies than principles.

It is a remarkable fact that the distinction of Whig and Tory, which tends to become effaced in the home policy of England, seems to preserve its full value with respect to America. The Tories on this point have learned nothing, and forgotten nothing; they are still with Lord Chatham, ordering himself carried to the House of Lords, and protesting with his dying voice against the proposition to recognize the United States. The United States always represent in their sight a rebellion which must be punished, a republic which must be humiliated, a rival navy which must be weakened. One would call it an article of faith of the *Quarterly Review*, *Blackwood's Magazine*, and their readers, that there is nothing good in the United States, that every American is a bankrupt, that the mob governs, that Lynch law is applied at the corner of every street, that the ridiculous and the odious jostle each other unceasingly in American society. The Tories once reproached Earl Russell for having abandoned "moral neutrality" by uttering a few words in Parliament on the abominations of slavery. On the occasion of the annual dinner of the Conservative Colchester Association, they attempted a great demonstration in favor of the South; Captain Jervis openly proposed there to break the blockade, to support the slave States, and thus to put an end to the sufferings of the cotton manufacture. Despite the lesson which had been given them by public opinion, in which, it must be admitted, so emphatic a policy had found no support, a number of the leading members of the party, Sir John Packington, General Peel, Major Beresford, Lord Derby himself, and Mr. D'Israeli have, some, encouraged the tendencies of Lord Palmerston, others, given out the impression that a Tory cabinet, not content with placing the South among belligerents, will manage ere long to give it a place among recognized governments.

We know what passed at the dinner of the Fishmongers' Corporation. This important body had invited Mr. Yancey, the Commissioner sent to London by Jefferson

Davis. There, in the presence of a sympathizing assembly, amidst unanimous applause, this representative of the slave States could not forbear exclaiming: "The word *America* no longer represents a united people; there now exist two American nationalities." Then, alluding to the name of *rebels* which the North pretended to apply to Southern men, he continued: "Thanks to this great English movement, promptly followed by France and Spain, justice and the sentiment of right have quickly effaced such a stigma from our brows, and here, at least, my fellow-countrymen are recognized as belligerents." He concluded by expressing the gratitude of the South for this prompt proclamation of its right: *Bis dat qui cito dat*—"Who gives quickly gives twice." And the assembly, which was not ignorant that the proclamation had been *prompt* indeed, responded by prolonged huzzas.

At the other extremity of the political world, two radicals, Messrs. Roebuck and Lindsay, have shown no more good will for the North. Mr. Roebuck has applied himself to recalling the insolence, the presumption, the recent insults whereby America has alienated all the sympathies of England. As to Mr. Lindsay, the former guest of the United States, where he held a mission, he appears to be one of those champions of free trade who inspire us with a horror of it by sacrificing thereto every other principle and every other liberty. He does not wish the blockade to be respected; he applauds the separation; he admits that the South can arm *a million men;* he demands, in fine, that England shall proceed to official recognition. We will add that the Sunderland electors, until then, most lavish of applause, had the good sense to become indignant on hearing this conclusion, and courageously hissed their representative.

My task would be too great were I to make the complete round of these electoral banquets, where so many members of Parliament met before its opening to give their profession of faith respecting American affairs. These professions of faith bear a general resemblance to each other, in that the fact of separation is admitted as definitive, and that sympathy for a generous cause is entirely lacking; but ordinarily the orators have taken care to predict the success of the South without counselling England to aid it. Among the prophecies of which I speak, I shall cite that addressed at the end of last September, by Sir Edward Bulwer Lytton to the Agricultural Society of Hertford County: "My young hearers of to-day will live long enough to see not two, but at least four independent republics, sprung from the United States." There is no feeling of hatred, moreover, among those who express themselves in this wise; their motives are in some sort geographical—nations too large never fail to become shattered. "I am far from thinking," he takes care to say, "that these separations must be prejudicial to the destinies of America, or to that principle of *self-government* in which consists the essence of liberty."

I need now, and also the reader, to hear some more generous accents. There have been men, thank God! who have raised their voices to recall the true cause and the greatness of the American conflict, men who have not waited to declare themselves until the sudden change of public opinion which we have witnessed should be first produced. Without speaking of Messrs. Cobden and Bright, to whom we shall presently return in connection with the *Trent* affair, I may cite Messrs. Latham and Gilpin, who have encouraged the North to show more and more that it is struggling against slavery, and have promised it the increasing sympathies of England. Mr. Forster exclaimed at Bradford: "It would be an eternal shame to England, were we to intervene for the South and for slavery. It must not be forgotten that we shall act in this manner if we violate a legitimate blockade, or prematurely recognize the Southern Confederacy, contrary to the law of nations."

I like the speech made by Lord Stanley a few months since, at the court-house at Lynn. It is not the first time that the son of Lord Derby has acted, not only as a superior but a truly liberal man. Although admitting the probability of a final separation, his language breathes a lofty and cordial sympathy. We feel that he esteems this great people of the United States, and believes in its future. He brands the spiteful and petty passions which are indulged in with respect to it, and would abhor the idea of profiting by its embarrassment.

If we listen now, at the same epoch, that is, before the opening of Parliament, to the members of the cabinet and the personages whose influence makes itself felt in the direction of public affairs, we shall remark anew this mixture of good and evil, this proclaimed indifference, this policy of provisory neutrality to which they seem to cling while awaiting better; then other men here and there represent the better feelings of the nation.

Lord Palmerston clearly showed his icy coldness with respect to the North when, in his speech at Dover, he spoke of the "fast running which signalized the battle of Bull Run." Later, at the Lord Mayor's dinner, the prime minister expressed himself more becomingly—he pledged his country to patience, mourned over "this difference of the most deplorable character between those whom we call our cousins and allies," and offered up the most ardent wishes for peace, refusing, however, to pass any judgment on the quarrel.

Lord John Russell was less prudent, because his mind was more liberal. He did not fear to pass judgment in the House of Commons on the quarrel, openly accusing and anathematizing slavery, while adding that, in his opinion, other reasons, those of supremacy, had played the chief part. At Newcastle he manifested real interest in the United States. "It would be a great misfortune," he exclaimed, "if this free government were to crumble away."

Mr. Gladstone has also spoken; his address at Leith will remain as a shining condemnation of the passions which so nearly gave birth to war. He recognizes the noble conduct of Mr. Lincoln's government, to which he wishes justice to be rendered, and considers it a duty to labor to maintain or reëstablish the relations, not of peace only, but of reciprocal affection between the United States and England.

I conclude on this point by citing a few excellent words, addressed by the Duke of Argyle to his tenants:

"Fears have been recently expressed on the subject of the inconveniences which must result to our country from the struggle which has broken out in America, and these inconveniences are deemed so grave that there is talk of asking the government to intervene. . . . I have too high an opinion of the good sense of the people of this country to believe that it will wish to exercise such a pressure on the government, and I should add that I have too great confidence in the firmness and intelligence of the government and parliament, to believe that they will ever consent to such a pressure. . . . We will not look at the question of what is called the right of secession. No country has ever existed, to my knowledge, admitting that a part of it had a right to secede and abstract itself from its domination. . . . If the Southern States, as they loudly proclaim, believe that slavery is by no means an evil which should be tolerated only and made to cease as speedily as possible, but a divine institution, a benefaction to humanity, which should be maintained and extended, and defended till death, then it is natural that the South should rise for its protection. But in this, as in all other revolutions, those who take part in it should be finally judged by the verdict of humanity. . . . We certainly wish most ardently that the struggle may promptly cease; but there is, I must acknowledge, another wish which should stand before this in our hearts —that the end of this war, at whatever moment it may come, whether sooner or later, may be worthy of the sacrifices which it has exacted, that it may coöperate in the civilization of the world and advance the cause of human liberty."

If every one wishes neutrality, if every one continues to wish for peace, I affirm at least that every one has not wished neutrality and peace *in the same manner.* One wishes them in the manner of the *Morning Post*, and another in that of the *Daily News;* one in the manner of Lord Palmerston, and another in that of Lord Stanley, Mr. Gladstone, and the Duke of Argyle.

The fact is, that of the two nations which coexist in England, the less good is the one which, for the past year, has directed or inspired the relations with the United States. Distrust, refusal of sympathy, the theory of belligerents, neutrality coupled with indifference, the unceasing discovery of new grievances, the perpetual threat of Southern recognition, the passionate, and in some sort eager exploitation of incidents which might lead to a rupture, the far from touching resignation to the horrible consequences which this rupture would entail—such is what has been seen among Englishmen under the guidance of this first nation.

What a change since the other nation has appeared! The victory, we have a right to affirm from this time, will belong to the England of the Bible, to that which the Southern journals have dreaded and anathematized from the beginning of the conflict. "We should be sure of winning it," they said then, "through cotton and free trade, *were it not for the fanaticism against slavery* which may put a check on the friendly disposition of the British government." They were not mistaken; to those who have examined it without prejudice, Christian and liberal England has never so far hidden itself that they have not felt its presence and foreseen its speedy awaking.

This will be one of the strangest and at the same time noblest struggles of our times. The cotton crisis on one side, the Gospel and liberty on the other. Which will win? The answer at first seems doubtful, but it will not long seem so. The true sympathies go to the North; no one can longer contest it. Before every thing, justice, before every thing, humanity, before every thing, duty! England will not be made an ally of Jefferson Davis; decidedly, this will not be done. The South, which has diverted itself greatly on the score of philanthropists, is in the way to learn at its expense, that their power surpasses that of the *Times* and of Lord Palmerston.

Through the sorrow which the attitude of England has caused us during the past year, we experience a secret consolation in verifying that Christian and liberal opinion, even when torpid, has nevertheless commanded respect. Despite cotton, despite free trade, despite the annoyances of a blockade which daily clashed with the interests and pride of the English, a blockade insufficient in the beginning, and which confiscated a considerable number of the ships of Manchester and Liverpool, there has been in the heart of this energetic community, a sentiment which nc one, let him have wished it as he may, has dared offend too strongly. Every thing has been attempted; but whenever there has been question of exceeding certain limits and really sustaining the South, an obstacle has always been raised, a *veto* has always made itself heard. England, in fine, has remained neutral, in spite of all the motives which urged her to be otherwise; the moral sentiment, upon the whole, has won a victory.

I wish no proof of this from what has passed in those manufacturing centres on which reposed the hopes of the South. By their advances, they had long relieved the slaveholders; the election of Mr. Lincoln had been welcomed by them with a sort of stupor; they trembled for slavery, the programme of secession was not perhaps unknown to them. Yet such is the power of abolition opinion in England, that even here retrograde tendencies have not succeeded in taking form. On the arrival of the new Minister of the United States, Mr. Adams, the Liverpool Chamber of Commerce received him with congratulations. When the incident of the *Trent* threatened to bring about war, a numerous gathering assembled at Birmingham, with the mayor at its head, and adopted a memorial in favor of arbitration. Again, the other day, the annual meeting of the Manchester Chamber of Commerce furnished to the "cotton princes" the natural occasion for supporting the policy of intervention. What did they do, on the contrary? They were unanimous in disavowing it. Not a person was found among them who deemed it proper to declaim against the blockade. Yes, at Manchester, at Liverpool, at Birmingham, at Southampton, the generous impulse of minds is also going forth; the true English opinion is reappearing; the public conscience feels itself wounded by the system of chicanery which has lately endeavored to turn to account, now the blockade, then the stone fleet, then something else.

I do not mean to say that, in a few months, when the sufferings of manufacturers shall have still further increased,[1] formidable impatience may not be manifested. It will be then, perhaps, exclaimed: "We detest the cause of the South, and we have proved it; but necessity has no law. Although we may have no right to interfere against those whose principles are our own, nevertheless the patience of our workmen is at an end. They are dying of hunger; the war in America must end; cotton must be restored to us; with peace, prosperity must spring up anew, and the consumers of the New World resume their place in the markets."

Such is the language which, doubtless, will some day be held, if the United States do not make haste to win decisive advantages; but, in the mean time, a very different language is held, and we should applaud it. England is becoming herself again.

I have spoken of Birmingham, Manchester, and Liverpool, I might have likewise cited London. Without designing, indeed, to mention here all the English meetings, how can I forbear recalling the first that took place in the most populous quarters of the capital? The one held at Lambeth, early in December, voted an address by acclamation, demanding that the difference of the

[1] Although great, they are not yet what they threaten to become in future. Cotton has not failed hitherto; Havre and Liverpool have even exported it to America. But the dearth will show itself ere long in all its horror, unless the maritime positions, of which the North have just taken possession, give an outlet to cotton, and the discouraged South cease to prohibit its exportation.

Trent should be submitted to an arbitration; the other, held at Mary-le-Bone more recently, adopted the following resolution:

"... It is incumbent on this meeting to express the sympathies of the working men for the United States in the gigantic struggle which they are sustaining for the maintenance of the Union; to denounce to the world the disgraceful arguments of the *Times* and its contemporaries, organs of the aristocracy in favor of slavery; and to commend to the energetic expounders of public opinion the scrupulous interpretation of the doctrine of non-intervention in the affairs of the United States, and, also, the measure which, by means of commissioners especially appointed for each State, submits to arbitration all differences that may arise."

If I do not approve all the tendencies expressed or supposed in this resolution, "addressed to the cabinet at Washington as being the expression of the sentiments and opinions of the working classes in England," I find it none the less remarkable that the working men thus rebel with energy against the policy of intervention which pretends to serve their interests. There is here a symptom of moral resurrection, the weight of which cannot be mistaken.

It was also among the working population that the meeting was held at Rochdale, where the speech of Mr. Bright and the letter of Mr. Cobden protested against a warlike policy, impatient of all delay and all arbitration, and accepting without a frown the chance of striking hands in the South with slavery.

Other protests are beginning to rise up on all sides. We know what was the Guy Fawkes of 1862: upon the effigy was read in large letters: *Jefferson Davis, dealer in slavery.*

Scotland has naturally distinguished herself. There, too, the great manufacturing cities have held to the honor of repudiating the tendencies which had been attributed to them. Glasgow, one of the first, has voted an address in favor of peace with the United States.

In blaming England, (and we are to blame her, though she has been better than her policy during the past year,) in blaming England, it is important not to forget that, despite her faults, she has always contained within herself an element of resistance to evil, the influence of which has made itself felt. The Anglophobic declaimers forget this, and the consequence is that they are not in a condition to offer any explanation of it.

Why, for example, has Mr. Gregory, the champion of the South in the House of Commons, himself recoiled during the last session, nor dared make his famous speech, so much talked of in advance? Why have the splendid offers of Jefferson Davis—freedom of trade, freedom of unborn children, and all that thenceforth ensues—not succeeded in making themselves welcomed in any measure or in any form? Why has the system of non-intervention definitively supplanted the militant feeble desires which preceded, accompanied, and followed the *Trent* affair? Why has the chicanery against the blockade given place to the most inoffensive measure which closes English ports to armed vessels, and is about to deprive maritime cities of the chance spectacle of a naval battle? Why would any one be sure, or very nearly so, of being foiled in parliament, who should say there: "The South must be recognized; at least an end must be put to this war; our manufactories are standing still; we have therefore a right to regulate the affairs of America." Why did the speech of Mr. Massey receive without delay, and in Manchester itself, this crushing response: "I believe that I speak in the name of nineteen out of twenty of our manufacturers when I declare that we do not wish the aid which Mr. Massey would like to give us"? Why the indignation at the idea of a war with the United States through commiseration for the sufferings of the cotton manufacture? Because the true sentiments of England may have been veiled for a moment, but have not been destroyed.

Upon the whole, were it necessary to state in a few words the inference to be drawn from this chapter, I should say that the English have been guilty above all of indifference. And this crime is not small! They, the standard-bearers of negro liberty, they who, in such a matter, had *charge of souls*, have for long months disappointed the hopes of the entire world; they have suffered much harm to be done in their name; little was wanting—and only the goodness of God has preserved us from such a misfortune—for them to have drawn the sword against Lincoln for Jefferson Davis; they have inflicted upon us, their friends, one of the bitterest deceptions that we have ever encountered in our career. What matters it therefore to us whether they have or have not had to combat designs conceived by other powers in favor of the violation of the blockade or Southern recognition? If they have opposed them, it was because it was their nature to do it. It was so truly their mission that we should hardly know how to give them credit for having fulfilled it. So long as they have not done something better, so long as their warm sympathies have not come to the encouragement of those struggling for a good cause, we shall not offer them the insult of praising them.

CHAPTER III.

TRUE MOTIVES OF THE CONDUCT OF ENGLAND.

It is the characteristic of legitimate conclusions that they deduce themselves, it being necessary only to point them out. Thus, everywhere in this study, as I need not weary the reader by repeating, the marvellous power of principles breaks forth to the sight. If Europe had obeyed them, if England had listened to them, what a transformation would there have been in the policy followed! As soon as the positions again become simple, difficult questions are resolved, the chances of war recede, crises lose their violence, the standard of morality becomes elevated. At the same time, let us not forget, interests recover the satisfaction to which they have a right. Nothing is so beneficent as justice, nothing is so *useful* (I underline the word) as integrity; between principles and interests, the opposition is never real.

Therein is the fundamental idea which I should like to see evolved from my work, although I do not dream indeed of establishing it doctorally. How many times already have we been led to its verification; men have thought to serve commerce, by trampling upon principles, and they have disserved it; they have thought to gain money, and they have lost it; they have sought to bring about peace, and they have gone on toward war. "The more we avoid interference, the shorter will be the struggle," this saying was not invented by cabinet theorists, it has come to us from practical men, from great English manufacturers. They have perceived by degrees that a war for cotton would give but little cotton, and would not aid in the establishment of American consumption. Of the two causes of commercial suffering in Europe, the failure of cotton, and the failure of the markets, it would do little toward relieving the first, and would surely aggravate the second.

This leads me to examine more closely whether it be true, as is pretended, that the interests of commerce and manufactures have been almost the only motive power of England in the policy pursued by her during the past year with respect to the United States. A great deal has been said about cotton and calico! calico has been concerned in the matter, I doubt not; but there has been something else beside; reasons, if not more important, at least more elevated, have contributed their full part in determining the attitude of the English people. It is only just to show this—it is both just and salutary; for the better it is known, the better will it be comprehended, and the better also will reciprocal animosities be calmed.

As to cotton, I am far from believing that a wise government ought not to take considerations of this nature into account. In a country where the working of cotton turns thirty million spindles, and gives the means of existence to nearly four million laborers, it would be a strange magnanimity that should take high ground above the sufferings of these men, women, and children. Material interests as much as you please! They translate themselves into physical and moral miseries. Cotton become scarce ends by being regarded in the same light as other provisions in a famished garrison. Here are workmen laboring but three days, two days, one day, perhaps, in a week; others who are without any work at all, and have no other resources than the gifts of charity.

Let us hasten to say that this charity is admirable, and that the resignation of the workmen is no less so. They themselves have recognized the necessity of introducing reduced days' work, *short time*, into the manufactories; they have murmured neither against their masters nor the United States, and we have seen in what terms they have addressed the Americans.

Government has only to follow their example. While neglecting nothing, as is its duty, to alleviate and abridge the crisis, it should comprehend that to endure such a crisis for such a cause would be to effect immense progress. There is here wherewith to tempt the best ambition of England. It is unceasingly repeated that this age is an age of cotton, that cotton rules, that cotton is king; the question is to prove these assertions to be untrue. Exposed to the most formidable temptation that a manufacturing nation can encounter, it would be glorious to look it in the face, and go straight forward on its way.

The United States, in this respect, set a great example to Europe. Their factories at Lowell are suffering no less than those at Manchester and Mulhouse. No matter; duty has spoken, a noble cause must be sustained; they will accept the suffering, all classes will submit to extended privations, and we shall see the uprising of a great people.

England, it may be believed, would have more easily consented to take part in the sacrifice; she would have admitted with a better grace the excellence of the end toward which the Americans were proceeding, if the unlucky adoption of a new tariff had not occurred to bring into discredit, as it were, in the nick of time, the incipient administration of Mr. Lincoln.

It was just at the very moment of the triumph of free-trade—a free-tradist myself and a free-tradist of yesterday, I have the right to speak—and to many the economical dogma which, after having prevailed in England, had just dictated the commercial treaty with France, took the lead of every other truth.

Although the Morrill tariff was not much more protective, in fact, than the new French-English tariff; nevertheless, its appearance, just at the rising in arms of the South, did incalculable harm in England. Even friends, I cite the *Daily News*, seemed also transformed into enemies.

Men accused Mr. Lincoln, forgetting how these events had transpired. While Mr. Lincoln was on his way from Springfield to Washington, he was asked, at a great meeting at Pittsburgh, what he thought of the Morrill tariff. He replied that it ought to be postponed till the next session of Congress. Eight days afterward, Congress adopted the bill without waiting for the ensuing session, and Mr. Buchanan signed it without waiting for his successor. One would have said that he was in haste to bequeath him one difficulty more.

The South, which men are seeking to make the representative of free-trade, need have said but one word to its docile servant, Mr. Buchanan, to prevent him from giving his signature. It must be remembered besides, that the tariff of 1842, one of the most protective ever passed in the United States, was supported by the vote of the South. It must be also remembered that the free-trade of the South has hitherto figured only in its plans, and in European negotiations. The tariff of 1857, adopted by the Montgomery Congress, does not pass for a model of commercial freedom, and Jefferson Davis has taken care to join to it exportation duties which are truly enormous.

I do not impute this to it as a crime. When we have great expenses on our hands, we must make money of every thing. This explains, let us say in passing, the conduct which has been maintained at Washington. Under the presence of financial embarrassments, the government has suffered itself to believe (how many enlightened countries commit the same error!) that by increasing the duties, the receipts would increase, whence arose the new bill passed during the war. It did not remember that, in custom-house matters, two and two never make four. But patience! adversaries of the prohibitory system are not lacking in the United States; it will not be long before the aggravation of the Morrill tariff, subjected to the test of trial, will be attacked on different sides. I would not be astonished if the Morrill tariff itself, a suicidal tariff, to use the expression of Mr. Motley, should speedily give way to a decidedly liberal measure.

But neither cotton nor the tariff can explain the unkindly, almost malevolent feeling which has repressed for long months the true sentiments of England. Whence comes this icy coldness? Whence came, at the first news of the seizure of the commissioners, these bursts of vehement indignation?

It must be admitted that it was the overflowing of a full cup. The point in question was to chastise Yankee insolence once for all.

The Americans, we admit, have often been very arrogant toward the English. They have shown themselves provoking and unjust. But what Americans? those of the North or the South? It would be rather strange to make friends atone for the wrongs of enemies. Now, whoever has penetrated beneath appearances sees that the North has never ceased to be attached to England at heart; it was the South that detested it. It was the South that, resting upon its cotton, believed itself able to brave every thing against it. It was under the rule of Southern men that those acts of violence were committed —the bombardment of Greytown, placed under English protection, the dismissal of the English ambassador during the Russian war, the occupation of the island of San Juan.

All this may be traced to Southern policy, a policy founded on the violation of international right, on the contempt for foreign nations, on the necessity of making conquests for slavery, an odious policy, of which the filli-busters of Walker were the worthy agents, and the Ostend manifesto the glorious formula. Mark that this policy had as its fundamental article, the hatred of England, abolition England, liberal England, conservative England.

By what strange mistake have our neighbors beyond the channel placed to the account of the North what belonged essentially to the South? Doubtless, the North too had been more than once implicated; it had more-over its democratic party in close alliance with the South. But under the surface, often rough, attentive observers discover something else. A moment's reflection will be sufficient to see that, once in conflict with the South, the North would seek in England its natural outside support.

To sustain the South in order the better to revenge the humiliations inflicted by the South, to grant the prayers of Mr. Davis and Mr. Mason in order the better to punish the system of which Messrs. Davis and Mason had been the most ardent representatives, surprises me, I acknowledge. It is a new example of the power of words. The word "United States," is enough with many; it was the United States by whom they were offended; it is the United States that must pay for the offence.

I shall not enter upon the examination of these real or feigned offences. I believe that England has self-respect enough not to show herself less patient toward America weak, than she did toward America strong. I think that she knows how to rank in their proper place, many pretended wrongs, veritable commercial gossip, words attributed to such or such a statesman, speeches made in the heat of an election, the passing and unimportant excesses of a noisy and democratic regime.

As to the concessions which she has made, far from considering them humiliating, I regard them as among her brightest claims to honor. Face to face to a quarrelsome government which, under the constantly dominant influence of the South, conducted the affairs of the Union, England has known how to show herself moderate. So much the better! She has given way, she says, eight times in twenty-five years. What does it matter? I ask for real reasons of regret. Would it have been better to break with America than to settle the questions of Oregon, Maine, and San Juan as she has done?

The fact remains unhappily certain, that the proceedings of the American government have been often of a nature to irritate England. We, Frenchmen, will not refuse to comprehend national susceptibilities. They have played a much greater part than has been imagined in the misunderstanding of the last year. They have rendered in some measure plausible the suppositions of those who say, "The act of Captain Wilkes is grave in our eyes, only because we see in it the inevitable and long foreseen conclusion of a policy hostile to England. Has not Mr. Seward himself made speeches in his time worthy of the most palmy days of American arrogance? Has he not designated Canada as the possible compensation for the loss of the South? The plan was fixed or nearly so. Knowing that we should be attacked, could we scruple much in becoming ourselves the assailants?

I understand the sentiment that is thus expressed; it may have existed, but is about to disappear. The *Trent* affair has rent asunder many veils, and laid bare many positions; the two peoples have seen each other, perhaps for the first time, in their true colors. Behind the blind transports of the moment, America has perceived the lasting affection of liberal Englishmen for the cause which she is maintaining; behind the declamations of the occasion, England has perceived the attachment of a friendly and sister nation. Henceforth, I hope, the monopoly will be left to Southern statesmen, Mr. Toombs, for example, of those malignant attacks in which he formerly excelled, when he declared on the floor of Congress that it was his ambition to cover the Atlantic with armed steamers in order to humble Great Britain.

I would go too far, doubtless, were I to affirm that many Englishmen, on their side, were moved by the desire of humbling the United States. It is notwithstanding incontestable that English policy has inherited the maxim from the last century, which clear-sighted men reject, but which has its effect upon the crowd, that the maritime preponderance of England exacts the abasement of the United States.

There are men in England who detest Americans as cordially as their ancestors did at the close of the Revolutionary war. There are some who regard as a great advantage the coexistence of two rival races, constantly engaged in strife, and annulling each other. There are some who have a vision of a protectorate in the South, or even a monarchical establishment under an English prince, with a national church and all its appendages; yes, the united kingdom of England, Ireland, and America appears to have mirrored itself before some imaginations.

All this must enter into the computation when we would explain the impulses of the public mind. I take care, moreover, not to stop at considerations of this kind. Although future danger of interference from the American navy may be taken in earnest by the majority of English statesmen, I do not think that such a motive had a marked influence on their attitude. It is more probable that, in the recent complications called forth by the war, they have found a natural occasion to put Canada in a state of defence, or to display the immense maritime resources of their country.

I cannot help believing that they have also found occasion therein to obtain another kind of success. The cabinet lived by expedients, the majority was reduced to the most alarming proportions. Lord Palmerston saw the session approaching without having yet discovered means to strengthen his position. Suddenly, an overwhelming majority presented itself; the Tories promised their support; the *Morning Herald* pledged it solemnly in their name, provided Lord Palmerston showed no weakness toward the United States; it was a party stroke, and the long parliaments of the American war seemed about to begin anew. With the war, all serious opposition, for the moment at least, would cease; the national excitement would give birth to a sort of unanimity; all reforms and all questions difficult of solution would fall to the second place.

If we add to this, that, unfortunately for Englishmen, they are far from examining their foreign with as much independence as their home affairs, that they are accustomed on this point to follow their government at first with almost blind docility, and to criticize later, too late, when the nation is at strife, and you will comprehend that the right of the parliamentary session and the triumphant majority may have contributed, unknown to the English people and the ministers themselves, to the rigidity that has been introduced into American relations.

But let us come to a more justifiable and also, I am convinced, more real motive. If there had been nothing but cotton, or the tariff, or the fear excited by a hostile navy, or the remembrance of a vexatious quarrel or unfriendly measures, or the desire of settling old accounts and preventing hostile designs, or the tempting chance of securing an election, neither the English nor their government would have acted as they have done.

Their great motive, their great excuse, shall I say, has been that, for many years past and with increasing violence, English institutions have been attacked in the name of those of America. The United States have become an engine of war, a battering-ram hurled unceasingly against their ramparts.

One might be irritated for less cause. What thence ensued? In the embarrassment of the United States, England saw at first only the embarrassment of a republic; in the failure of the American cause, she saw the failure of Mr. Bright and the radical party. The controversy has been continued in this manner through events and by events. The more the embarrassment increased on the other side the Atlantic, the more was the rejoicing, on this side, for having a throne and a House of Lords.

I, certainly, would not be the one to regret that the English republicans should receive such a lesson; I know of few enemies more dangerous to liberty. Let the constitutional monarchy be defended against them to extremity, let the levelling tendencies of the Manchester school be repelled afar; nothing is better or more lawful. I can even understand how the *Times*, somewhat exaggerating the natural instruction furnished by the American crisis, exclaims by way of conclusion: "If royalty did not exist, we would be forced to create it."

But, this concession once made to an enthusiasm which is far from surprising me, are we not justified in regretting that we could not have deemed it possible to be at once strongly attached to English institutions and strongly sympathetic with the American cause?

I seek in vain to discover the incompatibility of the two sentiments. What! are the friends of constitutional monarchy reduced to living by the failures of the republican system? What! if there should be somewhere a prosperous republic, would constitutional monarchy no longer have a right to subsist?

The men who have just entered their protest in England, thank God! against the fleeting errors of public opinion, are somewhat prouder and surer of their convictions. As much attached as any one to the institutions of their country, they know how to admit that other countries may have other institutions. If republicans succeed in resolving the true problem of liberty in Switzerland or America, they will be rejoiced instead of grieved thereby, and will be only the more devoted to their monarchy and parliament. To them, English institutions are not at the mercy of events, depending on the failure or success of some other form of government. With an assurance that is not devoid of pride, they contemplate their liberal loyalty, their aristocracy always ready to sacrifice its prejudices or interests at need, to decree Catholic emancipation or the abolition of the protective system, their powerful nation, in fine, securing the triumph of public opinion through elections, the press, and the jury, and they challenge the whole world to inspire them with the desire of political revolution.

Such has been the great motive of the English people. Let us add, to render it complete justice, that upon two essential points, sincere prejudices, as unconquerable as sincere, have formed an obstacle hitherto to the sympathies upon which America seemed able to count. These prejudices, the value of which I shall have to weigh carefully in the third part of my work, must be mentioned in this place, in order to take into account the sum total of the motive powers which have determined the attitude of England.

In the first place, the separation of the South was held at once to be definitive and irremediable. This admitted, a practical nation, which makes few theories and has great respect for facts, was naturally led to hold in contempt or even hatred, so many efforts essayed to attain a chimerical end. The war was nothing longer but a criminal and costly folly, in which it was impossible to be interested. "The Union is gone." Such was the oracle uttered by the *Times*, that political Bible of so many Englishmen. Thenceforth, all remained convinced that there were two nations in America instead of a single one; the great question was decided in advance in favor of the South; its quality of belligerent appeared reasonable, while waiting till it should be recognized.

When we set out with a conviction like this, we are usually little disposed to accept any thing which would call our axioms in question, and force us to recommence our calculations. Here is a fact accomplished ; let no one make any change therein, or we shall be disappointed.

A second oracle, no less infallible, was uttered, and its influence has been immense.—The North, it was said, is as indifferent to slavery as the South; the point in question between them is supremacy, political domination.

This once granted, the consequences unfolded of themselves. The great liberal and Christian party remained immovable, the men most known for their abolition sentiments openly refused to call or preside over meetings against the South. This forbearance was carried so far that prayers began to be offered for the success of the most iniquitous compromises, the peace conference, and the Crittenden measure. Through misapprehension of America, England had ceased to be England.

CHAPTER IV.

THE TRENT.

Our study would remain incomplete if we did not glance at the incident which lately had nearly produced a rupture between England and the United States. It is precisely because the *Trent* affair is ended that it is important to treat of it; we are sure of doing so now dispassionately. And what instruction it has to furnish us! Nothing could replace it in this respect. Here alone we have before us facts and not conjectures; here alone we see unfolded with freedom, and in some sort with sincerity, the policy adopted at the beginning of the crisis. Thanks to the *Trent* affair, we know where it leads, what consequences it accepts, and to what sentiments it appeals.

The *Trent* affair casts a brilliant light upon the value of principles and importance of interests which are sacrificed by mistaking them. As truly as justice begets peace, so truly does it lead to war—the expression is not strong enough—*to the state of war*, to lasting and long-lived hatreds, where right is trodden under foot and violence is done to sympathies.

I shall take care, therefore, not to neglect a subject of such prime importance. If the question concerned the past alone, it might be, perhaps, neglected, although the lessons of the past have their value; but the future is also in question. The *Trent* affair, which had nearly been the means of universal destruction, may be the providential means of universal safety. It has been, as it were, a great liquidation of the English policy in America. Matters have been explained, men have seen where they were going, practical conclusions have been abruptly brought into comparison with theories. The two countries, at the same time, have learned to know each other better; instead of the loose government which had been depicted to us, we have encountered at Washington an enlightened, prudent administration, very far from receiving its orders from the mob. In learning to distrust the descriptions presented to it, English opinion has reconquered its full liberty of judgment. Who knows whether the suppression of the rebellion be really impossible? Who knows whether slavery be not really in question? All sorts of interrogations are made, the awakening is effected, the true England has appeared.

It was time to awake. After having believed for a year that it would be called upon only to pout at America, it suddenly perceived that the question was to declare war against it; an *ultimatum* had just set out for Washington.

Between great, between sister nations, this was a strange beginning. It is scarcely the usage, as the word itself implies, to begin with an *ultimatum;* that is, to begin with the end. Usually, when there has been a misunderstanding, an act to be regretted, especially when this act involves a part of the right of nations which is still obscure, the natural beginning is a demand for explanation of intentions, and of reparation of wrong, without coupling it with an immediate menace of rupture.

I am not ignorant that Lord Russell by his recommendations, and Lord Lyons by his measures, softened, as much as possible, the odious character of the *ultimatum.* Public opinion, moreover, was aroused in Europe with unforeseen rapidity; the precipitation of the measures adopted at London was judged severely; the clause concerning apology was also abandoned in fact. But it is no less incredible that it figured in the original programme. Little children are made to ask pardon, the humiliation of apology is inflicted on countries without regular government, on Turks and savages; between nations which respect each other mutually, it is always deemed sufficient satisfaction to repair the wrong and deny the hostile intention.

Certain English journals have maintained that Europe approved of these summary proceedings! Just the contrary is true. On seeing such haste and so haughty a proclamation of indisputable exigence, on seeing the idea of an impious war accepted with so much readiness by some, and so much ill-dissembled joy by others, Europe declared without circumlocution or reserve, that if England were not miraculously rescued from her own enterprise, if she drew the sword against the North in the capacity of an ally of the South, she would destroy with her own hands her chief claim to the respect of the civilized world.

The language on this point was the same at Paris, Berlin, St. Petersburg, Vienna, and Turin. As they were unanimous in deciding the technical question of right against America, so were they unanimous in deciding the moral question against England. To recognize the technical right in favor of England, was to recognize the right of neutrals against her. Who is simple enough to be astonished at the eagerness displayed here by the other powers? But English demands gained little in general opinion by taking the wounding form of an ultimatum, even though the most courteous of ultimatums.

This form would be justifiable only in a single case—that of a premeditated insult to the English flag. The *Morning Post* is so conscious of this that it has endeavored to propagate, in England and elsewhere, absurd tales which for a moment almost passed for realities: The United States are seeking a pretext to declare war against England! This is evident from the policy of Mr. Seward! Being unable to succeed with the South, he has resolved to stretch a helping hand to it, and to seal the new friendship by a common invasion of Canada.

Thus, the question of right, insufficient to explain the despatch of an ultimatum, disappears behind another grave question. The act of Captain Wilkes ceases to be any thing else than the last of a series of hostile measures, designed to bring about a war. A little sooner or a little later—what mattered it thenceforth? Was it not better to foil American Machiavelism? Was it not wise to choose one's own time, instead of awaiting inevitable aggression?

To support these fine fancies, people were not content with accumulating a host of grievances and signs; they affirmed that the seizure of the commissioners on board the English packet had been deliberated in council, and thus, as it were, erected into a system. "See the *James Adger*," they exclaimed, "despatched to do in the very waters of Europe what the *San Jacinto* has done in the waters of Cuba!"

Now, it is found, not only that it had never occurred to any one to seize the commissioners on board an English packet, but that the *San Jacinto* had acted thus simply because, returning from Africa, she was totally without instructions, and furthermore, that the *James Adger* had been ordered to arrest the commissioners in European waters solely on the supposition that they had embarked in the *Nashville*, a vessel belonging to the rebels.

The question of right remains stripped of its covering, without the least aggravating circumstance of a nature to excuse the immediate despatch of an ultimatum. But the question was so important! the act of Captain Wilkes was of such enormity! Upon an ordinary infraction of international rules, we might have entered into negotiations, listened to explanations, if necessary, admitted an arbitrament, in fine, awaited the failure of the first measures before having recourse to extremities; but after an infraction so extraordinary, it was proper that the first message addressed to Lord Lyons should contain the conditional order to demand his passports!

Men must hold us in derision to use such language to us; they must suppose that we have forgotten our modern history, and particularly the history of Great Britain. Since they speak of *enormities*, I will recall the acts which merit this name, and, compared with which, the real but excusable error of Captain Wilkes bears the proportion of a peccadillo.

"We are no more immaculate than others," wrote the *Times;* and, having once made this confession, it thought itself entitled to reject musty old books and to repudiate expedients. It would be rather too convenient thus to throw off one's own deeds by beating his breast at the memory of his great sins of the past, while resolving by no means to pardon his neighbor the least of his sins of the present! There was once, according to the parable of the Gospel, a servant who owed his master ten thousand talents; the master had pity on him, and forgave him the debt. The same servant went out and found one of his fellow-servants which owed him a hundred pence, and he laid hands on him and took him by the throat, saying, "Pay me that thou owest."

I am sorry for England, but its enormities resemble those of Captain Wilkes as the ten thousand talents resemble the hundred pence. No one has ever thought of quoting English enormities as precedents; they are too disproportionate to the case in question. Such acts run no risk of becoming precedents, and there is not the least reason to fear that any one will dream of invoking their authority. Violence is violence, and right is right. It is upon the ground of right that we maintain that the *Trent* affair was a case of amicable complaint, and not of immediate recourse to an ultimatum; our arguments are not borrowed from the old doctrines of the English admiralty. By the side of our doubts, at least plausible, by the side of the honorable hesitation of Captain Wilkes, the true enormities would figure somewhat strangely. Since the subject has been broached, I will cite a few of them.

England has officially maintained the doctrine of closed seas, (*mare clausum*;) she has claimed that, as mistress of certain very considerable portions of the sea, she has the sovereign right to fix the conditions of neutral navigation therein in time of war.

England has fixed the ceremonial of salutation in these seas, in such a manner as to imply an acknowledgment of the inferiority of other navies.

She has seized sailors when it suited her on board American ships, hesitating neither to arrest individuals nor to render her naval officers supreme judges in the matter. At one time, by virtue of an exchange of orders in council and imperial decrees, the blockade (on paper) of the coasts of Europe, and the blockade (no less fictitious) of the coasts of England and all her colonies, were proclaimed at London, Berlin, and Milan. England exacted that every neutral vessel, before repairing to the Continent, should touch at her ports; while Napoleon, on his side, declared all vessels denationalized which had entered English harbors. It was then the United States, in consequent despair, passed the *Act of Embargo* and the *Non-Intercourse Bill.*

These are deserving the name of enormities. And it would be easy to swell the number; the story is long.* When America, weary at last of her system of embargo, commenced her war of 1812, more than nine hundred of her vessels had been seized. I add that at the peace of Ghent, Great Britain refused to withdraw her pretensions and disavow her doctrines.

Let us cease therefore to pretend that the act of Captain Wilkes is an enormity without equal. We know now how the matter stands.

There is in it simply a fact to be regretted, opening the way to a legitimate demand for reparation. Captain Wilkes, who erred, erred in sincerity, and nothing in his conduct justifies the excessive indignation which we have witnessed. The *Trent*, moreover, was really in the wrong; and, if opinions are divided on this point, it is no less certain that the evidence is not complete, since there is a division of opinions.

Behold, on one hand, an English packet whose fidelity to neutral obligations may be at least contested; on the

* See Ortolon, *Diplomatie de la mer*, tome II., pp. 95, 111, 121, 122, 128, 131, 133, 136, 137, 172, 173, 300, 326–331.

See also in the Blue Books of this year, the details of the Canstadt affair. This is quite another thing from the affair of the Trent.

other, an American vessel that has exceeded its rights. In such a case, the path is ready traced, and, to begin by a rupture, one cannot be wholly averse to war.

Do not fear—I shall cite neither Grotius, nor Puffendorf, nor Vattel, nor Burlamaqui. I am not a jurisconsult, although I have studied legal points like others, and the debates of the Council of State have familiarized me with this sort of discussions. Let us lay aside the rubbish of schools and use the language of common sense.

I begin by establishing one point—men are not contraband of war. With the exception of military men—and Messrs. Mason and Slidell did not act in this capacity—no person could have been lawfully seized, even supposing the packet to have been brought, according to rule, before a prize court. The doctrine of *Man-despatches* is the weak side of the American argument. In such a matter, it is not permissible to extend by force of reasoning, or even *a fortiori*, the categories fixed by the law of nations. "Despatches are contraband of war; therefore, and for the strongest reason, ambassadors, which are living despatches, are so likewise." This argument cannot be admitted. If Sir William Scott has declared lawful the seizure of ambassadors, it is not under the neutral flag, but under the flag or on the soil of the enemy. In fine, the principle involved here is of real importance; the question, in fact, is nothing less than the right of asylum, which would be endangered if the arrest of persons could be effected under the neutral flag. Here, let it be loudly proclaimed, all are secure, common criminals and political criminals, assassins and rebels. This is true, and it is important that it should be so.

Another point, too, should be conceded without hesitation: no one is authorized to execute justice with his own hands. The formality of a judgment is no trifling thing—it is the common guarantee of all civilized nations. I am far, indeed, from arraigning Captain Wilkes, who is among the most distinguished and most scholarly officers of the United States, and was the commander of one of the finest scientific expeditions ever made; I comprehend how he fell into the error—he has paid for our instruction. I comprehend also how strong was the temptation to arrest these commissioners as they passed before his eyes, announcing that they were bound for Europe to seek every possible means of destroying the common country. But the error of Mr. Wilkes was of importance. In his desire as little as possible to aggravate the inconvenience to the *Trent* and her passengers, with a disinterestedness for which he should receive credit, he took it upon himself to decide alone a question that belonged to the courts. It was something as if a policeman, on arresting a suspicious person, should say: "My friend, the magistrate lives a great way off; to take you before him will detain you, and put you to great inconvenience. Rather than subject you to all this trouble, I will give up the reward I should obtain for apprehending you, and proceed at once to chastise you myself upon the spot." It is essential that we should be inconvenienced for the sake of a regular judgment. The business of policemen and sea captains —pardon me the comparison—is confined to taking suspicious persons before a competent magistrate. I am not surprised that England and America should have been found agreed upon this point at the end of the reckoning. In England, the legal advisers of the Crown declared from the first that the vessel should have been stopped and carried before a court. In America, Mr. Seward acknowledged that this complaint was at once well founded and important. The English press and the American press—

the *London Times* and the *New York Times*—have had but one opinion in this respect, and Mr. Sumner, in his remarkable speech in the Senate, repeated in his turn, "The packet should have been seized and brought to trial."

Such have been the errors of Captain Wilkes. I have not sought to disguise them; they doubtless justified a demand for reparation: England owed it to herself to claim and obtain the liberation of the commissioners. But does this signify that all the wrongs were on one side, and that the conduct of the *Trent* was not blamable?

That despatches are contraband of war, we may dispense with demonstrating, for no author has denied it. Moreover, the Queen's proclamation is at hand, which interdicts, not the "fraudulent" transportation of despatches, but purely and simply their transportation.

Doubtless, if the despatches of the insurgent government had been confounded with the rest of the mail matter, no one would have thought of blaming the commander of the *Trent*, or of approving the cruiser who should pretend to open the mail bags and search for contraband of war. But matters had gone differently: Messrs. Mason and Slidell, with their families and despatches, had arrived with great display at Havana, and thousands of enthusiastic spectators had greeted the entrance of the *Theodora*, which bore them thither, with the Confederate flag at its mast. The commissioners knew so well that what they were about to do would give cause of complaint to the United States, that they had taken great care to assure themselves of the disabled condition of the *Columbia*, and of the departure of another American vessel, the *Keystone State;* they did not count on the *San Jacinto*, then returning from Africa. As to any doubts of the commander of the *Trent* as to the nature of the despatches which he was about to admit on board his vessel, he knew, with all Havana, that the commissioners had been presented to the Captain-General, (presented, it is said, by the English consul;) and he had seen with his own eyes the manner in which they were escorted on board the packet.

In the presence of such facts, had he not reason to call to mind the proclamation of the Queen, forbidding the transportation of despatches? Could he have reassured himself by the argument presented by a number of journals: "The Queen's proclamation is not a treaty, but a municipal regulation; it is binding only on us."

"By no means!" it is replied, "his reasons were far better. In the first place, a packet was in question; secondly, this packet was repairing from one neutral port to another; what would become of us if all mail packets were exposed to the visits of cruisers, even on the coasts of Europe, or between Dover and Calais?"

The answer is easy.

In the first place, packets, for the very reason that they have privileges, among others that of continuing their service in time of war, are bound to use especial care not to violate in any respect the rules of the most conscientious neutrality. Let special agreements, moreover, be concluded, to protect their sailing and exempt it from all restrictions.—I am willing; but such agreements are not concluded, and an agreement *to be concluded* cannot at present be binding on America.

The exception in favor of ships repairing "from one neutral port to another," will likewise figure in agreements *to be concluded;* in agreements already concluded, not the slightest trace of such reservation is to be found. The Queen's proclamation ought really to have mentioned this exception, if it exist; it would have then been known that the most hostile despatches, those best known and pointed out to the attention of the whole world, might be lawfully transported, provided they were taken from Havana. Why not enunciate in formal terms, these self-styled simple and self-evident facts? The evidence of the latter leaves it to be desired, since it has not been suspected by the legal advisers of the Crown, and since the English Government has not said a word of it in its demand for reparation. Mr. Seward was surely right in stating that, while all the powers desire neutral rights, they are still far from all desiring them in the same manner, and by virtue of the same reasons.

Let us come to an understanding—nothing can be better; let us inscribe the exception of neutral ports in a general agreement—no one will find fault with it. But, once more, let us not make of a plausible and probable, yet disputable and disputed opinion, an axiom in the law of nations, and let us not apply retroactively to the United States a rule which *may be established* with advantage in some future agreement.

I wish to say a word here of the speech so often repeated: "Intercourse will be no longer possible; navigation must be interrupted; there will be nothing to hinder the search of mail packets in the Straits of Calais or the Mediterranean!"

Affirmations like these will be best refuted by their absurdity. I know of no right which might not be easily converted into an enormity, if we amused ourselves by carrying it to extremes. Take the right of search, for instance. This right, you will admit, does not take the trouble to ask whether the contraband of war comes from a neutral port, for neutral ports are almost always those from which it is despatched. So long as the regions of search be not limited, so long as mail packets be not expressly excepted, so long, in a word, as the general treaty which we all demand be not negotiated. American cruisers will, strictly, have the right to search our merchant vessels on the very coasts of Europe.

They have this right, but they will not exercise it. Why not? Because there is still something in the world, thank God, called common sense, and because it is the special mission of common sense to set bounds between the exercise of right and its abuse. By virtue of common sense, the American cruisers, which make no search in the Mediterranean, will trouble themselves no more about despatches passing between Dover and Calais.

In fact, observe that packet navigation has never been obstructed, even in American waters; an extreme case, an embassy despatched with éclat, despatches of exceptional importance, a hostile act particularly dangerous, were needed for a single American cruiser (and this without instructions) to institute a search for a single time on board neutral vessels. I think, therefore, that we may let hypotheses rest, and feel secure concerning postal relations.

If the question were still of practical importance, it would be proper to examine here, from the stand-point of the existing war, the character of the ports of departure and arrival. The *Trent* was bearing despatches to a neutral port! Yes, but the American struggle has this peculiarity, that all the chances of the South are in Europe, and that its despatches sent to a neutral country are, of all others, the most important to stop on the way. The *Trent* had taken its despatches from a neutral port! Yes, but they did not originate there; they had come in the sight and with the knowledge of the whole world, from the very capital of the insurgents! Besides, what is Havana? Open a map, and you will see that Havana is near the lower end of Florida, at the point of intersection of the routes to New Orleans and Charleston. It is the rendezvous of all the small craft which have escaped the blockade, or are intending to run it. It is the admitted place of transshipment, the great harbor of the South. Vessels of light draught, gliding through the thousand inlets which riddle the Southern coast, arrive daily at Havana, or other points of the island of Cuba. They dare not go further. There, the vessels are fitted up anew, and what was begun by night under the Southern flag is continued in broad daylight under European colors. Read the story of Messrs. Mason and Slidell's adventures in the *Charleston Mercury*. They set out from Charleston in a dark, rainy night, on a small steamer, the *Theodora;* by favor of steam and the darkness, they escaped the blockade and landed at Havana; when, suddenly, the scene changed, the escapade became a triumphal march, commissioners and despatches were installed on board the English packet, regarding themselves safe from all danger!

I have written the preceding with the last despatch of Lord Russell under my eyes. Coming late, on the 23d of January, after long reflection, it seems to me of all things best fitted to confirm my principal observation; namely, the obscurity of the question at the moment of Captain Wilkes' action; and consequently, the relative innocence of this act.

The English Government has since studied the subject like the rest of us. Researches and experiences have been made between the first and the last note of the Foreign Office. If it had been as wise in the month of November as it is now, nothing would have been easier than to have enunciated the proposition on the spot, "There can be no contraband of war between neutral ports." M. Thouvenel alone has had the credit of adopting this position.

This axiom in itself is reasonable. I beg that it may enter ere long, in clear and formal terms, into international agreements. Only, I maintain that it has not been found in them hitherto, and that doubt was permissible in America, since error was possible in England. Do you remember the fairy tales, in which a frightful giant gives the hero an obscure riddle to guess on the spot under pain of death? Were the United States to divine at the first glance the diplomatic riddle of contraband of war, under penalty of entering into immediate war with England?

But the despatch of the 23d of January, while involving the argument of M. Thouvenel, develops before all another, which shows to what subtleties the discussion of a point of law may give rise, though declared, moreover, to be as clear as the light of day.

Lord Russell begins by laying down the principle that the South is a belligerent, and that the United States cannot regard it in any other point of view. This axiom established, demonstrates that both the two contending powers have the right to preserve relations with neutral countries. It thence follows that neutral countries are authorized to send them ambassadors and despatches, and that the contending parties are likewise authorized to send ambassadors and despatches to neutral countries. By what right can despatches addressed to neutrals be considered hostile?

This is admirable logic, but the United States have never admitted the South to be a belligerent, and I do not think that Europe, which adopts for herself this way of seeing, pretends to impose it on them. The South, therefore, is simply a rebel in the sight of Mr. Lincoln.

What become thenceforth of all the reasonings of the despatch of January 23d? Can an insurgent fraction of a country maintain lawful diplomatic relations with neutrals? What can these despatches contain which will not be treason? As it is true that the ambassadors and despatches of a belligerent have a legitimate end in a neutral country, so is it clear that the ambassadors and despatches of rebels cannot have a legitimate end therein. If you doubt this, interrogate your own heart, ask what were your sensations at this mission of Messrs. Mason and Slidell, sent to seek in Europe the ruin of their country.

What is my conclusion? That Captain Wilkes was right? I have said the contrary. My conclusion is that the question of right is not so clear as has been pictured, and that the wrong has been in some measure divided. It comprises, according to the expression of Mr. Seward, "rules imperfectly known and imperfectly understood."

The liberty and lives of Messrs. Mason and Slidell run no risk in any case. Supposing an arbitration to have been admitted, it is certain that the first condition would have been the transferral of the commissioners into the hands of the arbiter, and it is no less certain, (the commendable passion of Europe for the rights of neutrals is well enough known,) that the first act of the arbiter, whoever it were, would have been to command their liberation. The only means of exposing Messrs. Mason and Slidell to real danger, would have been to break with the United States. Transported into the interior, and remaining in the power of a people exasperated by its extreme danger, they would have been guarded, and well guarded, without doubt, by the honor of the Americans; nevertheless, it would not have been easy to banish all anxiety.

I have spoken of arbitration, not because I believe in

the necessity of recurring to it—a firm and amicable negotiation has always seemed to me sufficient for the arrangement of differences; but I have seen, like all others, in the pains that have been taken in advance to discard arbitration, the manifestation of a thought that the arrangement of the difference would give indifferent satisfaction.

This thought did not last; nevertheless it existed, and constituted one of the most deplorable facts of our time.

"Before all, no arbiters! A blow admits of no arbitration; we have received a blow! Arbitration is designed to resolve difficulties, only when the litigious question has not been prejudged by hostile acts; there has been aggression, war is begun, our territory is in some sort invaded! Where, moreover, are arbiters to be found? All Europe has declared its sentiments!"

Thus because a naval officer had been honestly mistaken, an insult, a blow had been offered; because the arbiters were too favorable to England, and England was too sure that they would decide in her favor, England hastened to except to them.

It is useless to recall the fact that many powers had not yet declared themselves, and might have played the part of arbiters: Sweden, Denmark, Portugal, Holland, Switzerland. To discuss these objections would be to do them too much honor. I have only wished to state them. A part of England seemed then to say—"Leave us our war; you would decide in our favor, but that matters little; you would set the commissioners at liberty, but that is the least of our cares; we want war and nothing else."

Mark that, five years before, in the Paris Congress, Lord Clarendon proposed the rule of arbitration as "a barrier to those conflicts which not unfrequently break out only because of the impossibility of offering explanations or of coming to an understanding." The question, thus introduced by the English Government, was earnestly debated, and so much importance was attached to it that the vote was postponed for two days, until Count Orloff could obtain by telegraph the definitive adhesion of Russia. Behold the unanimous declaration, to which the United States assented on the spot:

"The plenipotentiaries do not hesitate to express the wish, in the name of their governments, that States between which serious dissensions may arise, shall have recourse to the good offices of a friendly power, as far as circumstances permit, before appealing to arms."

On what occasion, I ask, will this salutary rule find application, if inapplicable here? The conflict was on the point of breaking out *because it had been impossible to offer explanations or to come to an understanding;* the dissension was *serious ;* the circumstances *permitted* recourse to a friendly power. Was Europe derided in 1856? Was there fear of losing an occasion of war in 1861? I express myself with the more freedom, that the England of 1862 is not that of 1861. Of these two Englands, the better, thank God, has just taken the lead.

That this sudden change is held for naught in London, and that men reason now, in the best possible faith, as if they had not been so lately disposed to fall upon the United States, to strike hands with the South, and to give the signal for an unnatural war which would have brought forth many others, I care not; but we who cling to peace and love the cause of liberty, are forced to have a longer memory, were it only to prevent the return of one of these experiences, so cavalierly glided over, in which civilization itself would be in danger of perishing.

To-day, thanks to the great change which has been wrought in Europe, and to which the public opinion of Europe has not been a stranger, a pacific course is established; the passions of yesterday have died out; the true English nation has greeted with enthusiasm the peaceful news from Washington; Lord Russell has hastened to accept the liberation without insisting on apologies, he has congratulated Lord Lyons for having so closely followed his private instructions and surrounded a discourteous proceeding with so much friendly courtesy, he has congratulated the American Government for having so nobly surmounted the difficulties of its part.

We, too, may congratulate the English nation and its ministers. That people is great in which faults committed are repaired in this wise, and in which the public sense of right thus makes itself obeyed.

Already, before the incident of the *Trent*, Lord Stanley had uttered this almost prophetic warning: "It is the duty of our government not to suffer itself to be irritated on account of accidental molestations, such as it must expect to receive in the course of such a struggle." At the very height of the irritation caused by the *Trent* affair, another voice was raised. A simple society appeared; and we felt at once that evil passions were about to recede before a superior power. For my part, I admire the victories of the mind far more than those of the bayonet or bullet. A few almost unknown men present an address to the prime minister, and the terrified world breathes again; although it is not yet known what will be the decision of America, it is thenceforth known that the cause is judged, for England has regained her path and will never more wander from it. How true were the words of the *Anti-Slavery Society:* "Such an undertaking on the part of England would not only be most humiliating, but would lamentably contradict her past efforts and former sacrifices for the liberty of slaves; it would expose her protests to the reproach of hypocrisy from the rest of the world; it would destroy her claim and close her lips henceforth to every appeal addressed to the intelligence and conscience of other nations. * * * * The members of the Society experience inexpressible horror and repugnance at the thought of seeing their country engaged in a war, the virtual end of which would be the defence of slavery!"

What Lord Stanley said in the political point of view, what the Anti-Slavery Society said in the moral point of view, all repeat to-day. Truth spreads quickly, and those who lately combated it with the greatest violence and disdain, are none the less eager to proclaim it from the house-tops. It is one of the traits of the English character that it is not long embarrassed by inconsistencies. Men stray from the right path, and return to it, perhaps only to wander from it again, and all this is accomplished with perfect assurance.

When you read an article from a journal, recommending patience toward America, rebuking those inclined to contest the blockade, and demonstrating that the manufacturing crisis proceeds from a previous excess of production more than from a scarcity of cotton, do not be greatly astonished to discover that this journal is the *Times*, or even the *Morning Post!*

So goes the world. If less care be taken in England than elsewhere to cover over changes of opinion, it is not because there is less change elsewhere. I like this lack of caution; it is to me a sign of strength and proof of frankness. At heart, the English, in expressing their present convictions, are fully conscious, and they are not wrong, that these convictions are their own. They have returned to them as one returns home, without needing to account to any one. The absence is forgotten, the journey to the land of illiberal policy goes for nothing: we are at home, what more would you have? Through accidental variations like these, is maintained the genuine and glorious consistency of the English people.

I wish to be just toward it, and I see that its return home has not been effected with giant strides. Some weeks before the session, there was reason to fear that both houses would witness the triumph of the friends of the South; Mr. Gregory was about to propose his motion; the Tories had their hands full of arguments against the blockade; the working population was at hand to bear upon the Government. The session opens, and what occurs? Lord Palmerston announces his intention of maintaining the neutrality, the Tories themselves do not venture to combat it openly; as to Lord Russell, he holds a language worthy of himself, contesting the proofs of the inefficacy of the blockade,* and insisting on the duty of making no movement that may seem hostile to the United States; the definitive separation, if it is to take place, must not look as if proceeding from the action of foreign powers.

Behold us far from the day when the duel was to commence between the two fractions of the Anglo-Saxon race, when two free nations, two kindred peoples, were about to destroy each other, to the great joy of their common enemies! We will not soon forget that fearful December! The vessel then crossing the ocean was far different from the peaceful *Mayflower* which, in the same month of December, two centuries and a half before, had

* It is known that one of his despatches officially recognizes the regularity of the blockade, and that the French Government has just held the same language.

anchored on the shores of America with its Puritans fleeing from English persecution—it was a vessel bearing the ultimatum of England!

And while it was on its way, while our hearts were wrung, and our minds terrified, by the prospect of the greatest political and moral disaster that could overtake our generation, the influential London journals took care to instruct us upon the character of the war, which they regarded as almost inevitable. "It will be terrible! It will begin by the recognition of the South, by the alliance of the South, by the assured triumph of the South!"

And when a rumor was spread that a despatch of Mr. Seward—the one written on the 30th of November, at the precise moment when the British cabinet signed its own—was of a nature to give hopes of a favorable solution, the *Morning Post* hastened to publish, in large type, the official contradiction of this news, which, nevertheless, was true. The spontaneous disavowal of all thought of insult, the declaration announcing that Captain Wilkes had acted without instructions, the express wish that the question might be treated on both sides in a spirit of conciliation, were considered of no importance.

At this moment, do not deny it, there was among many in England something of the eagerness which is displayed *in seizing on an occasion.* England, usually so slow, acted with unheard-of haste. Never have I seen a more striking commentary on the words of the Apostle, "Their feet are swift to shed blood."

America has just saved the peace of the world.

A government has been found at Washington, little resembling the picture that had been drawn for us, and a people, for the whole must be confessed, much more sensible and more fully master of itself than had been pretended. If certain Englishmen consider that the United States have not yielded enough, the vast majority in England and France think differently. We all knew that the Americans were not lacking in audacity; but we did not know that they were possessed of moderation; that, in a terrible position, and one calculated to call forth the passions of the mob, they could display the high wisdom and political bearing which has just won for them so much sympathy.

It would be difficult to exaggerate the progress which they have thus made in public opinion. For some time, at least, the public sense of right has set itself in opposition to the assistance destined to the South; the South feels the day of the commissioners' liberation to have been a day of mourning; it would have preferred the loss of a battle.

Independently of the advantages which they have reaped from it in successfully carrying on their present struggle, the United States have found in the upright and able solution of the incident of the *Trent* another kind of success. The true American policy—that which has always maintained the cause of neutrals and the liberty of the seas against England—has gained a brilliant triumph. This, General Scott announced from the first day: "I am sure," wrote he, "that the president and people of the United States would be only too happy to set these prisoners at liberty, unpardonable and unnatural as have been their offences, if by this they could encourage the commerce of the world." The note of Mr. Seward held the same language: "If I should decide this question in favor of my government, I would be obliged to disavow its dearest principles. Our country cannot make this sacrifice. * * * I express my satisfaction at seeing this question regulated in accordance with exclusively

American principles." This is the pure truth, and all the European publicists declared it at the same time with Messrs. Scott and Seward. It now remains to translate into immutable articles in the law of nations what has passed between England and the United States. The latter, we may believe, will not be the less eager to instigate the convocation of a congress commissioned to define contraband of war, to declare innocent all transportation from one neutral port to another, to accord to mail packets all the privileges which they require, to determine the bounds beyond which the right of search shall cease, and to examine the conditions of effective blockade.

Shall I justify, in conclusion, my elaboration of the subject? Those who, perhaps, are surprised at its extent, have not made the reflection—in many respects, we are right in saying that the American question must be decided in England. If the determinations of Europe have to play a great part in the conflicts of the North and South, the determinations of England will rule, or very nearly, those of Europe.

It was impossible, therefore, to treat the American question thoroughly without going to England and closely examining her sentiments and attitude. The *Trent* affair, which has brought every thing to light, has furnished us a means of inquiry which nothing could replace.

Shall I express my whole thought? I wished these pages to bear some small part in the attainment of an end which many lofty minds are now pursuing. The peace will be real only when it shall have sunk into the hearts of men; to be at peace, we must not only not be at swords' points, but must esteem and love each other; and to love each other, it is necessary to know each other. There is between the Old World and the New, especially between England and the United States, a mountain of prejudices and errors to be overthrown. Truth has one great power—reconciliation.

This is why I have attached importance to presenting in a book which will, I know, be translated and read in America, an impartial estimate of the character of the English people. I have admitted into it neither flattery nor hostility. It seems to me that it offers the picture of a generous nation that may for a moment have gone astray, have set itself against a cause that was not its own, and have been drawn into anger, passion, almost into war, but whose return to good has the energy and surety of the acts of the human conscience. The day that America shall see England in this light, namely, as she is, a vast improvement will be effected in the relations of the two continents.

To make them understand each other, there is no need to pile up phrases. Lying declamations can do nothing but harm; I have faith in truth.

I have also taken care not to adopt the truly strange explanation by which England is now endeavoring to set her late conduct in a favorable light. She lavishes eulogies on Lord Palmerston; she repeats in every key that no one really desired war; that the ultimatum, the demand for apologies, the precautions taken in advance against possible arbitration, the preparations for immediate war, the announced recognition of the South, were simply the surest proceedings to obtain peace.

May God preserve us from this sort of peace-makers! They pretend that they have ensured peace by their firmness! Let them tell this to those who have not followed their policy for the past year, and who have not foreseen, foreseen with absolute certainty, the occurrence of a *Trent* affair under some form or other, before spring. If this policy be left behind, if it have given way before a better influence, it is not fully enough proved that it may not some day reappear, to permit us to treat it with complaisance, and to glorify what we should curse.

No! you did not desire peace, for you believed for a moment in war, and this horrible chance was accepted by you with calmness. In the hour of distress of a kindred people, and for a difference easily arranged by pacific means, you left nothing undone to excite acute susceptibilities, and render the conflict inevitable.

Such is the real truth, on which it is useful to reflect in order that no one may take a fancy to plunge us again with cruel heedlessness into similar perils. That peace has been preserved, is due, next to God who had pity on you and us, to the good sense and patriotism of the American people. A distinction must be made here between *although* and *because.* Peace has been maintained, *although* England threatened it; it would have been maintained a hundred times more surely if the remarks addressed by England to Washington had been as amicable as firm in their tone, if she had entertained the same spirit with Mr. Seward's despatch of the 30th of November, if, at need, she had nobly condescended to admit the transfer of the commissioners into the hands of a third power. In any case, the liberation was certain; in any case, the interpretation of the right of nations in favor of England was certain; in any case, peace was certain. It is true that this last point would have disappointed some in England.

I agree entirely with those who believe in the excellence of firmness, and that tergiversations often bring about ruptures instead of averting them. It was fitting, moreover, of course, that England should admit of no other basis of negotiations than the immediate freedom of the commissioners or their remission into the hands of an arbiter; but this it had the certainty of obtaining, and of the two solutions, the first appeared more probable. The position of the United States was such that to avoid a serious quarrel without, especially with Great Britain, was an evident necessity. Far from yielding to fear, Mr. Lincoln took his resolution on the spot, even before it was suspected at Washington that a menace of war would be addressed to America. At this epoch of absolute security, which is derided, but which nevertheless arose from an honorable confidence in the sentiments of the English people, there was something else in the United States than those few popular demonstrations, which must have been necessarily called forth by the daring act of Captain Wilkes; in the face of these demonstrations, few in number withal, in the face of the thanks voted by one of the Houses of Congress, the true American opinion had its organs. The *New York Times* took care to declare at once that the vote of the House of Representatives left full liberty of action to the President, and that the question of right would be examined in itself. Other important journals also demonstrated, with the full approbation of the public, that if Captain Wilkes were in the wrong, the commissioners would be set at liberty. At that time, too, before there was the slightest suspicion of an ultimatum, the message of Mr. Lincoln preserved a significant silence on the *Trent* affair, and Mr. Seward voluntarily disavowed all instructions given to the cruisers.*

* It is said: "The American government might have acted still better; if it had spontaneously resolved to give up the commissioners, it would have done so before the arrival of the English note!" I would that it had done so, as I wrote to Mr. Lincoln at the first moment. But is it so difficult then to comprehend a hesitation on the form of doing so? Might not an arbitration have been preferred and hoped for, for in-

In truth, to attribute the maintenance of peace to the bellicose measures of England, we must have forgotten all that took place in December, at London and Washington.

America, we may affirm, has just rendered England the most brilliant service that ever one people rendered another. If war had broken out, it is certain that great calamities would have fallen upon the United States; but calamities no less great might have fallen upon England. I seem to hear Job's messengers, following each other in succession, each announcing a disaster.

America would have resisted; those who doubt it do not know her. The power which dared commence, with five frigates, the war of 1812, and which was by no means worsted in the end, would have accepted the struggle with all its chances. And who knows whether, commencing this time again with a few frigates, she would not have ended with a fleet?

The distress of the English manufactures would have reached its height. The civil war, proceeding thenceforth through the medium of slave insurrections, would have completed the destruction of cotton, and as to the American markets, they would have disappeared for a long time to come.

Even in case of success, what a calamity for England is this fratricidal war! It is their own blood that they

stance? The essential point is that the idea of making war, in order to retain Messrs. Mason and Slidell, did not for a moment enter the thought of the cabinet at Washington. Its despatch of the 30th of November, the reserve of the President's Message, the language of influential journals, all that passed, in a word, *before* there was the slightest suspicion of the threatening attitude of England, demonstrates conclusively that this attitude in no wise contributed to the maintenance of peace.

are shedding; it is their race that they are destroying; it is their influence in the world that they are sacrificing —the Old England assails the New.

And, by the same blow, she assails the liberty of the world; that is, her own cause, her reason for existing, her moral power on earth. From that moment, she ceases to be any thing more than the ally of slave-traders; she has abdicated her power.

Who will guarantee, moreover, that while she crosses the seas to make war, questions, capital questions, will not spring up behind her, for the solution of which there are those who will gladly profit by her absence? She is not altogether without enemies and envy in the Old World. Now, there is an Eastern crisis always ready to be revived, and which will be revived whenever there is need of it. There is also an English India, which revolted but the other day, and which already became restless, we are told, at the first news of the dispute with America.

Lastly, war gives birth to war. The war with America would have commenced as a duel, and ended, perhaps, as a mêlée. Those general conflagrations, which are our great peril, and which English policy studies with so much wisdom to avert, would thus burst, through its own act, upon terrified Europe.

Happily, all this is but a troubled dream. The friends of liberty and peace may be reassured; but are they to render thanks for this to England?

See how the truth of our formula is verified everywhere and always: as is the value of principles, so is the accordance of principles and interests.

It is the power of principles that has arrested the evil policy, the tendencies of which I have just recalled. In spite of the indifference of a noble people, in spite of accumulated prejudices, a sovereign and irresistible impulse has sprung up at the wished-for hour, and compelled a change of system. Let any one tell me what hinders, at bottom, the breaking of the blockade, the recognition of the South, the obtaining of cotton, cost what it may, if not the *impossibility*, I underline the word, the impossibility of giving the hand to the defenders of slavery.

And it will be some day found that principles have been the only intelligent guardians of interests. Justice procures peace, and peace engenders prosperity. Where was England drifting, so long as she disdained principles, and did violence to her best inspirations? She was drifting to ruin; the *Trent* affair, the ultimatum, the precipitate arming of a warlike fleet, with all the calamities which, hand in hand, were about to hasten after the rupture—such was the prospect a few months ago. What a change to-day! England has regained possession of herself, of her claims to honor, of her moral influence; the chances of conflict have disappeared, civil war in America is proceeding toward its solution, and as a recompense for the true neutrality, to the support of which she will henceforth rally, England may obtain a glimpse, at no distant future, of the reëstablishment of her commerce with the United States, while her Indian possessions will inherit a great part of the cultures destroyed by the folly of the South.

PART THIRD.

THE ERRORS CREDITED IN EUROPE.

CHAPTER I.

SLAVERY NOT REALLY IN QUESTION.

How will Europe, which professes to detest slavery, set to work consistently to treat with indifference the brave men who are struggling against slavery in England? How especially will England set to work to do this? There is but one resource in such a case—to endeavor to persuade both oneself and others that slavery has no part in the American struggle.

The friends of the South have not failed to do this. They have even attempted something better; they have sought to persuade us that to ensure the triumph of the South was to serve the cause of abolition! But this point, our credulity hesitated to accept, which is saying not a little. At most, it would only admit that this was serving abolition as Jeffreys served political liberty, as Louis XIV. and the Inquisition served religious freedom. Some crimes bring about reactions, some victories provoke vengeance: that this is true does not suffice to reconcile the human conscience to these victories and these crimes.

"Slavery is not in question;" such has been for a year the burden of letters from the South, the text of articles dictated and paid for among us by the South, the subjects of pamphlets and bound volumes printed in favor of the South. How often must an error be repeated for it to become truth? I know not. However it may be, this one has made its way, and we are to-day condemned to undertake its serious refutation. Well-informed men smile at our innocence; they know the Americans, they do not suffer themselves to be deceived by appearances, they are not dazzled by high-sounding words, they go to the bottom of things—and at the bottom of things, what do they find? The North, fighting for supremacy; the South, fighting for State sovereignty and commercial freedom, or perhaps, also, to satisfy the hatred inspired in it by the Puritans and Yankees: as to slavery, it is the pretext and nothing more—the shadow which a breath would disperse.

This is what they tell us with a shrug of the shoulders; then adding, for it is well to be cautious: "If by degrees the struggle against slavery gain place in the American war, it will be from the impulse of a bad feeling—a feeling of hatred and vengeance. It will not probably be claimed that abolition by way of reprisal has much right to our sympathies."

Admire here the power of principles! Men dare not attack them openly, they commit no infidelity to them which is not coupled with homage. They seek to keep up appearances on this point. "We, not encourage with our good wishes those who really oppose slavery! We, accord the shadow of a support, directly or indirectly, to those who really wish to maintain and extend slavery! Ah! you know us but little!"

There is no means, therefore, of escaping the pitiable comedy which we have witnessed. Some have lied; others more numerous, have admitted, in the best possible faith, that slavery is not the cause of the American conflict; others in fine, without denying daylight at mid-day, have reassured their conscience by saying (and no one will contest it) that the North sought the non-extension of slavery, but did not seek its immediate abolition; that there is a great distance between the Republican party and the abolitionists, properly called; and that consequently the North, not being abolitionist, is pursuing a political end and deserves no especial interest.

Before replying, which will not be difficult, let me express a thought which weighs on me. For thirty years, we have not ceased to reproach the North for its complicity with the South; yet, on the day when it repudiates it, on the day when, at the price of prodigious sacrifices, it utters the decisive speech, "Slavery shall go no further," on the day when it rejects that violent and gross policy which may be defined in a single sentence, *the policy of slavery*—on that day, we have for it only disdain, coldness, and distrust—on that day, we seem to have but one thought, to discover the weak sides of its conduct, to demonstrate that it does a generous deed without generosity, that its cause is not its cause, and that the election of Mr. Lincoln was wrought by men not in the least affected by the question of slavery.

Our time excels, I know, in thus blighting our rare occasions for enthusiasm; but such a course to me is revolting. I believe that by always suspecting, we become as blind and blinder than by always confiding. Of all dupes, the most miserable, to my mind, are those of scepticism. I do not like to put on spectacles to discover the faults of my friends; and if here and there something good be done on earth, it is repugnant to me to concentrate my attention on the less noble motives which must assuredly have mingled in it.

Having said this without dwelling on it, for my creed is well known, I enter upon the subject. These are the reasons for not admitting that slavery is concerned:

Mr. Lincoln, or his friends, have not been heard to utter a single time the word Abolition. They are fighting for the Constitution and the Union, and not against slavery. No important measure has been taken, no principle has been laid down; nothing has been done of a nature to move sympathies in Europe. A number of generals have refused to receive fugitive slaves, and have even returned them to their masters; but when General Fremont ventured to proclaim their emancipation, haste was made to annul his proclamation first, and to remove him afterward.

I feel myself the freer to reply, that I have felt myself sometimes very free to censure. Yes; every thing has not been perfect in the management of American affairs; in the presence of a colossal problem, the Washington Government has had its moments of wavering and error. But what is there extraordinary in this? Shall we cease to support men whom we cannot always approve?

To the service of great causes, it is necessary to bring, besides resolution and firmness, an abundant supply of patience, and, consequently, indulgence. I have not lulled myself with chimeras respecting the spirit which animated the North and determined the election of Mr. Lincoln. What did I say last year in my first volume? That this was by no means the work of the abolitionists, that it was by no means in question to destroy slavery, root and branch; but to begin at the beginning, to place before the progress of slavery an insuperable barrier, to limit the evil before destroying it.

I thought then that to limit it was something, that even in one sense it was every thing; I still think so to-day. Were there people ignorant enough of the position of parties in America, strangers enough to the march of social problems and the ways of the human heart, to dream it possible to destroy slavery at the first stroke? If there have been deceptions, there were also illusions! It is vexatious; but I do not see why the United States should be held accountable for the day dreams, to say the least, strange, which appear to have been current in Europe.

Their idea, which surely has greatness, is this: Slavery is a prodigious evil, morally and politically; if we remain chained to its cause, we shall perish; another step and we shall lose, with the esteem of the world, our last chances for uprising; it is necessary to break with the conquests of slavery, with filibusterism, with proceedings contrary to the law of nations, with ultra-democratic despotism; it is necessary to save our free institutions before they shall have been completely trailed in the mire.

All this is not abolitionism, I admit; all this may, perhaps, be said by men in whom still lives the detestable prejudice of skin, and who are affected much less by moral than political considerations. But what must be thence concluded? To make a prodigious effort in order to prevent one's country from falling into the pit digged by slavery—is not this to declare war on slavery? Do you doubt it? Consult the abolitionists themselves on this point; they will answer you. Although Mr. Lincoln may not be the representative of all their ideas, they know that their ideas will triumph through him. And the South knows it likewise. It was not mistaken; this election, though not an abolition one, bore abolition within its bosom; from the moment that the North refused to serve the cause of slavery on its knees, slavery was condemned to perish; it was no longer but a question of time.

For great revolutions, we must seek great causes, if we would attain the truth. I know of but one cause proportionate to the revolution which is being accomplished in America; the struggle against slavery is at the bottom; without being abolitionist, the Republican party of 1860 accepted, much more boldly than it imagined, the principle in virtue of which abolition will one day take place. It knew, better than it said, the way in which it was entering, and it entered it without hesitation. I pity those who do not know how to admire such an act; it seems to me that the history of Europe contains few that can be compared with it.

Alas! it is rather Europe which in this circumstance has deserted the cause of liberty! Supposing it to have been abandoned by the North; this would be no reason, it seems to me, for us to turn our backs on it. A fine conclusion, indeed, of the Pharisaical argument under which we have screened our selfishness—the North is not abolitionist enough, therefore we will not be so at all! The North is disposed to compromise, therefore we will advise her to make terms at any cost with the South! The adversaries of slavery lack enthusiasm, therefore we will favor its partisans! I do not exaggerate; to applaud decisions which confer on the South the position of belligerent; to admit its separation, that is, its triumph; to accept the chance of a war against the North and for the South without frowning—such have been, if I am not mistaken, the practical consequences of our scruples.

The passion for slavery is of recent growth in most of the Southern States. In the discussions which accompanied the foundation of the Union during the last century, Virginia and Maryland showed themselves no less convinced than Pennsylvania or Massachusetts, of the necessity of speedily putting an end to the slave trade, of preventing the introduction of slaves into new territories, and even of paving the way for emancipation. The leading men of the South, Washington, Jefferson, Patrick Henry, Wythe, George Mason, and many others, then held a language for which, at the present time, they would be tarred and feathered or hung by their fellow-citizens.

But if the disease be of recent date, it has nevertheless developed with unheard-of violence, and has now reached its crisis. Without going back to causes, among which figure in the first rank the growing demand for cotton and the invention of machinery to facilitate its cleaning, it suffices to establish the fact of its appalling progress..

The annexation of Texas was, as it were, the starting-point of the South, since which, it has not ceased to go forward—slavery, the progress of slavery, the dangers which may threaten slavery; these are its only anxieties.

It had taken care to stipulate that Texas should be, if necessary, divided into five States; wishing in this manner always to have the means of increasing its vote in Congress and protecting the "institution."

The admission of California as a free State was combated with ardor, and combated a long time; it seemed an injustice toward slavery.

The South indemnified itself for the loss by forcing the adoption of the forever odious Fugitive Slave Law. Next, it procured the repeal of the Missouri Compromise, wishing to open the North itself to the introduction of slavery. Next, with arms in its hands, and with the audacious support of President Buchanan, it opposed the free constitution of Kansas. Lastly, the Dred Scott decision came to signify to the whole Union that the day had arrived when it had to choose between a constitutional resistance to the crimes of the South and a general complicity with respect to them. It was then that the generous party was formed, which inscribed on its banner, "the non-extension of slavery."

Note, moreover, that in 1850, when California was admitted as a free State, a plan of separation was seriously discussed in South Carolina. It was the rebellion which we are now witnessing, ten years in advance; and I do not think that any one will take it upon himself to deny that its sole motive was the interest of slavery. But, in 1850, there was found in the Charleston Convention a prudent majority which, while also admitting the idea of a separation on account of slavery, was unwilling to attempt the adventure until South Carolina was certain that the rest of the slave States would follow in her train. The enterprise was therefore postponed.

Again, when Mr. Fremont was near attaining the presidency, South Carolina talked of seceding. To see a man hostile to the conquests of the "institution" at the head of the United States, was what she was determined never to endure. Fremont being defeated, (by very little,) the South Carolinians had not to put their designs into execution. They confined themselves to two things: on the one hand, to profiting by Mr. Buchanan and his cabinet to strengthen by every means the position of slavery, to invade the territories with the support of the administration, to endanger the Union, to corrupt institutions, to create in haste a condition of affairs from which escape would be impossible; on the other, to profit again by Mr. Buchanan and his cabinet to pave the way for the rebellion, to make provision for it in advance, to render in advance its suppression impossible, and, moreover, to announce loudly that if the voters of 1860 should dare to elect a president hostile to slavery, the dissolution of the Union would be proclaimed on the spot.

I have named the South Carolinians, because we must really regard them as the chief authors of the insurrection. There is in South Carolina and Georgia, as well as in the States formed from their original territory, Alabama and Mississippi, a passionate violence on the subject of slavery, which is not discovered in the rest of the South. Here is truly found the centre of the conspiracy. I could not have said of South Carolina and Georgia what I said just now of Virginia and Maryland; that, in the last century, the opposition to slavery and the slave trade was almost as lively there as in the North. The States who have been the first to give the signal for separation, were the last to accept the Union, and the motives of their hesitation at that time give but too clearly the key to their resolutions to-day—South Carolina demanded that the Constitution should recognize, in express terms, the legality of the slave trade. Mr. Pinckney himself declared without blushing that South Carolina would never accept the plan (of the Constitution) if it prohibited the commerce in slaves. Terms were made—and here commenced the sad series of compromises—the slave trade was sanctioned for twenty years. Such was the entrance of the South Carolinians; whoever recalls it to mind will have no difficulty in explaining their exit.

What has since passed explains it as well. I wish that those who dare affirm that slavery is not the cause of the present conflict, would be kind enough to interpret, apart from this cause, the discussions of the last few years. Not only has slavery always taken a constantly increasing part therein, but it has ended by remaining *alone* in debate—alone, I do not fear to go thus far. It would be necessary not to have read a line upon American discussions for the last ten years, to preserve a doubt on this point. The journals spoke only of slavery; Congress was divided only on the subject of slavery; elections, great and small, were made only with a view to slavery; internal and even external policy was preoccupied only about slavery; parties took form and opposed each other only by reason of views concerning slavery; the declarations and scarcely dissembled threats of the South articulated only grievances connected with slavery.

These threats have been heard during forty years, but constantly assuming a more precise character. The members of the South Carolina Convention recalled this to mind themselves not long ago. "Secession," said one of the members, Mr. Parker, "is no spasmodic and sudden effort. It has long been brewing among us." And Mr. Inglis added: "Most of us have had this subject for forty years under consideration." Mr. Keitt exclaimed, in his turn: "I have been engaged in this movement ever since I entered political life."

Animated by such a spirit, the ringleaders of the South, it will be comprehended, would make no scruples in proposing to break off the bargain with their Northern fellow-citizens, provided that slavery were menaced by them. On the presentation to Congress of petitions praying that the District of Columbia, the seat of government, might be free soil, the explosion took place; and directly, obedient to the angry commands of the South, Congress passed a series of ignoble laws, limiting its own action in every thing affecting slavery. On the adoption of liberty-bills in the Northern States, came a new explosion and new threats; the South would suffer no State to refuse its magistrates and prisons to the execution of the infamous law exacting the return of fugitive slaves. We remember, in fine, the struggle which took place before Mr. Lincoln's election, for the choice of the Speaker of the House of Representatives; for several weeks neither party would yield; and when finally the Republican candidate triumphed, the organs of the South were not slow in announcing the deep discontent of the slaveholders, as well as the terrible results which would ere long ensue from it.

So truly was slavery, and slavery alone concerned, that the question *par excellence* was that involving the fate of slavery—the question of the territories. According as this should be resolved in one direction or the other, the future of the "institution," every one felt, would be guaranteed or endangered. Thence, the bloody expeditions against free Kansas; thence, the sacking of Lawrence, in 1856, by the *Border Ruffians*, led by a former acting vice-president of the United States, Mr. Atchison; thence, all those scenes of barbarity, the sombre prelude to 1861; thence, all those solemn resolutions passed by the legislatures of the South. I quote that adopted by Alabama in January, 1860:

"The territories belonging to the United States are the common property of the people of the States. The people of the Slave States have a right to enjoy their property in slaves within the said territories, so long as they preserve this character, *and no law adopted by the territories can deprive them of such a right.*"

This lofty declaration, which is already well-nigh a declaration of secession, is found again in the platforms of the candidates for the presidency supported by the South.

Survey all these platforms, of the South and the North, of the ultra and the moderate parties, and you will find therein only the single, absorbing question of slavery—Kansas, the territories, fugitive slaves, and nothing else. Yet from these has been made the brilliant discovery: slavery is not the true cause of the American conflict!

What do we read in the platforms of the Republicans who supported Mr. Lincoln, and in the votes of their conventions? No extension of slavery beyond its present limits; no more admission of new slave States into the Union; the adoption of efficient measures against the slave trade; the important modification of the Fugitive Slave Law; the denunciation of the Dred Scott decision, which denied all rights to negroes and transformed all the free States into slave territory!

What do we read in the platform of the South which supported Mr. Breckenridge, and in the votes of its conventions? Slavery shall be national, and shall be recognized by the Constitution; it shall extend with the Union; no State can prevent the transit of slaves; the Fugitive Slave Law shall be made more stringent.

What do we see in the platform of the Douglas party? The right of the people of the territories to adopt or prohibit slavery; and, in compensation, doubtless, the acquisition of Cuba.

In fine, there is not a single party, even to that of Mr. Bell, which pretended to preserve an impartial balance between the South and the North, the Republicans and the Democrats, that has not taken care to immure itself within the question of slavery. The platform of the latter may be summed up in this wise: "The maintenance of the Union by important concessions to the slave States."

And observe, the threat of separation has always figured in the contest; so that it cannot be said that a new question has been substituted for that agitated at the time of the two last presidential elections. The question has remained and still remains the same: there are not two, there is but a single one. The South has demanded the extension of slavery, announcing that, if it were refused her, she would withdraw from the Union; the North has demanded the non-extension of slavery, and has valiantly accepted the chance, terrible though it were, of a disruption.

Do you wish for proof? Listen.

Mr. Butler, a leading member of the Senate, where he represented South Carolina, expressed himself in this wise in 1856: "If Fremont be elected, each of the Southern States will convoke its legislature, and take the necessary measures."

Mr. Brooks, the Member of Congress who caned Mr. Sumner, said in his turn to those who complimented him: "Trample under foot the Constitution of the United States, and form a Southern Confederacy, composed entirely of slave States. . . . If Fremont be elected, I am of the opinion that the people of the South should rise in their might above magistrates and laws, take the power in their own hands, and lay the strong grasp of free Southern men on the treasury and archives of the Government."

At the same time, the *Charleston Mercury*, an influential journal, declared that in case Mr. Fremont were elected, "there was not a public man in South Carolina, not one of its representatives or members of Congress, that would not be decided on a separation."

The Governor of Virginia held exactly the same language. Mr. Faulkner, of this State, the minister to France under Mr. Buchanan, exclaimed, a little later: "When that noble and brave child of Virginia, Henry Wise, declared as he did in October, 1856, that if Fremont were elected, he would seize the Federal arsenal at Harper's Ferry, how few at that time would have approved so bold a measure! It is the privilege of great minds to be in advance of their fellows."

The question was then no longer of Mr. Fremont, but of Mr. Lincoln. I have my hands full of extracts from the journals and official speeches of the time. Their uniform conclusion is, "If Lincoln be elected, the Union must not endure another hour."

Jefferson Davis, whose testimony will not be without value, said, in his address in 1859, to the people of Mississippi: "In case they elect as president a partisan of the doctrines professed by Seward at Rochester, dissolve the Union!"

On the 24th of January, 1860, Mr. Toombs, now a member of the cabinet at Richmond, made this speech in the Senate: "My State (Georgia) has made known its opinion. Nine years ago, it assembled a convention, and declared that its connection with the government depended on the faithful execution of the Fugitive Slave Law, and the full enjoyment of equal rights in the territories. . . . Free men of Georgia, keep your word, I am ready to keep mine! . . . Never permit the Federal Government to pass into the traitorous hands of the Black Republican party!"

Such was the attitude of the Southern senators and representatives. If a president opposed to the progress of slavery were elected, the disruption would take place. "You may elect a Northern president," exclaimed one, "but Virginia will resist his authority." And these furious declarations were applauded with enthusiasm, not only by Southern men, but by many members of the democratic party, by all who were in favor of slavery. Slavery must be saved at any price—they would sacrifice to it, if necessary, the Union, the Constitution, the greatness of the Republic! So true was it that the only anxiety was for slavery.

Once more, I cannot transcribe every thing for fear of wearying the reader; it seems to me, moreover, that my demonstration is complete. Let me be permitted only to give a few lines of the speech delivered in December, 1856, by Mr. Wise, the Governor of Virginia; I recommend them to the attention of Englishmen:

"If pacific means do not suffice, a little blood-letting, gentlemen, will reduce the fever. . . . The true seat of American dissensions, the true cause, the true root of our evil, is the influence of Great Britain. . . . I fear sometimes that the constant intercourse between New and Old England has rendered the sympathy of the former for the latter more lively than her affection for us."

This is called speaking frankly. The love of slavery and the hatred of England, which everywhere attacks slavery—this is really the basis of Southern feeling.

The Republican party was therefore forewarned. It knew beyond the possibility of mistake what would be the immediate results of a liberal election. It must be granted, that if these men were not sustained by a moral principle, if they were not obedient to the law of duty, their conduct becomes inexplicable. One does not sacrifice, without sufficient reason, his tranquillity, his fortune, and the fortune of his country. How am I to comprehend the election of Mr. Lincoln, if opposition to slavery were not its cause? I go further; how am I to comprehend the existence of a Republican party? In what does it differ from that of the Democrats, which maintains the system of concession to slavery?

Slavery or liberty! The question was put in these terms. All the citizens of the United States, all without exception, understood it in this wise, before and after the election. All in the South who were in favor of liberty, voted for Mr. Lincoln; (when, by chance, in some parts, they were at liberty to express such tendencies;) all in the North who were in favor of slavery, or disposed to make concessions to it, voted against Mr. Lincoln. The election was so far from *sectional*, as Americans term it, that a Northern man in favor of slavery would have been accepted with enthusiasm by the South, and a Southern man opposed to slavery would have been welcomed with no less enthusiasm by the North.

Never, surely, was a grander problem set before a people. Mr. Seward reduced it to an admirable formula, when he spoke of the "irrepressible conflict." *

The conflict remains to-day in the civil war what it was in the constitutional struggle of the political meetings. If it were otherwise, why is there not a single free State on the side of the South? Why is there not a single cotton State on the side of the North? Why are the Border States themselves divided in proportion to their attachment to slavery? Why have Western Virginia and Eastern Tennessee, for the sole reason that they have fewer slaves, detached themselves from their States in order to separate from the rebellion?

And let not this rebellion be called insane; in view of slavery, in the sight of men who consider nothing but slavery, and who, to save it, are ready to immolate every thing, even their country and their oaths, the separation had become a necessity. There is an infallible instinct which warns social iniquities that the

* This is his phrase, which deserves to be preserved, since it was the almost constant text of the debates which preceded the election: *The collision between the two systems of labor in the United States is an irrepressible conflict between two opposing forces.*

moment their power is circumscribed, their death-warrant is signed. They are condemned to go on increasing under pain of perishing. Can you conceive of stationary slavery, stationary in the country of incessant progress? Every thing around it is growing, while it has ceased to increase. How long will it be before it will have ceased to exist? See free States springing up at the North and West; what will become of it, imprisoned in insuperable limits, shut out from the territories, the list of States which belong to it definitively closed?

Mr. Sumner has said with great reason, "Such is the nature of slavery, that it can only exist where it rules." A vital question was therefore at stake, and nothing had power of changing its nature—promise what you like, pile up guarantees, interdict yourselves the right of interfering in any manner with the internal institutions of States—it matters little; slavery ceasing to reign, will cease to live; forbidden to go forward, it will go backward rapidly.

It remains for me to examine what has passed since the election of Mr. Lincoln; I find it the exact confirmation, and counter-verification, as it were, of all that happened before. Slavery remains the sole question. The cotton States continue their threats, the partisans of compromise endeavor to effect negotiations.

And what do we find in these schemes? Did the peace conference, which sat at Washington under the presidency of Mr. Tyler and the influence of Virginia, have any other thought than slavery? Did it propose to proclaim free trade? No one dreamed of it there for a moment; no one thought of it until after the attempt to deceive Europe by substituting pretexts for reasons. The minutes of the Peace Conference may be consulted; nothing will be found in them which does not relate to slavery in the territories, to fugitive slaves, to amendments calculated to render the Constitution more favorable to slaveholders, to the maintenance of slavery in the District of Columbia, to the transit of slaves through free States, to the sojourn in free States of planters with their slaves, to the suppression of incendiary attacks against the doctrine of slavery, to the abrogation of liberty-bills.

These were the things then debated at Washington; and if a few stipulations were proposed besides, designed to recognize the right of separation, I need not say that circumstances rendered such manifestations inevitable. At the same time, a respectable man, Mr. Crittenden, with whom compromises are somewhat of a specialty, offered motions in Congress, designed to reëstablish peace, the sole object of which was slavery.

I have turned over with some care a large volume containing the debates of the Missouri Convention in 1861. I was curious to see what the representatives of one of the largest of the Border States had to say among themselves, under the impulse of events. I have examined it thoroughly; and, apart from a few dissertations on the right of separation, and, consequently, on State sovereignty, I have discovered nothing but discussions, often very interesting, and arguing a remarkable development of local life, but relating solely to slavery.

There was another document to be consulted; namely, the act whereby the insurgent South appropriated to its use the ancient Constitution of the United States. What changes have been introduced in this? Two, only. The first, the necessary consequence of the political principle proclaimed by the revolution, ensures State sovereignty; the second, the expression of the fundamental idea of the South, recognizes and protects slavery in all the States, as well as in the territories which may be acquired by their confederacy.

The South has been praised for having put aside all "false delicacy," and called things by "their right names." It is certain that it has fully deserved this praise. Although restrained by the necessity of not too greatly exasperating public opinion in Europe, although sacrificing to this necessity the slave-trade, warmly defended at Montgomery by the South Carolinians, it has unfurled its banner, and if we do not read thereon its true device, it is our fault and not its own.

Not only does it summon to itself all the slave States, which are still missing, while it would not accept a free Státe at any price, but it defines in the clearest terms that article of its constitution which ought to have aroused the conscience of the nineteenth century.

Hear the *Richmond Enquirer:* "Hitherto the defence of slavery has encountered great difficulties, because its apologists (for they were merely apologists) stopped half way. They confined the defence of slavery to negro slavery alone, abandoning the *principle* of slavery, and admitting that every other form of slavery was wrong. Now, the line of defence is changed; the South maintains that slavery is just, natural, and necessary, and that it does not depend on the difference of complexions."

Hear Mr. Stephens, the Vice-President of the Southern Confederacy, and the most eloquent of its orators. His Atlanta speech, which I am about to quote, is a manifesto, and a manifesto accepted by his fellow-citizens; for it was after this speech that he was reëlected to the eminent position which he fills: "Though last, not least, the new constitution has put to rest *forever* all the agitating questions relating to our peculiar institutions. . . . Slavery was the immediate cause of the late rupture and present revolution. Jefferson, in his forecast, had anticipated this as 'the rock upon which the old Union would split.' He was right. The prevailing ideas entertained by him and most of the leading statesmen of his time were, that the enslavement of the African race was in violation of the laws of nature. . . .Those ideas, however, were fundamentally false. They rested upon the assumption of the equality of races. This was an error. It was a sandy foundation. . . .Our new government is founded upon exactly the opposite idea; its foundations are laid, its corner-stone rests, upon the great truth that the negro is not equal to the white man; that slavery, subordination to the superior race, is his natural and normal condition. This, our new government, is the first in the history of the world based upon this great physical, philosophical, and moral truth. . . .The negro, by nature or by the curse against Canaan, is fitted for that condition which he occupies in our system. This stone, which was rejected by the builders, 'is become the chief stone of the corner' in our new edifice."

We see that there are two schools in the South, and that Mr. Stephens, not going so far as the *Richmond Enquirer*, confines himself to negro slavery! But with what enthusiasm he speaks of it! How we feel that to him and his Southern compatriots it is a duty to be accomplished!

By the side of this official manifesto, all else grows dim. I will therefore suppress the numerous quotations which I have at hand, and content myself with recalling the fact—the remembrance contains a lesson—that Mr. Calhoun, the most important politician, perhaps, that the South has ever produced, did not fear to affirm already in his time, that "slavery was the surest and most stable basis on which to establish free institutions." Mr. Hunter, of Virginia, expressed the same idea in a figurative shape: "The keystone which caps and sustains the powerful arch on which our social system reposes, *is made of that block of black marble called the African slave.*"

Is doubt still possible? Suppose even, which is false, that the North has not risen against slavery, we are forced to admit at least that the South has really risen for slavery. It is the first time, they have taken care to tell us—it is the first time in the history of the world that a great movement has been made in the sole end of proclaiming and securing the sacred rights of slavery. This is a rebellion without grievances or pretexts; it has but one thought—slavery is menaced, slavery may perish, the new President will not give slavery the protection which it needs, majorities will be formed constantly more hostile to slavery.

Yet European opinion has wavered!

We are told of other questions which give the key, it is said, of the present crisis. Let us examine them.

"At the bottom of the electoral struggle which resulted in the presidency of Mr. Lincoln, there was not slavery, but supremacy!" This is often repeated in Europe, and has an air of profundity. I seek for things behind the words, and find nothing.

What means the supremacy of the South?—the extension of slavery. The South, moreover, willingly accepted Northern men, and Mr. Buchanan, the Pennsylvanian, suited it admirably, because he served the purposes of slavery; because, with him, it could organize expeditions against Central America and Cuba; because, with him, it could continue the slave trade; because, with him, it could impose slavery in Kansas on a people that rejected it.

Discover, if you can, any distinction whatever between

the question of slavery and the question of supremacy! You will not succeed. If it were otherwise, the electoral platforms, I think, would have accorded some place to this question of supremacy. If it were otherwise, would there have been an important party in the North—the Democratic party—voting for Southern candidates? Who can make you believe that the supremacy of the South was desired by Northern democrats? Their policy was more natural—they accepted the candidates of the South because they accepted the extension of slavery.

"Well, be it so," it is said; "the question is not of supremacy, but State sovereignty."

What does this mean? Was the South to be oppressed? Was any one about to meddle with her peculiar institutions? Was *self-government* to be infringed upon in any wise? Had Mr. Lincoln announced his design of attacking that portion of sovereignty constitutionally devolving on individual States? The attempt is vain; it will not be easy to transform Mr. Lincoln into a despot, rending, with his own hands, the constitution of his country; or to move our compassion for the servitude with which the South was bowed down or threatened. It possessed, by virtue of its constitution, the privilege of electing more representatives than its white population would have permitted; it had, in fact, since the foundation of the Union, made twelve presidents out of nineteen; twenty-one speakers out of thirty-three; and sixty-one presidents of the Senate out of seventy-seven, including presidents *pro tem.* The minority, it had made the law.

Ah! if by the words, "State sovereignty," you mean the right of the South forever to rule the North, and its right to withdraw when this government escapes its hands, into the bargain, I have nothing to say; in this respect, the questions of supremacy and State sovereignty were both involved. But who does not see that the claim to rule was confounded here with the cause of slavery, which perishes, as we have said, as soon as its interests cease to rule? The supremacy and independence of the South again was only slavery. If this had not been so, every one would not have said and felt it. There is a popular instinct in great crises which is never mistaken.

In our eagerness to put ourselves on the wrong scent and reassure our conscience, we have carefully gathered up the small reasons and let the great ones go. The small reasons are real ones; the error does not consist in pointing them out, but in assigning them a place which does not belong to them.

I will apply this remark to the most general, most popular explanation of the Southern insurrection.

"There is in it," it is said, "an antipathy of race. The incompatibility of temper between the North and South already troubled the patriotic soul of Washington, who trusted to time to resolve the problem. Time, however, has wrought no solution, the problem remains entire, the mutual hatred of the Cavalier and the Puritan, the man of leisure who leads the life of a gentleman, and the man who works for his livelihood in the fields, the factory, and the warehouse—this long-lived hatred must some day have brought about a rupture. It has done so; why should we cast the blame on slavery?"

Why? Because, so long as the question of slavery was not raised in its present form, the differences of the North and South, which, doubtless, were not less, brought about no secession. The threats of secession commenced on the day when slavery had reason to believe itself in peril; the threats of secession were realized on the day when this peril became certain.

It is convenient to forget this, and to expatiate on the

definition of the distinct types found north and south of the Susquehanna. If you say that the cotton planter detests the Yankee, you are right in some measure. The *Times* correspondent, in his journey through the South, gathered manifestations of feelings not precisely amiable: "Would that the accursed vessel that brought those d——d Yankees to America had foundered on the way! We could get along with these fanatics, if they were only Christians and gentlemen. Give us whatever government you like, even tyranny or despotism, but nothing shall compel us to remain united with the brutal and vulgar rabble of New England!" Such is indeed the expression of hatred as it is felt now in Charleston. In the eyes of the South Carolinians in arms for slavery, New England, I say it to its honor, can be naught but the incarnation of evil. Freedom of speech, freedom of the press, habits of labor, every thing that wounds the susceptibilities of slaveholders, is found in these primitive States, peopled by Roundheads. The attack comes from there, the enemy is there.

But the enemy—let not the English deceive themselves!—is also in England. Among Americans, I perceive much less antagonism of races than of principles. Take away slavery, and the motives for union will a thousand times prevail (South Carolina and Georgia excepted, perhaps) over those for separation. In the South and North, I see the same religious faiths, the same charitable institutions, the same national glory, the same great men adopted by all, the same historic memories, the same language, the same literature, the same interests, the same parties. Let us add that the same institutions have been practised and loved in both North and South; they still exercise such an influence over the Southern people, that after having seceded to protect their slavery, they have deemed it impossible for them to imagine forms of government other than those of the United States.

I am not ignorant that, under the influence of over-excited passions, and to flatter the English, of whom they had need, the South Carolinians may have uttered the cry which, according to Mr. Russell, must have caused the shades of George III., North, and Johnson, to leap for joy: "If we could but be governed by a member of the royal family of England!" But let them not trust too much to this. If the planters cast a look of envy on the landed aristocracy and gentry of their cousins, if they love English customs, if they pride themselves on their descent from old English families, England, notwithstanding, will do wisely not to dream of the establishment of a constitutional monarchy under a prince of the house of Hanover. Republican manners have struck root deeper than is imagined, even on the shores of the Gulf of Mexico; the opposition of the South and North is less absolute than is said. Apart from slavery, no question would have separated those united by so many ties. The honorable correspondent of the *Times* was much nearer the truth when, forgetful for a moment of the compliments paid to England, and remembering, as a man of heart, the great cause of humanity which England patronizes, he exclaimed, of the conversation held around him by Southerners: "My ears were shocked at hearing this subject discussed in the English tongue."

Such are the principal explanations of the insurrection; the rest are not worth the trouble of naming. Has not the attempt been made, after all, to attribute considerable importance to the tariff? I do not believe that, even in the South, a single man could be found willing to maintain that this question had any share in the last election, or that it was thought of when secession was proclaimed. It is easy to arrange antitheses in Europe: "Here the agricultural interest, there the manufacturing interest; here protection, there free trade." Without denying the opposition of interests, I believe much more in their unison; and as to the chimerical part attributed to the tariff, the planters think like me, for, by the confession of Mr. Stephens, their mouth-piece, the tariff which was in force when they seceded was the result of their own votes.

There was, then, but one question in 1860—that of slavery.

"But," it is objected, "the republican party, by its own admission, does not pursue abolition, properly called; it thinks only of non-extension."

Yes, certainly; and what do you conclude from it? Non-extension contains abolition; it leads to it necessarily. For many years, the problem has been put in these terms; some demanding extension, others rejecting it, all knowing that this first point once resolved, the rest must follow. Two roads start from the same point; the question is to know whether we will take the first or second; the whole journey is comprised in the choice. Will it be said that the travellers who thus proceed in contrary directions, are only separated at first by the distance of a few steps, and that this signifies nothing? But the separation will go on increasing; directions alone are important on earth.

Now, the electors of Mr. Lincoln have done a great thing—they have changed the direction hitherto adopted by their country. That they may not have had, with respect to slavery, the profound hatred and energetic determination which might have been desired, I do not dispute. I believe that the greater number were impelled less by the need of protesting against a moral evil than by the desire of combating a political one. This is true; yet, notwithstanding, without having the design to exterminate slavery, they had a design whose greatness cannot be contested, since they thought to limit it, since they cast their suffrages for the man who had expressed himself thus: "If I were in Congress, and the proposition to prohibit slavery in the new territories were under discussion, in spite of the Dred Scott decree, I would vote for its prohibition. . . . . We must endeavor to overthrow this Dred Scott decision."

The Republican party in general was not abolitionist; it was anti-slavery-propagandist—pardon me, for once, so barbarous an expression—without abolishing, it wished to check it. And where is the abolitionist in Europe who would not have leaped for joy if any one had foretold to him, three or four years ago, that the extension of slavery was about to be checked in America? For myself, I confess that I have long desired this, and nothing else. And I have never thought myself modest in making such a wish.

Behold us at the heart of the argument; let us endeavor to form a just idea of the present sentiments of the North, the intentions of Mr. Lincoln and his cabinet, and the movement of public opinion with respect to slavery.

I begin with the abolitionists. They did not make the last election, although they contributed their share to it; they do not direct the policy of the North, although their influence may make itself felt there. We would wrong the United States, were we to attribute to the abolitionist party the monopoly of generous sentiments on the subject of slavery. Yet, in the presence of this great cause, so long misunderstood, but which is now advancing with giant strides, it is impossible not to think with respect of those valiant men who have stemmed the current of interests and accepted the hatred of the multitude; who, without even speaking of their martyrs, have sacrificed their repose, their influence, their political prospects, to devote themselves to the defence of the oppressed. Woe to the country where the name of Garrison, of Tappan, of Wendell Phillips, shall not be honored!

I know what reproaches a considerable number of American abolitionists have deserved. There are some who, like Parker, rebel against the Gospel in which, strange to say, they fancy that they discover the sanction of slavery. There are others who seem not to be fastidious with respect to means—to trample the Constitution under foot, to emancipate the blacks after the manner of John Brown, to accept if necessary the horrible chance of negro insurrections—there is reason to suppose them ready for these.

I shall not dwell on the point. As a system, abolitionism is dead. It has died the death of noble causes, by the very effect of its own triumph. What is the use of an abolition party, when the whole North is about to become abolitionized?

This does not mean that the North has already become so. Let us beware of that feverish impatience which refuses men time enough to be sure of their own minds! When we do an honorable action, we never know how far it will carry us.

The election of Mr. Lincoln will carry the North a great way, as Europe must comprehend. But time again is needed. On the morrow of the election, or, if we will, on the morrow of the fall of Sumter, whatever might have been the patriotic unanimity of the North, it nevertheless included, side by side, the victors and the vanquished, the friends and the opponents of Mr. Lincoln, the Republicans and the Democrats. Thence arose a complicated position, the difficulties of which were evident.

If the Republicans themselves were then far from measuring the full scope of their triumph, the Democrats mingled with the indignation caused by the revolt of the South, a persistent tendency to compromises. The party of Mr. Douglas certainly cared little to enter into direct conflict with slavery, and the party of Mr. Crittenden in the Border States cared still less to do so—Mr. Crittenden, who published descriptions of fugitive slaves in the newspapers, with the promise of "two hundred dollars reward."

Composed of such elements, the public opinion of the North could not be impelled at the first onset to decisive measures; a considerable party was necessarily found, obstinate in dreaming as long as possible of the return of the South and negotiations with the South, and determined not to give umbrage to the staggering fidelity of the Border States.

Sentiments of this sort were several times manifested with extreme violence. Abolition presses were destroyed, and abolition meetings dispersed or hissed down in Ohio, Illinois and Massachusetts. The watchword was "Unión, not abolition." For the Union, for the Constitution, lives by thousands, and dollars by millions were promised and given; for the destruction of slavery, was promised neither a dollar nor a drop of blood.

This is the fact; I do not seek to paint it in ideal colors. If I do not greatly admire it, neither does it succeed in rousing my indignation. Is it not in accordance with the necessary progress of human events? Does it ever happen on earth, that a nation engaged in a laudable work maintains itself on the level of its principle? Our works are always greater than we.

The North, moreover, is more conscious than is supposed of the goal toward which it is advancing. This intelligent and reflective people is not ignorant that abolition is at the end, only it wishes to do one thing after another. To-day, war; to-morrow, . . . For the war, all are needed; we will therefore put aside every thing that can divide us. The question of slavery makes its way naturally, necessarily, as a carriage glides down the inclined plane on which it is placed. The American people, let us not forget, placed it upon this inclined plane, when, in spite of threats, and in the face of an appalling crisis, it resolutely, to resist the excess of evil, adopted the nomination of Mr. Lincoln.

In setting forth the moral position of the North, I defined Mr. Lincoln's position in advance; he represents with marvellous fidelity, the country by which he was elected.

A Kentuckian by birth, and the fast friend of two able Kentuckians—Messrs. Holt and Crittenden—who urge him to circumspection, Mr. Lincoln is evidently not a stranger to that fever of compromises which seems to run in the American blood. He will go on to the end, but he will proceed thither step by step. A slow gait is most in conformity with his nature. The declared enemy of the progress of slavery, he would fear too hastily to approach the problem of abolition.

I do not impute this to him as a crime, for I feel as much as any one with what prudence the strongest conviction should be armed. A special prudence, moreover, is almost always imposed on men by high position and grave responsibility; considered from high or low, by the head of a State or by the first corner, questions do not, and should not, present the same aspect. But, aside from this legitimate prudence, there is, it seems to me, a natural, and in some sort innate, tendency in Mr. Lincoln to seek the middle course. In his great electoral campaign, he made no absolute pledges either for the abrogation of the Fugitive Slave Law or for the abolition of slavery in the District of Columbia; while manifesting the desire to remedy the wrong, he did not for a moment lose sight of the difficulties and inconveniences of the remedy. No one was more anxious than he to respect State sovereignty and avoid whatever might give the government a "sectional" appearance.

Although, as far as I am concerned, I prefer the most decided characters and entire convictions, I am not blind, notwithstanding, to the advantage, in the present circumstances, of so moderate a President. I experienced a feeling of respect—I, who so ardently desire the abolition of slavery—when I saw Mr. Lincoln, taking his oaths and the Constitution in earnest, hesitate for several hours to sign the law of Congress which declared free all slaves of rebels employed in arms against the North. He finally signed it, and he did right; the condition of war confers certain exceptional rights on the head of the State, who is also the head of the army. To fetter the movement would have been a great mistake, but to precipitate it would have been a still greater one. It belonged to the President, above all, to strive to maintain intact the unanimity of the North by avoiding to wound the Border States, which will be henceforth faithful, by too abrupt measures, and also by regarding the feelings of the Democratic party, which is daily becoming more favorable to the cause of emancipation, but which cannot in a moment leap over the space which separates it from the Republicans. Enough for the day is the evil thereof; in proportion as we advance, in proportion as the public opinion of the North shapes itself in the direction of progressive emancipation, Mr. Lincoln can take measures impossible at the outset.

Mr. Lincoln has acted with reason and humanity in refusing the negro regiments offered him by the refugees of Canada, as well as in averting as long as possible measures calculated to stir up slave insurrections in the South.

Mr. Lincoln has endeavored to strengthen his cabinet in its resistance to the ultra abolitionists. Has he never gone too far in this direction? I will not deny it. The removal of Mr. Fremont, though we may not be in a position to judge fully of it in Europe, has grieved the friends of liberty among us.

But how many redeeming measures have there been! Mr. Lincoln, let us not forget, has abolished the Fugitive Slave Law, in fact;* has given the most liberal orders concerning negroes to his generals; has announced, in fine—and this is prodigious progress—that diplomatic relations will be opened with the two black republics, Liberia and Hayti. These first acts give hopes of others; I await them with full confidence.

It was not useless to give instructions to the generals. Several among them, seeming to mistake the high end of the American movement, and carrying to extremes the desire of taking away all abolitionist character from the war, had well-nigh transformed their soldiers into slave catchers, and their camps into prisons. Slaves, alas! had been put in irons, whipped, and restored to their masters! One hardly dares think of the consequences

* The recent execution of the Fugitive Slave Law in the District of Columbia and elsewhere, proves that Count de Gasparin was unfortunately mistaken in supposing it a dead letter.—Tr.

of such deeds. Thank God! they have become henceforth impossible; the August circular has regulated the matter in the most liberal manner—to receive fugitive slaves, to employ them in the quality of free men in exchange for wages, to reserve the regulation of the indemnity due the master, if the latter be not a rebel—such are the principles laid down by the minister of war.

General Fremont went further. His proclamation, which Mr. Lincoln has modified, went beyond the limits set by Congress, and constituted, consequently, an excess of power which the President was right in repressing, notwithstanding the generous feeling which Mr. Fremont had inspired. He had other faults besides; an ostentatious body-guard, extravagant expenses, lack of administrative capacity — such are the reproaches which have been brought against him. It is added, but this is a question which it does not belong to us to examine, that, despite his eminent skill as an engineer and explorer, he was a bad general; that he had failed to send timely aid, either to the heroic Lyon, the defenders of Lexington, or the main body of the army overwhelmed at Springfield; that, in fine, the principal expedition of the war, that of the Mississippi, was imperilled in his hands.

Once more, we are not the judges. Mr. Fremont has energetically protested against the report of Adjutant-General Thomas, which served as the basis of his recall, and which events have taken pleasure ever since in contradicting on all points. Perhaps Mr. Fremont has been unjustly sacrificed; however this may be, it is difficult not to regret that the most rigorous act of Mr. Lincoln should have happened to fall upon so excellent a man. The *Pathfinder* enjoys an immense popularity in the United States, in which is associated Mrs. Fremont, familiarly called "*Our Jessie*," whom the army of Missouri has seen marching by the side of her husband. Mr. Fremont represented, in the eyes of Europe, a liberal and generous tendency, which has been believed, doubtless without reason, to be involved in his disgrace.

It added to the prestige of Mr. Fremont that his recall reached him at the moment when he was in pursuit of the enemy, and almost on the eve of a battle. His Springfield proclamation is stamped with a patriotic sadness, with which it is impossible not to be touched. In taking leave of his enthusiastic and exasperated soldiers, the sole thought of the general was how to appease their wrath, to maintain discipline, and to transmit intact to his happier successor, this army, sure of obtaining the victory.

There are words here that quicken the pulses of the soul, words such as we have heard too seldom from America during the past year. It has therefore been incumbent on me to pause at this incident, and briefly to narrate the feelings of Europe on seeing this general removed in the very face of the enemy. If there be error, as I am inclined to believe, it will be repaired; if Mr. Fremont, despite his eminent qualities in other respects, be scarcely capable of commanding an army, he will none the less remain one of the loftiest characters in America, as his conduct at the moment of his disgrace will remain one of the glorious facts of our time.

In any case, I am happy to say that his removal cannot be explained by the motive that some have affected to suspect in it. It was not in the capacity of abolitionist that he was set aside; for, on the one hand, he had accepted the modification introduced by the President into his proclamation, and, on the other, the minister of war who proposed his recall was a more pronounced abolitionist than himself.

One would say, indeed, to hear some persons, that Mr. Lincoln's government had been signalized by no progress, with regard to the liberty of the negroes. I recalled a few facts of this sort, just now; but there are others which must be mentioned.

On the 4th of December, a letter of instructions was addressed by the Secretary of State to General McClellan, which leaves room for no misunderstanding with respect to fugitive slaves: "Instead of imprisoning them," says Mr. Seward, "we should imprison those who pursue them."

A fugitive slave was arrested in Washington, conformably to the celebrated Fugitive Slave Law. The government ordered his immediate liberation.

The instructions given to the naval expeditions destined for the South, contain these explicit commands: "You are at liberty to accept all services, whether of fugitives or others, that may be offered to the National Government. You are to assure loyal owners that Congress will secure them a just compensation."

Congress, on its side, has not remained inactive. It has ordered an inquiry concerning certain slaves still imprisoned in the jails at Washington. It has several plans before it, the openly abolitionist character of which cannot be contested. Called by the last message of Mr. Lincoln to the discussion of grave questions, all relating to emancipation, it does not appear far from entering upon more decisive measures than were announced in its Confiscation Bill.

One fact among others permits us to measure the distance already passed over since the election of Mr. Lincoln. It will be remembered that, under his predecessors, the slave trade was in full prosperity. In the space of a year, more than a hundred vessels had been fitted out from the ports of the United States, and if there had been a few prosecutions here and there, they had never been followed by any severe sentence. This was the time when Mr. Slidell, one of the commissioners seized the other day on board the *Trent*, offered resolutions in the Senate, requesting the President to signify to the other powers that America would no longer furnish her quota of cruisers on the African coast. To-day, things have greatly changed: for the first time for many years, the captain of a slaver has been sentenced to death for the crime of piracy. Still more, despite the repugnance inspired in Mr. Lincoln by the penalty of death, despite the unheard-of efforts of the friends of the condemned for his life, his execution has taken place. We may judge by this that the epoch of acts of violence against English cruisers, of enterprises against Cuba, of Ostend conferences, and of programmes signed by Messrs. Buchanan, Mason, and Slidell, in favor of an unlimited extension of slavery, are left behind.

The progress of public opinion is rapid, and the description which I just gave of the position of parties in the North, will soon cease to be correct. A work is being silently accomplished in the heart of American society, the results of which will not be long in appearing. The conviction that slavery is the great criminal, that slavery must perish, and that without this there is nothing really done, is continually gaining ground. "There is a moral principle in our war. Whence came our debasement? Why is the uprising of our people now necessary? Slavery has done it. Slavery is the arch rebel, the great traitor, the sole traitor, in reality; the whole rebellion is contained in slavery." Such are the ideas and words, unpopular or distrusted at first, which are now in every one's mouth. The Democrats themselves are inclining to this side. It seems absurd to all to contend purely and simply to restore the condition which gave rise to the civil war. If nothing else were wished, of what use has it been to elect Mr. Lincoln, brave a destructive crisis, sacrifice thousands of lives, and add millions to the public debt?

The good sense of the Americans thus acts its part by coming to the aid of their conscience. The moral nature of the conflict, confused at first in the eyes of many, constantly reveals itself more and more in its majesty. It is with this as with all generous causes—it grows and strengthens as it goes on, *vires acquirit eundo.*

The influence of the war has been decisive in this respect. The balls that pierced Ellsworth and Lyon slew the prejudices among thousands of men which still beset their minds and hindered them from clearly discerning the scope of the last presidential election. It is henceforth impossible for the war to end without giving to slavery the blow that must destroy it, sooner or later. Charles Sumner eloquently expressed this thought in the late Republican convention at Worcester: "Contemplate the war, study it on all sides; you will always see slavery as the sole cause of its evils." Never were the words of the Roman orator more applicable: *Nullum facinus extitit nisi per te, nullum flagitium sine te.* Slavery is the cause of the war: it is its power, its end, its aim, its all. It is often said that the war will put an end to slavery; this is probable, but what is still more probable is that the abolition of slavery will put an end to the war!

The popular excitement is such that there is reason sometimes to fear too hasty movements. The warmest abolition feeling is propagated in the immense army of the North, and whole regiments have been seen marching through Northern cities to the John Brown song:

> "John Brown's body lies mouldering in the ground;
> His soul's marching on."

We remember the strange speech of Colonel Cochrane, and the still stranger approbation which was so openly given to the Secretary of War, Mr. Cameron, when the question was nothing less than that of urging the arming of the slaves. It is possible, doubtless, that the power of events may carry America thus far; social revolutions often carry a blind force within themselves, to which the wisest can offer but a weak resistance; but the friends of the negroes will be the first in this event to deplore such impetuosity.

I readily comprehend why Mr. Lincoln exposes himself to the reproach of ultra moderation, rather than endure the yoke of the Jacobins of abolition. When General Phelps, in his address to the people of Louisiana and Mississippi, proclaimed in strong terms the hatred of Anglo-Saxons to slavery, he might be accused of going a little too fast; nevertheless, there was nothing in this directly to instigate negro insurrections. Any thing that should go further would be strongly opposed.

There is a party in Congress which would not recoil before extreme measures, and which would gladly ensure its success in the beginning by obtaining the removal of General McClellan. Mr. Lincoln acts like himself, in resisting this party, in striking out a part of Mr. Cameron's report, in replacing him by a more conservative minister, in giving his support to the young commander-in-chief, in declaring himself ready to adopt measures conducive to emancipation, without accepting those which would engender civil war.

Do you remember that admirable speech of Mrs. Stowe: "Great pity makes us pause." Yes, at the thought of servile war (she said this to England, which did not yet comprehend prudent progress, but confounded it with inaction)—at the thought of servile war, great pity should make us pause; pity for the whites and pity for the blacks. Picture to yourself three or four millions of negroes, roaming over the plantations with fire and sword in hand! It is the only calamity, perhaps, that may be compared with slavery. Ah! let us not ensanguine the cause we love; let us not dishonor the flag of abolition; let us remember that such is not the method of the Gospel!

If any thing were capable of justifying the Southern rebellion, it would be these negro insurrections. "You see for yourselves," they say; "we are fighting for our lives, and the honor of our wives and daughters; emancipation among us would be necessarily a second St. Domingo."

Those who cling to the honor of the North and of abolition, should strive before every thing not to authorize such language. If a few negro insurrections take place, it is, perhaps, inevitable; the responsibility of them at least must not rest on the friends of liberty. Their work—and I praise Mr. Lincoln for having so well comprehended it—is a work of love and peace. They know that to organize negro insurrections would be to condemn this unhappy race to a remediless degradation. Emancipations effected in this wise never lead to true liberty; look at Hayti, and compare it with the English West Indies!

Who knows, besides, whether slave insurrections would not bring about a violent reaction in the North itself? Perchance the Federal armies would with their own hands suppress these criminal attempts on the lives of fellow citizens, friends and relatives. In any case, the public opinion of the whole world would turn aside with horror; at the story of the massacres, we should begin to curse freedom. Do we not know that liberty suffers more from the errors of its partisans than from the attacks of its adversaries?

Then a crime is a crime; we must always come back to this. By the side of this conscientious reason, all arguments of utility grow dim. No crime, at any price, for a holy cause! Such is our cry; America will hear it.

Let it not be maintained, moreover, that slave insurrections are impossible. I am not ignorant that the South, with the boasting imprudence which characterizes it, lately argued against the North the tranquillity of its negroes, thus making a weapon of the very peace ensured it by the moderation of Mr. Lincoln. The Southern journals have talked loudly of negro battalions, full of ardor, and anxious to give a good lesson to the abolitionists.

And how could the negroes of the South help showing enthusiasm? A slave has the feelings which he is commanded to have, until the moment when his true sentiments are at liberty to break out. Will they never break out? God only knows. I suppose at all events that the people of Virginia have not forgotten the insurrection of 1831, Nat Turner, and the two days' massacre. Denmark Vesey and his accomplices are doubtless still remembered at Charleston. They were numbered by thousands; their heroic silence wearied the executioners; the whole State was a prey to terror. Yet madmen now exclaim that slave insurrections are impossible.

I have pointed out the danger of going too fast; I shall no more deny the danger of going too slowly.

As it is honorable to resist radical measures and repudiate the aid of slave insurrections, so it would be shameful still to retain in the heart any lurking thought of compromise. That there may be such thoughts in the North it would be absurd to deny; to obtain the restoration of the Union as it was is the ideal of a few. Happily, their projects are outgrown and forever repudiated by the public conscience, and their success, were it for an instant possible, would call forth an irresistible reaction.

Inquiry should long since have been made concerning the slaves imprisoned at Washington. The cautious language which is still used at times toward the shorn majesty of slavery, the twisted language which is used sometimes as if to steer clear of the great issues of the American movement, are not of a nature to call forth sympathies.

Sympathies are the first of all powers in such a conflict. Simple ideas, clearly expressed, alone make converts. The United States now have soldiers, vessels, and munitions in abundance; what they lack most of all is the energetic manifestation of the idea for which they are struggling. Their regiments need to be reënforced by ideas. No one must be longer deceived therein, either in the North or the South, in America or Europe. Justice must be made manifest. The war must be in the eyes of all a holy war, "a war which we can pray for."

The United States will triumph only when they shall be right with God—forgive me the expression. Their cause is good; it will be better when they shall have thoroughly comprehended it themselves, and presented it in its true light. God awaits this moment. There are infamous laws to be revoked and acts of ignominy to be effaced. This can be done without adopting plans of radical abolition, and without instigating slave insurrections. It can and should be done; else God, I fear, will use the South as an avenging rod, and, in one form or another, the chastisement will endure until all traces of the old complicity shall be blotted out, and until the North shall have written her motto upon her banner.

Sufferings and reverses play the part of Providence on earth. The plagues of Egypt continued so long as Pharaoh refused consent to the deliverance of the children of Israel. The first important act of emancipation was not passed at Washington until after the battle of Bull Run. The liberation of slaves was not proposed at Athens until after the Chæronea battle-field, and the orator who made the motion had the right to say, "It is not that I propose it, but Chæronea."

I am not among those who pretended that the North is "advancing backward" toward the abolition of slavery. I have maintained, on the contrary, and believe myself to have proved that it *willed* its non-extension, that it accepted the terrible chances of the crisis, in order to effect this step, prodigious in itself and the guarantee of all the rest. But these new steps would have cost it too much; it was not prepared for them. The parties which are coexistent in its bosom, and many of which would not even accept the first measure, since they rejected Mr. Lincoln, still embarrass his progress. This is quite natural, and gives no reason for either astonishment or indignation. As, however, all progress must be accomplished, the last as well as the first, God sends trials which may be needed to overcome resistance. Who knows whether this appalling war may not work a mysterious and profound change in the South itself? Who knows whether, forced to be regardful of their slaves, forced sometimes to entrust arms to their hands, the planters may not learn unwittingly that slaves are men, and that the doctrine of Mr. Stephens is blasphemy?

As to the North, what proves but too well that its prejudices are not all destroyed, is, that we see no marked change in its conduct with regard to free persons of color. Where are the States that have ever really admitted them to the exercise of political rights? Where are the churches, I am ashamed to say, that have taken energetic and public measures to reëstablish in their bosom equality according to the Gospel? Where are the manifestations of public opinion in this direction? Where are the meetings, the pamphlets, the editorials, the sermons? Herein—let no one mistake it—lies the special crime of the North, the persistent, and in some sort legitimate motive of European distrust. To reform our own conduct is the first condition to be fulfilled in seeking to correct the vices of others. I do not say that nothing has been done, and I shall take occasion hereafter to show that some advancement has been made in the right way; I will say at present that, in admitting the diplomatic envoys of Liberia and Hayti, in introducing two negroes as ambassadors into the White House, Mr. Lincoln will do something. Nevertheless, there is better to be done—other negroes in great numbers are waiting for generous hands—patriotic and Christian hands—to introduce them at last into the churches, the schools, the electoral colleges, the public vehicles. A great reform must be accomplished.

It is difficult to conquer one's self; but America is now called upon to attempt difficult things. I prefer pointing out the great, the true reform, without circumlocution, to losing myself in the examination of the twenty projects which she has to-day under consideration. There are petitions addressed to Congress; there are plans drawn up by military committees; there are individual propositions.

The common feature of all these projects is abolition by means of the war. The exceptional rights to which the war gives birth furnish, indeed, a natural occasion to surmount certain constitutional difficulties. The slaves are one of the resources of the South (until they become one of its most cruel embarrassments); their presence in the field confers on the South a liberty of action which the North does not possess—those levies of men effected without injury to agriculture. Why not strike the enemy where he is most vulnerable?

As soon as the Federal armies advance toward the rebels, the inevitable question is put: "What shall we do with the slaves?" They flock into the camps and offer their services. It becomes impossible to postpone the solution of all these unfinished problems until the close of the struggle.

Now, the solution has been furnished by one of the loftiest and most generous of American minds—John Quincy Adams. "From the moment," said he in Congress, May 25, 1836; "from the moment that your slave States become the theatre of war, the war power becomes extended, and Congress may, in particular, fix an indemnity for slaves."

On June 7th, 1841, Adams, after several years of reflection, maintained that an universal emancipation of the slaves might be accomplished by means of the exceptional powers engendered by a state of war. Finally, April 14, 1842, he exclaimed in the House of Representatives: "The law of nations is this: In time of war, military authority takes the place of all municipal institutions, including slavery. Then, not only the President of the United States, but the Commander-in-Chief of the army has power to order the universal emancipation of the slaves."

I comprehend, certainly, why men hesitate, and think this universal immolation of rights at the feet of army generals, too radical. Exceptional measures are usually as dangerous as convenient. The definitions of Adams, taken as a whole, may be contested. Nevertheless, it remains evident that certain powers are indispensable to military commanders; they should be authorized to deprive the enemy of his advantages, and whatever serves their operations almost always becomes lawful by this reason alone. Besides, the experiment has several times been made; General Gaines and a number of others, twenty or thirty years ago, employed slaves, emancipated them in virtue of the right of war, maintained that no one had a right to find fault with it, and were sustained, even when the South ruled the Union.

This, moreover, is only a means of resolving local difficulties. As to the general question of abolition, I am at rest. Whatever may be the measure adopted, the social transformation will run its course. I have always found it impossible to feel any anxiety on the subject of slavery. Since the election of Mr. Lincoln, I *know* that it has received its death-blow, and I am not of those who believe the cause lost because men hesitate or postpone it overmuch. One thing is evident—the word Union formerly signified "slavery," it now means "liberty."

Every thing is comprised therein. That among those who voted for this change and are laboring to accomplish it, there may be some, many perhaps, who have not comprehended the import of their action, cannot surprise me; the most glorious revolutions of humanity are wrought in this wise. It is rarely that the workers have full knowledge of their work. And what matters it? Is their work therefore less great? If many men have wished but half that they have done, have they done it the less for this?

This is the beginning of the end. I desire no other proof of it than what is passing in the Border States. I have spoken already of the remarkable deliberations of the Missouri Legislature, and have said that the interests of slavery were still its ruling anxiety; but what was true in 1861 will be no longer as true in 1862; the progress of minds is rapid. Kentucky is advancing still faster; a bill is talked of there, confiscating the property of rebels, "including slaves." The convention of Western Virginia, which has created the new State of Kanawha, is discussing plans of gradual emancipation.

Thus everything is going forward. Those abolitionists are very timid who tremble for their cause! Are they then unconscious of the power of truth? If Mr. Lincoln experiences some hesitation, honorable in principle, and which, moreover, will not last, why should it alarm us? Things are here more powerful than men, positions of more importance than programmes.

I feel myself endowed with an abundant stock of patience, because I have great confidence. I cannot succeed in imagining any hypothesis, union or separation, victory of the North or the South, intervention or non-intervention of Europe, resolute or timid policy of Mr. Lincoln in the matter of Slavery—no, I cannot fancy a single one which must not end in liberty. There are impulses which are irresistible. Do not pause at appearances, nor yet at intentions; look higher than man. Justice is there; she will make herself served by those who love and by those who mistake her, by those who comprehend her and by those who shut their eyes to her light.

CHAPTER II.

WE ARE, BEFORE EVERYTHING, TO AVERT CIVIL WAR.

I DETEST war as much as it is possible for any one to do, but I am accustomed to lay the blame on those who make it, and not on those upon whom it is made. When I see a party in America, devoid of all scruples, long engaged in making ready for an armed struggle, which not only is treasonable, but, as all admit, has little to recommend it in its cause, it is not for its opponents that I reserve my indignation. It is useless to exclaim: "No blood! no civil war! cease this slaughter among brothers!" We must say this to Charleston before saying it to Boston or Cincinnati. This government, this nation infamously attacked, which is striving to preserve its flag, its institutions and its greatness, and which, by admirable good fortune, is at the same time preserving the interests of liberty and justice, does not seem to me committing an act of monstrous ferocity.

For seventy years, it has lived united under the same laws and the same oaths; the Congress which assembled at Washington on the 2d of last December, was the thirty-seventh of the United States; to the thirteen original Stars, twenty-one others have been successively added—yet you wish a great people to consent to a mutilation effected by rebellion. France and England had not consulted themselves when they appeared to recommend to Mr. Lincoln that political and moral abdication styled "a peaceful separation."

If the United States had not picked up the gauntlet, Mr. Lincoln would have had to devote his whole time to the signing of orders of evacuation—the order to evacuate Fort Sumter; the order to evacuate Fort Pickens; the order to evacuate Key West and the Tortugas. Then, doubtless, for one need not fear to show himself somewhat exacting toward people so accommodating, the South would have claimed Maryland as a Slave State, as well as Kentucky, Missouri, and above all Washington, the capital of the Union. The surrender of Washington was the logical conclusion of the noble principle of non-resistance which we extol in Europe when Americans are in question.

Mr. Lincoln has not certainly been lacking in patience. Every one remembers his inaugural address. He announced his resolution to make no aggression, but simply to act the defensive. Well, aggressions took place. The people of Charleston knew full well that the garrison of Fort Sumter could commit no aggression on them; they had been even expressly forewarned of it. The national government, carrying the spirit of conciliation a great way, claimed to do nothing more than furnish bread to a handful of famished soldiers; yet the insurgents assailed Fort Sumter, and deliberately destroyed all chances of peace.

Gentleness, I repeat, had been carried a little too far. Action! action! such was the unanimous cry of the North. It demanded, and with reason, some proofs of energy, after so many of forbearance. A month of apparent inertia was a long time, especially in the face of the military preparations which were being multiplied on the south of the Potomac.

I add that Europe, which had not yet invented its theories of support, was beginning to manifest its disdain. The North had therefore a foretaste of the disgrace that awaited a people incapable of resistance, which should suffer itself to be insulted and dismembered without a word. The correspondence of the English journals were filled with prophecies of this sort: "The North has lost all its vigor; luxury, and the worship of the almighty dollar have rendered it incapable of the least sacrifice. There will be no war; the republican party will drop its candidate."

This was the beginning of a series of predictions, all contradicted by the event; which does not hinder the oracle from remaining as sure of itself as before, and from deciding again to-day, with unparalleled assurance, what *ought to* happen four months hence. I say this in passing, for my quotation had another purpose; I wished to call to mind the tone in which the words were then spoken: "War will not take place!" Those very persons who have since unceasingly reproached the North for the mad cruelty of its resistance to the South, were preparing last year, in March, to demonstrate, by the absence of war, that the North had no blood in her veins and was deserving of nothing but contempt.

I prefer, for the government of Mr. Lincoln, the reproaches of this year to those of the last. This year, esteem has reappeared; we have resumed the habit of treating the United States as a great people; the idea of recognizing the South is no longer so lightly entertained. Ah! if there had been negotiations at the time when the unarmed North found herself face to face with the armed

South they would have been conducted in a strange manner! The very facility with which the title of belligerents was then conferred on the insurgents, testifies to the disposition of Europe when she believed in the resolution of the South and the benevolent resignation of the North. All this has greatly changed, believe me; and has changed because of the drawing of the sword. If now the day should ever come when overtures shall be made, either by Jefferson Davis or by the European governments, they will be honorable overtures; rendering homage to the great movement which proceeded from the election of Mr. Lincoln; manifesting the value of principles; establishing, in fine, or at least pretending to establish, the bases of a progressive emancipation.

Energy and self-respect are therefore of some use. Their first result was to call forth a burst of patriotism in all the free States, and to give courage in the Border States to majorities in favor of the Union.

It is injurious to listen to so many cold railleries against a people which is struggling and suffering to maintain its threatened unity. The idea of unity, the idea of country is great—it is worth the blood it costs. To suppress rebellions, to resist the diminution of territory is to fulfil a duty. Woe to us, if we ever cease to see in it an interest of the highest order. For my part, while deploring civil war, I should have put on mourning for the United States, had they refused to fight, bowing the head to the threats of the South, and asking its pardon in some sort for having dared to make, despite its prohibition, a constitutional election. After wars courageously sustained, there may be a glorious peace; after disgraceful submission, there is nothing but shame and death.

Other governments, I know, have yielded to the force of circumstances; none have yielded to mere threats.

Were Scotland to secede and take possession of the national property, forts and arsenals; were she to send ambassadors to the continental powers; were she to revive letters of marque, and cruise the seas, burning English merchant vessels; were she to proclaim her design of raising the rebel flag over Buckingham Palace, all England would rise, without fearing for an instant that this war would be deemed perverse or fratricidal. When shall we cease to have two weights and two measures.

That a war like that of America should be pursued in a peaceful spirit; that all thought of conquest, subjugation, or reprisals should be put aside; that Mr. Lincoln should never lose sight of his maxim: "We are fighting to establish order, and, with order, liberty—the liberty of the conquered will remain as intact as that of the conquerors," I am profoundly convinced, and I shall return to the subject. I applaud, in this connection, the humanity which, despite the inflexible logic of principles, has prevented prisoners of war from being treated as traitors, and the shedding of blood outside the battle-field. But the necessity, the duty of fighting are none the less evident to me for this.

Instead of betraying his solemn oaths, and precipitating the United States into final dissolution and the contempt of the whole world, Mr. Lincoln has fulfilled, sorrowfully, slowly, too slowly perhaps, the high obligations imposed on him by circumstances; suffering has appeared to him preferable to death; he has refused to humble the stars and stripes before the arrogant banner of slavery, unfurled in the face of the nineteenth century; he has deemed war, civil war, fratricidal war, better than this abasement. What right have we to cast the stone at him?

I fear sometimes lest we become hypocrites. We veil our faces at the mere thought of a country depraved enough to oppose an insurrection, to enlist troops, to increase taxes, to impose on itself and others a commercial crisis; one would say that we had never seen the like! Well! I will make a full confession. Would you know what wars appear to me *impious?* Those of ambition, and love of power. Wars of conquest are quite as criminal, though in a different manner, in the sight of my conscience, as are some civil wars.

CHAPTER III.

THE SOUTH HAD A RIGHT TO SECEDE.

I SHOULD have blushed to dwell upon the subject treated of in the preceding chapter; the crime of armed defence does not appear to me one for which it is fitting to justify the United States too much at length. The new subject which I broach here exacts more elaboration. The right of secession has given rise to so many misunderstandings, it involves political questions of such importance that we cannot legitimately refuse it attention.

It is to the honor of our times that questions of principle never become entirely blotted out. Whatever may happen, by the side of, or rather, above transient contentions, the immutable problems of morality and right make their appearance in the end.

We are sometimes astonished at the place which the American government reserves to the question of abstract right!

Nevertheless, in this it only renders justice to the importance of the argument, and singles out the features of general interest to all nations. There is more here than a matter for judicial dissertations or even for curious researches into the nature of the Constitution of the United States; there is resistance to a subversive doctrine, incompatible with order, and, above all, with liberty.

This has been imperfectly understood in Europe. The cabinet at Washington has seemed to us to devote its attention to a petty side of the difference of which South Carolina has given the signal.—What is the use of these judicial and almost pedantic dissertations? Yield or fight, but do not amuse yourselves in demonstrating that to us for which we care but little; namely, that the right of secession does not exist. Secessions are great facts, violent in their nature, which may be readily assumed to be illegal in the beginning; you waste your time in proving it!

This is a mistake; the South is troubled concerning its legitimacy; the right of secession is discussed with lively interest everywhere, and particularly in the Border States. There must be some reason for this state of things. For my part, on seeing a whole people attentive to this constitutional and moral problem, I hesitate to decide from afar that it has gone astray. It seems to me unjust, or at least unfriendly, to reproach the federal government for the importance which it places on questions of this kind. It is a remarkable fact that they have been always regarded with great attention by the statesmen of the United States; there is, as it were, an American tradition which ensures them respect.

Mr. Seward remained faithful to this tradition, when he addressed his first instructions to Mr. Dayton. "You cannot be too decided in making known the fact that there never has been, nor ever will be, the least idea of permitting a separation of the Union to take place in any manner whatsoever. . . . . The thought of a dissolution of the Union, peaceably or by force, has never entered the mind of any impartial statesman here, and it is full time that European statesmen also renounced such an idea."

I applaud the American government for having given to the question of right the place which belongs to it. A sentiment of which we know little in Europe, the Anglo-Saxon respect for law, thus manifests its power. Yes, at the very moment when force alone seemed at stake, principles were not forgotten.

This may pass for folly in the eyes of many. To contend in the name of the right, to defend a constitution, a national flag, the past and future of a great country—this is nonsense, they say! The true way is to count the chances and see where they lie, who can longest keep the field, who will receive in the end the support of Europe—as to compacts and pledged oaths, what intelligent nation cares to-day for things like these!

Thank God! there is a nation, and an intelligent nation, which cares for them infinitely. I say it to the honor of the United States; they are giving us a lesson which we scarcely expected to receive from this direction. Even though slavery did not form the basis of the contest, we should be interested in the North, since it defends the right, since it rejects the anarchical doctrine which pretends to protest by secession against a constitutional election.

Lord Stanley not long since nobly called this to mind: "Let us not blame that in America which we have always done and are still doing ourselves—making war to retain a portion of our territory."

The question thus presented, aside from any principle, will be better understood among us. Why should we wish the United States to show themselves more indifferent than we to the territorial greatness of their country?

Of course, I do not believe that no separations will ever prevail. "Never!" says Mr. Seward, but there is no such thing as never in human affairs. To carry the denial of the right of separation so far as to affirm the eternity of institutions, would be madness. It would give cause to say that extreme right is extreme injustice, *summum jus summa injuria*. As it is true that in strict justice, individuals have no right to secede nor countries to fall asunder through caprice, so it is certain that a persevering determination, which firmly sustains a struggle and survives it, will end by conquering for itself a place on earth. By the side of the right of secession which the United States contest, and which they are right in contesting, there is the right of revolution; pardon me this comparison of terms ill fitted to exist together.

As, in the end, modern governments rest on the consent of the governed; as it is impossible to hold garrison eternally in disaffected countries, it thence follows that when the separation has become a revolution, violated right (for it is none the less violated, and it is of importance that this should be understood) submits to the presence of triumphant fact. It will be certainly necessary to let those go who can be no longer retained except by the lasting use of force. Free institutions would perish in the effort, through enemies or despots, were they carried on in these conditions of persistent struggle. By this course, a republican government would speedily become transformed into a military despotism.

This is a reservation which I am anxious to state in explicit terms. Although I have little respect for the right of revolution, I perceive that, under penalty of admitting two other rights still more odious, the right of foreign intervention and the right of permanent domestic oppression, a disruption becomes inevitable in the end, when it is desired with real earnestness by whole populations.

But this exception once admitted, (and the repudiation of the common country will rarely appear among great peoples, nothing less than an exceptional cause like slavery can render possible a fact so monstrous,) we will lay down the general rule, the importance of which seems too often forgotten in our times, that there is no such thing as the right of secession.

I hear it affirmed in an oracular tone that the new jurisprudence of nations does not permit the use of coercive measures! Every rebellion constitutes a government *de facto*, and every government *de facto* is a legitimate government! To tell the truth, even, we are no longer justified in speaking of rebels! The contract which holds the divers parts of a people united, deriving its validity only from the consent of each one, as soon as this consent is wanting, the contract ceases to exist!

I have a great mind to offer no other refutation of these heresies than a striking comparison borrowed from a recent speech of the Duke of Argyle. "We will not regard the question," said he, "of what is called the right of secession: no government has ever existed, to my knowledge, admitting the right of separation within itself. There is a curious kind of star fish in the waters of Loch Fine, which I myself have caught several times, and which effects the most extraordinary and adroit species of suicide. On drawing it from the water and attempting to remove it from the hook, the fins immediately drop off, the body falls in pieces, and of one of the most beautiful forms of nature, nothing remains but a few fragments. Such would have been the fate of the American Union, had its government accepted what is called the right of secession. Gentlemen, we must admit in all justice, with respect to Americans, that they are fighting for things that are worth the pains, and that the national existence is one of these things."

Yes, the national existence. This idea alone contains the unanswerable refutation of what is called the right of secession.—But is a confederation a nation? is it not rather an assemblage of nations? We are reminded of the celebrated definition of Montesquieu: "A community of communities."

We touch here upon one of the most important mistakes made by European opinion with respect to the United States. M. de Tocqueville himself seems to have but imperfectly understood that, under this somewhat ill chosen name of Confederation, the American Union presents the remarkable phenomenon of a state *sui generis*. Judging it from its title, and starting from the true principle that the bond of simple confederations is unstable, he decides that if ever any portions of the whole should secede, the separation could be in no wise opposed.

Now, no name like that which is here in question, can cover things so dissimilar.

There are in the first place, and it was of this fact that Montesquieu was evidently thinking, confederations which are nothing else than leagues. Antiquity had its Amphictyonic Council and Achean League; the middle ages had their Heptarchy, and Lombardic, Suabian and Hanseatic confederations: the modern world has seen the ancient Low Countries, and now sees the Germanic confederation. These are truly "communities of communities." The general government is well nigh null and void; the centre of political life resides in the members. Each of them is a complete State, possessing the totality of political rights, and often the right of maintaining diplomatic relations with foreign countries in an extended measure. Confederations, understood in this wise, the only confederations, to tell the truth, which deserve the name, are almost always models of political impotence. Good to attain certain particular ends, such as defence for a limited time and the development of commercial interests—good, in a word, as leagues, they are incapable of strong resistance and of duration. It is difficult for them to cope with great centralized states; and, as to arresting by force the separation of their members, it is evident that they could not think of it, provided the design of separation were resolutely adopted.

Switzerland, under its ancient compact, presented already another kind of confederation. The idea of a league began to give way before the idea of a nation. The central power was invested with real authority; the cantons, although preserving an extended sovereignty, nevertheless abandoned to the diet some of their essential attributes. Moreover, the mere fact of a popular representation gave to the collective whole, a cohesion which the confederation of princes could never have succeeded in attaining.

Let us take another step. The present compact of Switzerland furnishes us the remarkable realization of a third form of confederation, much more centralized than the last. The *referendum*, that ancient guardian of cantonal sovereignties, has entirely disappeared. We see, moreover, assemblies sitting at Berne, whose decisions have the force of law; a federal council which governs in the full meaning of the word the interests of all the cantons. The latter remain, notwithstanding, and their individual existence is not impaired; only they have divested themselves of authority in behalf of the centre. Duties, political treaties, foreign affairs, general legislation, supreme jurisdiction, currencies, weights and measures, all these belong to the central power. Let a canton take it upon itself to pass a law ignoring the principles laid down in the compact, and this law will be annulled; let it attempt to throw off its federal obligations, and it will be occupied on the spot.

This is an entirely new fact in politics, which I am not surprised that Montesquieu did not foresee; it did not suffice for this to have read Thucydides, and to have studied the democracies of Greece, the republics of Italy, or the States General of Holland. Yet there is as great a distance between the confederation of the United States and the present confederation of Switzerland, as between the latter and the rude outline of an alliance which serves as a basis to the Germanic body.

We have a light and easy manner of solving questions while dispensing with their study. In the first place, the word confederation is enough. Next, the United States were born of rebellion, and cannot pretend to put down rebellions; they sprung from secession, and secessions are legitimate on their soil!

As to the last argument, we will find few states in the Old or New World which would be authorized to defend themselves, were the right of defence reserved solely to countries innocent of revolutions. The secessionists of 1860 have only to follow the example of the secessionists of 1776, to conquer their independence step by step and then force a recognition from the whole world; until this time, we demand in the name of justice that the United States be not interdicted the use of force against a rebellion, which is doubtless more momentous than that of the last century, solely because it is in support of an odious cause and cannot put forward the shadow of a grievance.

The word confederation remains. We have already perceived that it is far from corresponding always to the same system, for modern Switzerland escapes the definition of Montesquieu. What are we to think of the United States? Are they a confederation according to the old formula, or a confederation according to the new formula? Are they perhaps something different—a nation in which the central preponderance is still more strongly implied?

There have been two republics of the United States; that which preceded 1787, and that which followed the great constitutional reform which then took place. This momentous change appears, in truth, to be held for nothing, and considered null and void. Yes, before 1787, the United States were a simple confederacy. In 1774, the thirteen colonies represented in the Congress at Philadelphia, adopted certain "Articles of Association." In 1778, they made "a firm league of friendship." This was really a confederation, with its powerlessness and anarchy. You will seek in vain at this epoch for an American *nation.* Each state acted for itself alone; there were refusals to go forward, refusals to levy taxes, refusals of the soldiers to obey their generals. It was impossible to execute the decisions of Congress, impossible either to raise men, or to improve a highway or canal, or to pay the state officials, or to discharge the interest of debts, or to resist civil or military insurrections. The negotiation of the most insignificant treaty encountered barriers of interests on its way; wars of tariff appeared in the horizon. Under this system of sovereign States, in which Congress voted by States, under a pure confederation, in a word America had nearly died shamefully, miserably, beneath the cold hand of local selfishness.

At this crisis, illustrious patriots raised their voice. An Assembly was convoked in 1786 at Philadelphia.

Washington, John Adams, Monroe, Madison and Jefferson were present. A plan of confederation was fixed upon which profoundly modified the political organization. By the side of the Senate, to which each State, whether great or small, was to send two members, was placed a House of Representatives, elected in proportion to the population of each State. And this important change was not the only one; a President was appointed to direct the general polity; his attributes and those of Congress were made extensive; lastly, under the name of the Federal Supreme Court, a centralized judiciary power was commissioned to decide the differences which might arise either between the States themselves, or between a State and Congress, concerning the interpretation of the Constitution. To Congress alone was henceforth to belong the right of peace and war, the negotiation of treaties, and the regulation of tariffs. It was also authorized to levy taxes and contract loans.

In this manner was accomplished a most important revolution, of which we make too little account when we apply to the United States the vague term, confederation. The federal organization anterior to 1787, that unique assembly in which all the States had an equal representation, that simple committee, charged with the execution of decrees stamped in advance with impotence, all these gave place to an organic Congress of the nation, to a President, to a central power, in fine, whose attributes equal, and in some respects excel those of our European governments.

This was a novelty on earth. The most original feature, perhaps, in the *rôle* of the United States was that of having propounded and resolved the problem of founding a perfectly strong, perfectly united, perfectly national power, without sacrificing the independence of either States, commons or individuals. Among us, centralization is a Moloch to which new victims are offered up without ceasing; our modern governments have been hitherto created only at the expense of the provinces, commons, and private consciences. The American solution is more liberal—it begins by ensuring the liberty of the individual, by absolutely denying any religious jurisdiction to the State; it next provides for the liberty of the commons, by abandoning to them the complete administration of their interests; it maintains, in fine, the entire freedom of the States, by refusing to interfere in any wise with their private institutions. But, at the same time, it positively remits to the President, the Supreme Court, and Congress, all that concerns the general affairs of the nation. Never was religious or administrative centralization more invalid, never was political centralization more complete.

This distinction, which appears so simple, and which Europe has hitherto so little understood, has never been objected to in the United States. When Jefferson, in 1786, proposed his amendment, designed to reserve the local sovereignty of the States in the most express terms, and to declare that what they had not delegated to the central power, they preserved themselves, the acceptance was ready and cordial.

No one, in fact, ever thought of lowering the States to the rank of provinces or departments. To compare an American State with a French department is one of the greatest political solecisms that it is possible to commit. There is no analogy therein of any kind; I see naught but difference. But to conclude from this difference that the United States do not exist as a nation, that they are a confederation according to the formula of Montesquieu, is to be still more grossly in error. Self-government exists in the United States, the commons, the churches, we will add, the individuals; but centralization exists in Congress. We have gone beyond the *Articles of Confederation.*

Is America an agglomeration of States, or is it a people? This is a question of supreme importance, which we are not justified in deciding, as we do, with the negligence of disdain. It is easy, moreover, to become informed on the matter. We have not here before us a remote origin, in which there is full scope for hypotheses; the foundation of the United States is recent, almost contemporaneous; it has been effected in broad daylight, and the commentary is found by the side of the text—a commentary written by the founders themselves.

Now, on the question which I am investigating, there is not the slightest disagreement among them. Consult, for instance, Patrick Henry, one of the adversaries of the Constitution of 1787; hear what he will tell you: "That this government is a consolidated government, is evident. The Constitution says, *We, the people*, instead of saying, *We, the States.*"

The constitutional revolution of 1787 is contained entire in these few words. Formerly, they were the States; the Continental Congress was simply a representation of the States; it could act only on their recommendations; its functions, as has been said, were essentially diplomatic; it was therefore reduced to the necessity of negotiating with the States for obedience to its decisions; it was unsuccessful in treating with foreign powers, and England, on making peace, disdainfully refused to conclude an agreement with this league of rival sovereignties which did not form a people. Now, the American nation governs its general affairs.

Let us, for a moment, consider the sphere of the central power.

It acts directly, observe, on the citizens of individual States, having over them even the power of life and death. The individual States have neither army nor navy; they are authorized to levy troops to repel invasion only in case of urgency, or when the national army cannot intervene. They have not the right, like the Swiss cantons, to sign certain treaties with foreign powers. They do not coin money. There are national customs, national imposts, a national debt, a national army and navy, a national Supreme Court. The nation has its laws, its ambassadors, its fortifications and garrisons on the territory of individual States. The new territories are placed under the guardianship and authority of the nation. Despite the States, among the States, the nation accomplishes its work, the political work which devolves on it exclusively.

As to laws which are merely local, the States alone decide them; they regulate their own institutions, on condition, of course, of respecting the principles laid down by the general Constitution. They have their senators, their legislators, their governors, their courts; in a word, they manage important interests with admirable liberty. Observe, once more, that the United States have invented a form of government, hitherto unknown in the annals of mankind; it is neither impotent, like ordinary confederations, nor despotic, like our centralization; it proclaims at once the administrative sovereignty of the States and the political sovereignty of the State.

The State and the States—such is the great formula which America has brought for her share to the great political work of our race. They have little comprehension of the originality of this discovery who gravely inform us that Virginia or Alabama retain their sovereignty in presence of Congress, like Prussia or Wurtemberg, in presence of the Germanic diet, and who persist in seeing nothing in the Federal Government but a simple agent of the States, whose commission may be withdrawn when it ceases to inspire confidence. The Supreme Court, that unappealable authority on the subject of constitutional interpretations, arrived at very different conclusions when it held this language after the adoption of the compact of 1787: "These allied sovereignties have transformed their league into a government, and their congress of ambassadors into a legislature."

Such is the truth. If the States subsist, the State has taken a consistency which it lacked under the deplorable system of weakness, disorder, and bankruptcy, which was that of the Confederation, properly called. As things stand, it is this which protects an individual State against another individual State, which in certain circumstances protects the citizens against their own individual States, which interdicts this individual State to establish a monarchical constitution, which forbids it to pass laws violating the obligation of contracts, bills of attainder, export or import duties. It is this alone which accords naturalization to emigrants. It is this alone which receives oaths of allegiance. It is this alone which is recognized by foreign powers. Peace, war, commerce, finances, the navy, the army, the mails, the legislative, executive, and judicial functions—it is to this alone that all these are remitted. It possesses Federal property on the territory of individual States. The President is not limited to the command of the national army; he also commands the militia of the individual States, when he summons them to the service of the Confederation. In a word, provincialism is foreign to the organization of the United States; the United States are a nation.

This was doubted by no one for a whole generation. But, later, the doctrine of State sovereignty began to take form in the South. It was a gross political heresy; but no matter, it was a convenient weapon to use, if necessary, for the defence of the "peculiar institution.".

Nothing is more striking than this offensive and defensive alliance between slavery and the doctrine of State sovereignty. The leaders of the South, as we have seen, were not long in catching a glimpse in the future of the possibility of a separation. They could not long conceal that, face to face with the gigantic progress of the North, in contact with free discussion and liberty, the countries petrified by slavery could not forever escape the liberal contagion. Their only chance, and they exhausted it to the utmost, was to impose their yoke by force of threats and violence, to transform by main strength their minority into a majority, to force upon the Union an ultra policy, to win at any cost new territories for slavery. But they were not ignorant that there would be perhaps a limit to this kind of success, that resistance to slavery might be some day awakened in the North, and that on this day they would need a theory ready-made. Américans, as we have remarked, have derived from their Anglo-Saxon origin an instinctive veneration for law, which forbids them ever to neglect demonstrating to themselves that they respect it, even while treading it under foot.

Thence arises the mother-doctrine of State sovereignty, and its legitimate offspring, the right of secession. It is easy to follow them in their growth, from the moment when Mr. Calhoun proclaimed his doctrine of the right of secession; that is, the faculty reserved to each State to annul certain acts of Congress; from the moment when the South, irritated by the admission of California without slaves, reserved to itself in formal terms the right of secession, to the moment when Jefferson Davis, accomplishing what Mr. Calhoun had announced, based the secession of the slave States upon their sovereignty.

That the South should have invented such theories, may be conceived; that Europe should have admitted them, it is more difficult to comprehend. We must acknowledge, notwithstanding, that we have, in general, admitted to the rank of axioms, the sovereignty of States and their right of separation.

In other terms, we have drawn up, for the use of America, the theory of inevitable and contemptible death; the theory of forced powerlessness. We have gravely printed in our journals that the American Constitution does not authorize the Federal Government to employ coercive measures.

We must conclude from this that General Jackson held unconstitutional language when he threatened to make the South Carolinians return to their duty at the point of the bayonet. The United States would possess this privilege, that they alone of all known governments, would have no right to defend themselves; rebellions might take place among them with safety; *amicable dismemberment* (an admirable expression!) would be the supreme law of the country.

I had rather hear it said, without oratorical pretension: "The American Government is a government outside of the law." Has Europe, which has sought for the last year to apply to it a system which she would desire at no price for herself — has Europe, which has thus endeavored to bring it back to the state of shameful anarchy, suppressed in 1787, really measured the extent of this principle, which at least deserves the credit of orginality—the principle of pacific separations? If she has not measured it herself, she has placed Americans in a position to form a just idea of its significance; they must have seen for some time how far a nation falls which is bound to accept division and, in some sort, dissolution at the first summons. It has been shown to them, it seems to me, that, the principle of separation once at work, they need hope for little consideration.

I like better this letter from an English merchant, settled in Philadelphia: "If it be an acknowledged fact that there is here neither State nor government, and that a fraction of the United States can secede whenever it chooses, it is time to pack our trunks and go where there is a State and government." I would advise all the people of America to *pack their trunks* at the same time, were so monstrous a theory admitted. Thank God! it will not be admitted; the government at Washington has entered its protest, despite our counsels. This pointed and necessary protest will remain inscribed by the side of the pretensions of the South and the explanations of its friends. We will consent at length, perhaps, to place America in the domain of the common law, and not recommend to her a moderation contrary to nature—we, who would be so greatly surprised if, in the event of an Irish insurrection, Mr. Lincoln should pledge the Queen not to oppose the right of separation.

It is sometimes asked why the Constitution of the United States did not explicitly declare itself against this right of separation! I think that such a clause would be vainly sought in ancient and modern constitutions, in those of Europe and those of America. There are some things so evident that they are never laid down. It is never laid down that the infringement of sworn oaths is forbidden. Neither is it laid down that the National Government is permitted to employ force against those who attack it by force. The authority of the highest law would be in no wise increased by adding thereto: "We also decree that this law shall not be violated."

Under what pretext can the United States be reproached for not having taken a ridiculous precaution, without precedent in history? Those who wish to modify the American Constitution have a way provided to do it; they have only to obtain a majority of two-thirds of both Houses of Congress, and a ratification by three-fourths of the whole number of States. Apart from this means, I know of none but bullets. But as bullets constitute force, right is no longer in question.

Let men cease to couple two words which mourn to see themselves united; *right* and *secession;* the discussion will be more honest for it. So long as secession pretends to be nothing more than it is—an act of rebellion and violence, an attempt at revolution—we avoid inoculating the social body with a principle of dissolution; as soon as it becomes a right, on the contrary, dissolution begins.

The South already perceives this itself; at the beginning, in spite of excited passions, it sees its principal State, Virginia, divided into two hostile portions. If, to its misfortune, it should succeed; if its confederacy should be finally established, I will not give it ten years to become reduced to dust and ashes. In virtue of what principle will it prevent first one State from going off, and then another? What reply will it make to the county which wishes to constitute itself an independent State, or to the discontented township which is no longer willing to live with the county?

Our time, fertile in anarchical theories, had not hitherto discovered this one. Had the United States accepted it, they would have sunk to the rank of the Mexican States, distracted on all sides, and condemned to civil war in perpetuity.

For long years, the adversaries of the United States in Europe have prophesied this state of permanent revolution and anarchy; they take delight in believing that North America will be ere long a fit peer for South America. It is doubtless to facilitate the fulfilment of their predictions that they are attempting to introduce into the heart of the Union a system which would effectively produce an armed struggle after every presidential election, a secession after the adoption of every bill.

It is time to admit that, if the North cannot consent to the peaceful withdrawal of the South, it is not only, nor above all, because it needs the South or needs the cotton of the South, but because it needs *to live.* To admit the right of secession is to renounce being a people; and to renounce being a people is to sign its own death-warrant.

It cannot "let the South go," for every thing (I do not use the word by chance) — every thing would go with it. Every thing would go with it, not only because each fragment would become isolated in turn: to day, California; to-morrow, the West; the day after, New York or Pennsylvania; not only because war would become endemic—war for the boundaries, war for the territories, war with the fellow-citizens of yesterday, war with friends and enemies—but because the right of secession is anarchy, and anarchy marks the end of nations.

To the support of what I have just said, it would be

easy to multiply qnotations; all the American statesmen, Washington, Jay, Hamilton, Marshall, Madison, Kent, Story, Webster, and many others, have rejected the doctrine which ends in the right of secession. Jefferson alone, the enthusiastic founder of that bad school of democracy which had nearly drawn on the United States to their ruin, and the decline of which has been proclaimed by the election of Mr. Lincoln—Jefferson alone used now and then a different language. In 1803, he wrote on the occasion of the acquisition of Louisiana: "If these people should come to find it greatly to their interest to separate from us, if their happiness should so far depend on it as to resolve them to brave the inconveniences of such a crisis, why should the Atlantic States dread this event? Why should we, in particular, their present inhabitants, concern ourselves with such a question? . . . . We think that their union is necessary to their happiness, and desire that it shall be maintained; events may determine otherwise. . . ."

We recognize in this letter, on one side, the diplomatic adroitness of the leader of the State seeking to anticipate objections and facilitate a vast increase of territory; and, on the other, the political tendency of the leader of a party, instinctively preparing for the South and the ultra democracy the means of subversive action which they would yet need.

Washington expresses himself differently. Who does not know his celebrated Farewell Address?—"Be, before all, children of the same confederation, American citizens rather than the citizens of such or such a State. Let the Federal Constitution be your ark of safety. . . . Remember that it cannot subsist without authority strong enough to protect it against factions."

Moreover, he elaborates this idea, which was constantly present to his mind: "The unity of government is a main pillar in the edifice of your real independence. . . . As this is the point in your political fortress against which the batteries of internal and external enemies will be most constantly and actively directed, it is of infinite moment that you should properly estimate the immense value of your national Union to your collective and individual happiness; that you should cherish a cordial, habitual, and immovable attachment to it, accustoming yourselves to think and speak of it as the palladium of your political safety and prosperity; watching for its preservation with jealous anxiety; discountenancing whatever may suggest even a suspicion that it can be in any event abandoned; and indignantly frowning upon the first dawning of every attempt to alienate any portion of our country from the rest. . . ."

The Message of 1833, of President Jackson, contains the following words: "The right of the inhabitants of a State, at their own good pleasure and without the consent of the other States, to throw off their most solemn obligations and imperil the liberties and happiness of the millions of men who compose the Union, cannot be recognized. To say that a State can separate at will from the Union, is to say that the United States are not a nation."

The illustrious Henry Clay, of Kentucky, held no less decided language; here are a few sentences from a speech delivered by him in the Senate in 1850: "If Kentucky were to-morrow to unfurl the banner of resistance, I would not fight under her flag. The submission which I owe the Union is absolute; that which I owe my native State is only relative."

To all these witnesses which have arisen at the different epochs of the crises, but a single man of importance can be opposed—the theorist of secession, Mr. Calhoun. Behold with what vigor he is attacked! Here are a few words from Mr. Webster, respecting his doctrines: "I maintain, 1st, that the Constitution of the United States is not a league, a confederation, or a contract between the people of different States acting in their sovereign character; but a government properly called, based on the adoption of the people, and creating direct relations between itself and individuals; 2d, that no State has the power to dissolve these relations, that nothing can break them except a revolution; that, consequently, there can be no separation without revolution. . . ." The apologists of the South have attempted to lengthen the too short list of the partisans of secession by inserting therein the respected name of Madison, under the pretext that this statesman took the responsibility in Virginia of the resolutions of 1798; but without entering into the history of this incident, it will suffice to recall the fact that, when interrogated in 1830, Mr. Madison made the most solemn and explicit declarations to the contrary—declarations which he never ceased henceforth to reaffirm. The resolutions of which he was the author were designed, he said, to amend the Constitution by addressing themselves to the American nation, and by no means to individual States. No one has expressed himself more openly than he on the score of the right of secession.

I am unwilling to quit this great subject without recalling the fact that the question is not only American—it is *human*, pardon me the expression. We too are concerned in it; the old contest between right and anarchy has just taken a form appropriate to the events of the day. Under the vague labels of consenting governments, popular sovereignty, and the principle of nationalities, all sorts of doctrines glide in; we shall do well to pay close attention to them—we liberals, who are unwilling to become revolutionists.

Let us remember that the triumph of injustice is an unhealthy spectacle. The seed falls to the ground and disappears, and we think no more of it; but the day will come when it will bring forth fruit.

Thus it is with violence done to right. The human soul receives the germ of anarchy, and becomes accustomed to the evil. That definitive success, indeed, should win itself acceptance, is well; under pain of having recourse to intervention and the holy alliance, internal revolutions must prevail; but that revolutions should be respectfully greeted through principle, and in advance, terrifies and saddens me.

To hear some men, there are no longer rebels here below; on the sole condition of being somewhat numerous, whatever may be their cause, they always deserve another name. Thus, right becomes absolutely effaced before force.

There would above all be no longer any rights for republican governments. Could there be a rebellion against a republic? Would a republic be authorized in maintaining its own existence? Would it not be acting against its principle in using constraint? Should not the will of the people prevail?

Every one will doubtless comprehend, without need of my explanation, the full scope of such a maxim. All free governments would be more or less accused and convicted of irremediable weakness, of powerlessness to retain seceders and to punish rebels. To yield and to yield again in virtue of a constitutional vice—such would be their destiny here below. Instead of yielding to majorities, and submitting to laws which they had combated, and acts which displeased them, minorities would have two resources always ready—the right of revolution and the right of secession.

Such a theory would leave nothing further to be done; the code of anarchy would be complete.

CHAPTER IV.

THE SOUTH, THOUGH CONQUERED, WILL NEVER BE BROUGHT BACK INTO THE UNION.

WE will lay theories aside; the partisans of the South are themselves beginning to renounce them. They are much less anxious at present to sustain secession as a right than to demonstrate secession as a fact. Think of it as you will in the point of view of principles and philosophic speculation, it is done, and it will stand; to reëstablish the Union is henceforth impossible; the North, in continuing the struggle, is yielding to the demoniac suggestions of wounded pride; it is ruining itself without a justifiable end; it is committing suicide without a real chance of success.

Such is the opinion which the friends of the South are laboring to propagate in Europe, and in which they succeed but too well. I meet men everywhere who ask in dismay: "How will this end?" Without any hostility with respect to the United States, they nevertheless accept with incredible facility the idea of Southern recognition. Is not this a necessity? What can we do in opposition to a deed accomplished? Do you wish the North to set about subjugating and occupying the cotton

States? Do you wish to make of them a Poland or a Venice?

No, a thousand times no. But, as I have said, my knowledge of the subject is less extensive than that of those who speak in this wise. They settle questions which to me are still obscure. They foresee, with a certainty which astonishes me, the future attitude of the Southern States. As to me, I wait; it seems to me a surer method to cling to what is just than to seek for what is probable. Political clear-sightedness is subject to error; integrity never goes astray. What do we risk in pursuing the right cause? When it shall have failed, it will be quite time to turn the back on it. Here, on the same side—a rare fact!—behold positive right and natural right, legality and humanity—why are we in such haste to declare that their triumph is impossible, and that the only rebellion that ever dared write the word "slavery" on its banner, is certain to attain its end? Instead of adapting our opinions to suit chances, would it not be better to maintain our opinions in spite of chances? It is so pleasant to live under the shelter of principles! Our course will become so simple when we have no longer to ask ourselves with anguish which must succeed—when the only question put is, "Which is right?"

I have followed this rule from the beginning of the American conflict, and I have found it right. More than once have I regretted that Europe had not done the same, preserving and expressing her sympathies, calling that which is right, right, and that which is iniquitous, iniquitous. What will happen now that our too able policy has swelled the proportions of the insurrection? I know not. It is not my design, therefore, to prove here that the reëstablishment of the Union will take place; it is enough for me to prove that it is not impossible.

Without going very far back in history, or quitting our own country, we see that many *impossibilities* have been done. When the first coalitions were formed, prudent men doubtless ranked among impossibilities a victory of divided and exhausted France over all Europe united against her. When the revolutionary anarchy was at its height, it was declared with some show of reason that a regular administration, and peaceable relations between the different classes, would never be seen in France. The hatreds which separated them seemed indeed more difficult to conquer than are those of the North and South.

Let us study, then, impartially, the chances of reëstablishing the Union; if the difficulties are great, justice and liberty are accustomed to overcome difficulties; the force that dwells in them is never taken sufficiently into account. They level mountains of prejudice, they blot out animosities, they harmonize interests, their soothing resources are miraculous.

There is, I admit, a form of union which has become well-nigh impossible; I mean the ancient form. And this is great progress. Thank God! there are no longer means of reëstablishing what then existed—that complicated and unnatural condition, that guarantee of slavery by free countries, that incessant uneasiness of the public conscience, that unstable equilibrium maintained by force of acts of cowardice and compromises, that debased policy in which America was straitened for want of room, in which she was stifled for lack of air, in which she would have perished, had she not, by a bold effort, freed herself in time.

This, the founders of the United States might have established in the last century; struggling with a disastrous war, with anarchy, with bankruptcy, seeking in vain around them for forces proportioned to their design, they thought it their duty to alienate no one, and to submit to the conditions of the slaveholders rather than lay down their arms before Englishmen. But to-day, after the experiences of the last administrations and the present rebellion, to restore what has just crumbled away, in fine, would be a criminal folly, the spectacle of which, it is my firm conviction, will be spared us.

Whatever may be the temptations of the future—and they may be great at some moments—the time for compromises is assuredly past; supposing, which I by no means admit, that there should ever be found a government at Washington to accept them, there would be no longer found a people in the United States to regard them; useless paper rags, they would fall into the mire, and no one would think in future of stooping to pick them up.

Lord Russell said at the Newcastle dinner: "If the South were to return voluntarily to the Union, the quarrel would be renewed, for slavery would remain." I cannot admit the hypothesis; I much rather believe that in case overtures of peace should be made and received, they would be based on progressive emancipation, and the stipulation of an indemnity in favor of the masters. Despite the support which a portion of the Democrats and politicians would doubtless give to plans of negotiation, it is indubitable that the reëstablishment of the Union will not take place by this means.

If the reëstablishment of the Union take place, it will be simply because, the war once ended and the South conquered, there will be found more Union sentiment and interests in the South than is generally supposed. There will be union because there is unity.

During the war, hatreds become exaggerated and

passions excited; it seems then as though the blood spilt would never permit reconciliation, as though there were really two peoples contending, two peoples strangers to each other, who have had and can have nothing in common. This is not only the language of the leaders, it is the truth of the moment. It is certain, and the government at Washington ought not to conceal it, that the separation is more real to-day than at the hour of the disruption; the separation is *consolidated*—I find no other term—by the habit of living apart and hostile; the difficulties of reestablishing the Union have gone on increasing. It was justifiable to maintain in the beginning that the rising of the South was nothing but a rebellion, fomented by the ambition of a handful of agitators; this is no longer true to-day. The South, a part of the South, at least, has come by degrees to desire what it, perhaps, forced upon itself at first; the South desires the separation—it desires it with fierce and passionate energy.

I do not seek, it will be seen, to disguise perils and favor illusions. The reëstablishment of the Union is difficult; it remains to be known whether it is impossible. Upon this point, I still have doubts, and for these reasons;

If we set aside the transient excitement which belongs to the struggle, and which will give place after the struggle to sentiments of a different nature, we will see that all of the Southern States contain a Union party. What is its importance? Those more able than I will tell you; for my part, I do not feel that I have the right to be so positive. I confess my ignorance, but at the same time I insist on recalling the manner in which the disruption was proclaimed. Nothing could less resemble an unanimous conviction, a popular impulse. We do not need, in studying this miserable spectacle of a rebellion in behalf of slavery, to have present to our minds the calm resolve displayed by the founders of the United States.

Last year, the violent course adopted by South Carolina at first encountered naught but blame. Numerous Southern journals declared themselves opposed to this excessive precipitation. I read in an influential sheet of Georgia, *The Augusta Chronicle and Sentinel:* "We are quite sure that every movement designed for secession and the formation of a new government proceeds, so far at least as Georgia is concerned, only from the quasi-consent of its people. It is time that this usurpation of power had an end, and that the people were consulted. . . . Before the Convention takes it upon itself to ratify a permanent constitution, let it submit it to the vote of the people. . . ."

The vote of the people is what the ringleaders of this insurrection, self-styled *popular*, avoided with significant care. Everywhere, despite the principles of democracy, the ratification by the people was set aside. An able and unscrupulous minority had seized the reins; the majority submitted to the yoke; nearly all the men who would have been naturally called by their social position or character to exercise an important influence, remained in the shade: we seek in vain for their names at the foot of the Charleston proclamations.

The people were still more hesitating. It will be remembered that but just before, in most of the States, they had rejected, with a nobleness of feeling of which it is just to take note, the infamous laws passed by the legislatures for reducing to slavery the free blacks who should not immediately quit the South. It is a striking fact that the governors were everywhere more violent than the legislatures, and the legislatures everywhere, in turn, more violent than the people. When the Alabama Convention was elected, the number of voters was minimum, and out of this small number, two-fifths supported the candidates opposed to secession; had the ordinance of secession been submitted to the people, it would have been rejected. In Virginia and in Texas, the opposition was still stronger.

Observe that the cities played a great part in this movement; the country, much more Union in feeling, was set aside. Let not too much, therefore, be said about the *national* insurrection of the South! It certainly had not this character in the beginning; if it has assumed it since, under the influence of the passions excited by the struggle, it may easily lose it again under the influence of opposite sentiments. The discontent caused by ruin and reverses, the irritation against a government which has taken it upon itself to act without consulting the people, and has precipitated events and accumulated deceptions—all this will suffice to subdue a factitious ill-feeling, and to restore life and speech to veritable majorities.

I by no means affirm that this will be so; it will be at least granted me that it has some chance. Who will dare affirm, moreover, that the struggle of classes will not then intervene to complicate the position of the South, and that it will not give strength to the partisans of the Union? According to the last census, there are not found in America more than four hundred thousand slave-holders, large and small; the number of large slave-holders is under a hundred thousand. There exists, therefore, a considerable number of whites who are strangers to the interests of slavery.

We have a right, I think, to doubt the unanimity of the South. Without even taking into account, which is wrong, the four millions of blacks who should have, and some day will have a voice in the matter, we are justified in believing that, should unexpected defeat once occur, should its illusions be rent asunder, should the rude hand of reverses replace each by reality, there will not be found in the Gulf States a population animated by the same desire, ruled by the same passion, and pursuing the same end.

It will, perhaps, be objected that hypotheses are not facts. I grant it; but hypotheses are not alone in question; certain facts have already appeared. Wherever the national army has regained its footing, sentiments in favor of the Union have been manifested on the spot. Scarcely had the fleet touched at Hatteras, when numerous delegates from the neighboring counties assembled there in convention, and disavowed, in incredibly forcible terms, the secession sentiments attributed to North Carolina. Scarcely had General Dix set foot in Eastern Virginia, when Accomac and Northampton counties enthusiastically declared themselves in favor of the Union. Scarcely had the Federal power become somewhat strengthened in Missouri, when numerous Unionists from Arkansas took refuge there. Scarcely had the success of the Northern troops permitted Western Virginia to express her true thought, when she constituted herself apart, and joined the United States.

An analogous movement has been called forth in Eastern Tennessee; the return to the Union numbers partisans there who declare themselves with daily increasing boldness. Wherever it is possible to declare one's self a Unionist without danger of the gallows, I do not see men lacking to do it. Even in Alabama, even in Georgia, even in South Carolina, even in Richmond, under the eyes of the insurrectional government, unequivocal symptoms betray the presence of a party in favor of the Union. The Border States are interesting subjects of study in this respect. We know how little hesitation was shown by Kentucky in rejecting the idea of a separation. As to Maryland, if you consult her outside the streets of Baltimore, you will find in her a strong general tendency in favor of the Union; nowhere have so decisive majorities been seen as those which declared themselves this year in Maryland for the Union candidates.

I am not ignorant of the objection that may be raised, that majorities called forth under the pressure of an army of occupation are always suspicious. Are we forbidden, however, to draw any inferences from these facts? Are we not authorized to suppose that the material defeat of the secessionists will involve a moral defeat, that faith in their cause will then die out, that the former dream of an independent South, prospering through the conquests of slavery, will at length fall in ruins? Our dreams never fall alone, they draw down with them many convictions, many passions which we deemed immortal.

Those who extol the impulse of the South, and wish to make us believe in its unanimity, should explain to us the indifference of which proof was given when the ratification of the new Constitution was in question. In Georgia, for instance, the journals of the country pointed out several counties in which scarcely a hundred voters presented themselves at the polls, and others, where the votes in favor of secession scarcely prevailed over those against it.

If the North succeed, and it will succeed, perhaps, in suppressing the factitious and transient state of exaltation in which the South is now found, a much more real attachment for the common country will be discovered at the bottom than men are now disposed to admit. For nearly a century, the sum told, they have lived together, under the same constitution, with the same destinies, by no means devoid of greatness.

Such a history is a bond. More than one glorious memory, more than one illustrious name, causes the hearts of men to beat alike in the North and South. Far from discovering there two peoples naturally hostile, I cannot help seeing a single people, and a people whose unity seems founded on indestructible bases. Not only is there unity of language, unity of origin, unity of race, and unity of religion, but it would be difficult to find, apart from slavery, any serious cause of antagonism. The solidarity of interests is evident—there is no rivalry, the agricultural South completes the manufacturing North, the rich cultures of the South have need to prosper of the capital of the North, the entrepôts of the North, the vast commerce of the North.

It is puerile to raise up a few differences of character and manners, and transform them into causes of disruption. There is no great people which does not comprise such contrasts within itself; they do not endanger unity, they strengthen it, on the contrary, by introducing therein the element of diversity. Then the people of the North and South, with their emigrating habits, are much more closely intermingled than is confessed. How many families number members at the present time in both contending sections?

The geographical unity will strike every one who looks at a map of America. Seek natural limits, possible limits—you will not find them. A great arterial communication, the Mississippi, passes through the central valley where beats the heart of the people; numerous branches, canals, and railroads, establish a momentary contact between the most distant portions of the territory.

The necessities of defence are to America a supreme law of unity. If the South, which talks about independence, wishes to remain independent, I advise it not to set itself apart; it will soon be obliged to place itself, in consequence, under the protection of some European power. As to the North, once separated from the States which make it a whole, it is in danger of being like a dismantled fortress, which may be entered henceforth by the breach.

Nothing less than the blind passions of slavery could close one's eyes to truths like these. Who will dare say that these eyes will not be opened? If the leaders at Richmond be overthrown, will not the day come when reasonable and patriotic Southern men (and these are not lacking) will perceive in what sort of a path they have been forced? Seeing on one side that the golden dream of Southern greatness is but a dream, recognizing on the other that the Yankees are not so ferocious, so thirsty for oppression and vengeance as had been said, feeling both the final ruin of their country and the greater or lesser domination of Europe approaching with rapid strides, will they not become reconciled to those who will restore to them greatness, independence, and prosperity?

Two sentiments subsist in the South—the American sentiment and the republican sentiment. Its monarchical tendencies exist only in the imaginations of our newspaper correspondents. As to the affection for Europe, see with what painful earnestness the South and the North, united at least in this, lately witnessed the progress of the plans of Spain, first in St. Domingo and then on the very continent of the New World? The shudder which runs through America to-day from one end to the other, reveals its unity to itself.

This unity appears to me so deeply seated that I persist in believing in it for the future, even though it should be necessary to renounce it for the present. I can scarcely admit that the patriotism of Southern men will always consent to betray and deliver up America. Weary of the yoke of wretchedness and violence which is now weighing upon them, will they never turn their eyes toward those free institutions which have given them so many years of prosperity and greatness? When they know, beyond the possibility of doubt, that, in destroying the United States, they have not done the least thing toward founding the glorious Southern empire, that their slavery has none the less received its death-blow, that a permanent war is ravaging their frontiers, that a foreign power is entering and ruling among them, that their ruin is becoming definitive, that their downfall is about to be accomplished without remedy, will not an irresistible reaction take place?

Either the destinies of America will suffer shipwreck, or the union of the South and the North will be reconstructed; sooner or later, more or less completely, this reconstruction will arrive. Great nations are not formed by chance, nor is their destruction so easy, thank God! as is imagined by cabinet politicians. Artificial unions may be broken, two countries brought together despite themselves—a Belgium and a Holland—may be separated; but under the name, United States, I discover a real, vital, natural fact, which has a great chance of becoming reëstablished sooner or later, and the final ruin of which, should it take place, would make itself long felt on earth.

There exist, it seems to me, three great means of reëstablishing it speedily—negotiation, the abolition of slavery, and political liberty.

I use the word *negotiation* for the sake of brevity, although the dignity of the United States will not permit them to treat officially with rebels. But, outside official action, overtures may be made. It is not absolutely impossible that the war, instead of terminating by the victory of one and the defeat of the other, may end by an arrangement. Suppose that the South, discontented with its present government, alarmed at the progress of the North, ceasing to count on the support of Europe, knowing, moreover, that this support would by no means consolidate the "peculiar institution," remits the power to more moderate and less compromised hands. After the fall of the Richmond cabinet and the influences which have hitherto prevailed in the South, it is conceivable that, under some form or other, proposals of peace may be communicated to Washington.

We have the right to look them in the face to-day without disquietude. Doubtless there are still those who, if it were said, "Reëstablish the action of the Fugitive Slave Law, and pass anew the Missouri Compromise, according to slavery all the territory below 33° 30′, and you will obtain the restoration of the Union," would accept the offer with enthusiasm. I have read writings published in the North since the rebellion, in which the *moral pressure* of citizens who give refuge to fugitive slaves was denounced almost with anger. Nevertheless, we are advancing, and provided the war lasts longer than men in haste imagine, it will be at length universally recognized, even in the bosom of the Border States, even in the bosom of the Democratic party, that, to reëstablish the Union and maintain slavery, is not to reëstablish the Union; that to end the war and leave the great enemy standing, is not to end the war.

This is the opinion which is gaining ground, and which it will be difficult to brave. If peace become reëstablished before the annihilation of the Southern armies, the arrangement will probably rest on this double basis; the complete reëstablishment of the Union, and the progressive abolition of slavery. Why should not the United States, in this case, offer to indemnify the slaveholders of the States which shall decree emancipation? Why should not a general amnesty, without exception, prevent reprisals? Credit, for a moment abolished, would resume its value on both sides; confiscations would be revoked; the costs of the war would rest equally on all, since they would form a part of the national debt; in fine, the disbanding of the troops, the reëstablishment of the regular working of institutions, the resurrection of Southern cultures, the encouragement given to the introduction of free labor into the Cotton States, the proclamation and practice of commercial freedom, would give equal satisfaction to interests too long hostile.

This is an Utopian vision, I fear. It seems to me, however, that I should have failed in a duty, if, among the chances of reëstablishing the Union, I had omitted this one.

I adopt a less contestable hypothesis, supposing the complete victory of the North, and the submission of the South. How can this forced submission give place to a cordial union?

The abolition of slavery presents itself anew to the mind. Since slavery has been the essential and almost the only cause of separation, the Union will be reëstablished only on condition of retrenching slavery. To use the American expression, liberty must be declared national, and slavery sectional. Slavery leads to isolation; the instinct of preservation counsels this; in contact with free discussion and liberty, it could not but perish.

It will, therefore, be requisite to take at once, in the interest of the Union, a decisive measure that shall deliver the future from the horrible evil which has entailed so much suffering on the past and present of America. This is absolutely necessary; whether the war be terminated by decisive victories or by an amicable arrangement, the destruction of the great enemy cannot, under any pretext, be questioned.

I do not pretend that the immediate freedom of the blacks must be proclaimed; I admit circumspection, transitionary measures, whatever may serve to soften a formidable crisis for the South. But it is essential that the principle of emancipation be laid down with firmness.

The principle once laid down, every thing becomes modified among the Southern people—passions, ambitions, and interests. Great social revolutions have this peculiarity, that it is only necessary for them to become certain, to bring forth at once excellent fruits. They will not be completed, perhaps, for twenty or thirty years; nevertheless, from the beginning, they influence minds and transform positions.

Slavery about to end is no longer wholly slavery, and its monstrous legislation falls to the ground by piecemeal. The indispensable appeal to free labor introduces a new element among the Southern people. The course of parties is no longer the same, political chances present themselves under a different aspect.

We have pointed out the influence of surroundings; in changing the surroundings of Southern men, their sentiments by degrees will be changed. They lack nothing, in order again to become leading members of the Union, in order again to win perhaps new titles to the rank of which they so long preserved the monopoly—they lack nothing, except to be themselves delivered from the crushing yoke of slavery. Their cause, which seemed to serve them for a moment, had ended by destroying them; they were in danger of perishing in its ruin. But let a liberating hand restore to them their instincts as citizens of a free country, and noble men will rise up among them, the world will cease to hate them, their success will again become the success of the human race; far from fearing their conquests, we shall begin to desire them. What a future will then open to the South! These States, with such fertile soil and so magnificent a climate, will go onward at last toward their true destinies. European emigration, which turns aside with horror from an accursed land, will flow into it from every side; liberty will beckon to its companions; prosperity and peace will hasten thither; the South—I borrow the expression from a Northern orator—the South will become like a terrestrial paradise.

Among the methods which lead to unity, I know of none of equal value to this—to resolve all questions. Questions unresolved divide men; questions resolved draw them together. So long as it is possible to struggle against a social progress, evil passions will rise and coalesce against it; as soon as all chances of success have disappeared, a sudden calm succeeds the storm. The aspect of things becomes at once transformed; other interests, other habits, other alliances, other hopes arise; books, journals, pulpits hold a different language.

When a great question is resolved, a host of small ones are found resolved at the same time; these can be decided in no other manner: the French revolution was needed to abolish seignorial rights.

Study history, and you will see the value of the method which I point out. Here is a divided country rent by the war of hostile classes—how shall unity be established in it? By giving it the civil code. Here is another country where creeds are at strife—how shall unity be established in it? By separating the Church from the State.

We can never know how many fruitful results are

comprised in the bold solution of a single question. Yesterday, the Emperor of Russia emancipated his serfs; to-morrow, Russia will have political liberties, universities, schools, and journals; to-morrow, the spirit of reform will attack its administration and police.

I have spoken of political liberty; a powerful means will also be found therein for a return to the Union. After the defeat of the South, there must be neither victors nor vanquished. It is the admirable privilege of free countries that the words *subjugation* and *conquest* are to them terms destitute of meaning. A conquest would leave deep wounds, which it would be very difficult to heal; the suppression of a rebellion leaves no such traces. After as before it, I see equal States, equal citizens, a government resting equally on all. After as before it, the independence of the States is maintained, their representatives sit in Congress, parties contend for their votes, their influence is exercised over the general direction of affairs.

To have been brought back to duty dishonors no one, especially when former rights have not perished in the struggle. Let us not always be too forgetful of the power of reconciliation possessed by liberty. Who is definitively the conqueror? Neither a man nor a party. The constitution is the conqueror; and it prescribes the law that the conquered shall resume possession of their rights as citizens. Come, vote, your right has not perished; we know neither subject peoples, nor subordinate republics; you have no other master than the supreme compact by which we are all bound; after having cut down the chief criminal, which is slavery, we invite you to enjoy with us the blessings in store for free nations; come, aid us; come, oppose us; come, take your broad and glorious place among a people which is your own!

It seems to me that such language must find its way to many hearts. By the side of compromised and hardened men, the South contains a far greater number of others who have yielded to impulse. If their present hatreds are ardent, the history of civil wars shows us that hatreds no less ardent have become assuaged after peace. Civil and political equality closes many wounds.

Let no one reproach me for preserving such hopes. I am sure of nothing, but I am obstinate in hoping. In the interest of the North as in that of the South, I do not despair of seeing them ere long place their different genius at the service of the same institutions. The principle of abolition once laid down, the North and South once delivered from the burden which is crushing them, I see them united both by their resemblances and differences, completing and finally appreciating each other. Certainly the place of Southern men will not be small in the country which they have sought to disrupt; the sympathetic qualities which distinguish them have indeed their value. They have spirit and ambition—they are the Gascons of America. Now, the Gascons have never ceased to take a powerful part in the government of France, although France has massacred the Albigenses, although the *langue d'oïl* has many a time trodden the *langue d'oc* under foot.

Northern men were then hard; at this time things are different. It is necessary that they should be different.

The first condition of the reëstablishment of the Union is that the North, victorious, (I suppose this hypothesis,) give proof of generosity. No refusals, no recriminations, no inequalities, even temporary! Think no more of the past, make haste to blot out those measures of confiscation which grieve your friends, do not say to yourselves that the rebellious South has done the same; to reëstablish the Union is more difficult than to destroy it; it needs more forgetfulness of injuries, more magnanimity and more virtue.

I hold this language with confidence, for I know that the North is far from being exasperated, as is supposed.

At the present time, there is already talk of amnesty. It is true that there is also talk of excepting the principal leaders; their exemplary punishment is demanded as the necessary sanction of the law which they have violated, of the blood which has been spilt on their account. This is the first impulse; which will give place, I am sure, to a better thought. The glory of the United States will be precisely that of not having shed a drop of blood on the scaffold after having poured out so much on the battle-field. There is herein a greatness, a guarantee of the future, a moral recompense, in a word, far superior to that which would be obtained by the vaunted measures of political justice. The leaders will be far more thoroughly annihilated by pardon than by punishment. The magnanimous conduct of the North will thus manifest a feeling of confidence which must make proselytes. Behold it! it is master of itself, and, although determined to suppress the rebellion, it is far, very far from hating the rebels. Who does not see that it even experiences a touching pity on their behalf, choosing rather to prolong the war and endanger its triumph, than to let loose slave insurrections? There should be calmness in justice; the cause of right should be defended in a spirit of peace. The other day, on the announcement of the conflagration at Charleston, a subscription for the sufferers was opened at the New York Exchange. Those who took the lead in such a patriotic act of charity did much, whether they knew it or not, for the future reëstablishment of the Union.

Lastly, I will not leave this important subject without recalling two measures which I have mentioned before, and which must contribute a great part toward bringing back the South. The first is the abrogation of the ultra protective tariff, the broad application of the principle of commercial freedom. The second, the principal one, I should say, is the offer of an indemnity designed to second progressive emancipation. Apportioned over a term of twenty years, that is to say, he time necessary to complete the emancipation, this indemnity will not exceed the resources of a powerful people. Two hundred millions of dollars thus appropriated for twenty years to this work of peace would assure to the masters a compensation at least equal to that accorded by England and France, would place resources at the service of a difficult transformation, and would retain in the bosom of the Union, the most infuriate of its adversaries.

I have shown that the reëstablishment of the Union is not impossible, I might have shown that it is almost necessary; for if the difficulties of union are great, those of separation are none the less so.

It is easy to write the word *separation;* to realize the thing is assuredly less easy; we have no longer an Alexander VI. to trace a line of demarcation. To whom shall be given Washington, situated in a slave country? With whom will the other Border States remain? Will Tennessee, Virginia, and North Carolina drag by force to the South those fractions of their territory which have just rallied to the support of the North? Will free Kansas be delivered up, a bleeding victim, into the hands of those who surround and covet her on every side?

Will the inhabitants of the West, of the States that form the valleys of the Mississippi, the Missouri, and the Ohio, be told that they must renounce the mouths of their rivers, that New Orleans and Texas are to belong to another country, a hostile country, a country which Europe will ere long, perhaps, have under her protection?

Picture to yourself this great American republic, mutilated, separated from its southern boundary and its ports on the Gulf of Mexico, deprived of Louisiana, which it had purchased from France; of Florida, which it had bought of the Spaniards and Indians; of Texas, whose debts it had paid, regulating both well and ill these accounts with an insolvent neighbor, securing the indemnities due for Federal properties, for repudiated credits, for reciprocal confiscations! The North and the South—this is soon said; but where does the North begin, and where does the South end? Does the North end at the Potomac, which cuts in two the faithful State of Maryland? Does the South stop at Tennessee, beyond which the rebellion of slavery has found partisans? The fact is, that from the Gulf of Mexico to the great Canadian lakes, we find the same nation. On the day when it shall be wished to separate the North and South, it will be necessary to trace I know not what uncertain line through the loyal States, through the rebel States, through the slave States, through rivers, through railroads—a line which would place a custom-house with a body of guards at every point of this vast frontier.

Tell me not that there will be peace, that the absolute freedom of commerce will be proclaimed, that custom-houses and guards will consequently be useless, and that the weakness of the frontiers will occasion no inconvenience. Who does not see that such a division is war,

war always and everywhere? European commerce sometimes wishes the realization of this bad dream! It talks of amicable separation, of pacific separation; it has the appearance of believing that by merely putting peace into words, it will put it into things! Things are less accommodating than words. From the state of distrust to the state of war, it is never very far. Now, what will be the remediless distrust between the mutilated United States and the rebellious South, transferred into a government? I waive all that pertains to slavery; I suppose that the South, forced in any case to resign itself to progressive emancipation, will make up its mind to continual escapes, to provocations coming from the North, to abolition appeals from the Northern press. But will the North, in turn, make up its mind to see the influences and the busy action of Europe installed in the very heart of the American continent?

Let us see things as they are. The South, miserable, ruined, dependent, forced to lean on some one, will seek and find a protector. This will be a great misfortune to America, and, I do not fear to say, a no less great misfortune to Europe.

The moment has not come to insist on this point. What I have just said suffices to show that questions are not suppressed with phrases, and that the fine formula, "an amicable separation," resolves no difficulty. The United States will resign themselves to it in case it should become absolutely necessary; I am the first to counsel them this sacrifice; but I would speak falsely should I present to them an assured peace as the consequence of such a resolution. By force of wisdom, it might perhaps be attained. Perhaps the wisdom of Europe would also aid in it, and the South would be left to itself. However this might be, nothing would be concluded, and it might be even maintained that a new problem, no less perilous than the old, would begin to propound itself. The attempt would be made, which would indeed be something, to live on good terms; the peril of standing armies and huge expenditures would be escaped; nevertheless, this peril would threaten to reappear from one moment to another, and the day that a European intrigue should penetrate the South—that day of itself would rekindle the war.

Once more, there is less arbitrariness and chance in the formation of national territories than is affirmed. It is not the will of man nor the caprice of treaties that has made by itself alone a France, a Switzerland, an England. The laws of geography are something, although they certainly are not every thing. Now if there be a country whose unity is written on the soil itself, so that, on looking at a map, we can scarcely comprehend its being broken into fractions, it is precisely the one which we are considering. The same chain of mountains runs through it from one end to the othér, its eastern plain is interrupted by nothing, its interior plain is one vast valley, the valley of a single river, running from Canada to the Gulf of Mexico; its homogeneousness is obvious; there is in it evidently an organic life, which it is unjustifiable not to take into account. I marvel at those who demonstrate to us at length the impossibilities of union, and do not perceive the difficulties of separation. To accept the latter as a last resort, may become necessary; to seek it as an ideal, is indeed what I cannot comprehend.

I know of but one thing more detestable than separation; it is conquest. To subjugate, to hold garrison, to reduce the Southern States to the condition of provinces, to send and long maintain among them governors from

Massachusetts or Illinois, to enter upon the system of subject republics, to proclaim a lasting suspension of constitutional rights—what are we to call all this? We know what Venices and Polands cost Europe, what they cost, not in money or soldiers alone, but in honor and liberty. An American Poland or Venice would be far worse. To give itself the pleasure of crushing the South, the North would begin by immolating its own institutions. This would be true suicide.

Let us not disguise it, men are found in the North who have accepted the idea of a conquest, with all its consequences. Many others go forward toward it, without too closely examining things, saying to themselves in vague terms that great circumstances call for great measures, and that if it be necessary to make a few transient sacrifices, America will not shrink from them.

These so-called transient sacrifices are of those which bear in history the name of revolution. A thousand times rather separation, with its inconveniences and dangers, than the death of the United States! They would die on the day when, making themselves conquerors and oppressors, they should assume a system appropriate to this *rôle*, a military dictatorship, a large standing army, exceptional laws.

There is no medium—after the defeat of the slave States, and past the very brief moment when the reëstablishment of political and material order will exact the adoption of transitory measures, it will be necessary to govern these States either as a conquered country or as free members of the great republic. Lay aside the plans of military colonization, and other follies, which the press has put forward; have faith in liberty!—it has often done and will do miracles. When the South, delivered from the terror which is weighing upon it, delivered also from the illusions by which it has been lulled, having no longer to occupy itself with slavery, the destiny of which will have been fixed before the end of the war, will find itself called to participate as before in the votes of Congress, it will not perhaps bring to it the best possible spirit; I think, however, that this spirit of opposition will become rapidly modified under the influence of a position radically changed.

In fine, it is the nature of governments to exist with greater or less opposition. This one, if it hold out, will contribute to maintain the unity of the North, and will play the part of an increasingly feeble minority; it will be swallowed up in the rapid development of free States, territories attained to the rank of States, and all endowed with liberty.

But it appears to me more probable that, under the light yoke of the constitution and laws, happy in regaining their original independence, the inhabitants of the South will rally in great part around their country and flag. The old questions will have disappeared, new interests will appeal to hearts, parties will become transformed, and as nothing will recall the defeat, as reprisals will be absent, as the traces of civil war will be carefully effaced, as the victors will have no right that will not belong to the vanquished, a better triumph than that which is won, sword in hand, the triumph over prejudices and hatred, will come perhaps to crown a policy as skilful as generous.

I know of no other counsel to the United States—to conquer first, to bring back afterward; to bring back by the opportune solution of the problem of slavery, by the immediate and bold reëstablishment of liberty.

I add that if, in spite of abolition, and in spite of liberty, a violent resistance be maintained in a few States, if nothing be found there but sullenness and opposition, if the state of war be reawakened there unceasingly, if it become necessary to return there from day to day, rather than hold garrison in these States, it would be fitting to abandon them to their evil destiny. At no price should permanent occupation be admitted.

I should have foreseen an extreme case, which appears to me, I acknowledge, far from probable. But no matter, though improbable, it is not impossible. There is a corner of America, the same in which the rebellion was born, the corner formed by South Carolina, Georgia, Florida, and Alabama, which will remain, perhaps, in insurrection, and will not rally to the Union, despite the defeat of the South, and the repossession by the Federal troops of the fortresses and arsenals. Perhaps it will not limit itself to making opposition in Congress, or even refusing to be represented there; perhaps perpetual disturbances, a lasting agitation, will manifest the determination of a people resolved to remain alien and hostile.

Then would be the time when the United States, consolidated on their essential frontiers, in possession of the mouths of the Mississippi, having besides denied by force of arms the right of separation, certain thenceforth of escaping the system of amicable dissolution recommended to them by so many pretended friends, might address the following language with honor and security to the four or five refractory States: "We will not sacrifice to you our principles and institutions; we will not hold garrison among you, and enter upon the system of standing armies; we will not pretend to constrain you to be free and happy. Go then, attempt to live alone; some day, we will see you return to us."

CHAPTER V.

THE SOUTH WILL NOT BE CONQUERED.

There are causes for which it is to our honor to fight, without troubling ourselves too much about the chances of success or reverses. A principle is involved; this is enough for us, happen what may! And this is the way in which great things are accomplished; the principle is maintained, and success comes into the bargain. Such is the fate which awaits the United States, should their war become more and more what it was not enough at first—a war of justice. Not only will European opinion declare itself with increasing warmth,* but they will meet Union elements in the conquered South, which will facilitate the task undertaken. Besides the Germans of Texas, besides the inhabitants of the mountainous regions in North Carolina, Tennessee, Virginia, and Alabama, they will see all those return to the old country whom the defeat of the South will have disenchanted or affranchised, all those whom abolition, steadfastly advancing, will have brought face to face with a new future.

* I am happy to cite here one of the most eminent minds of Europe, the great economist and logician, Stuart Mill. He has just defended, in a much remarked article in *Frazer's Magazine*, the same theories which I maintain here.

But still it is necessary to conquer; and here is a contested point. The champions of the insurrectional government at Richmond, who display so much activity among us, do not content themselves with affirming with imperturbable coolness that the conquered South will not return to the Union; they affirm with no less coolness that the South will not be conquered.

It would be easy for me to oppose to these bold affirmations, which were much bolder two months ago, the recent victories of the Union. I shall do nothing of the sort. The issue of the conflict is still in the hands of God, and I do not feel the right to say that no disaster can arise. I, who believed in success when few believed in it, have not ceased to believe in it now that few doubt it; but success may be more or less slow, more or less surrounded with difficulties and reverses. I shall not therefore imitate my opponents, but shall employ a more modest language. Not feeling any vocation for the character of prophet, I shall take care not to recount here in advance events that are about to happen. I marvel at people who are so sure of their facts! The future has not the least obscurity for them, it has much for me. I confine myself to protesting against the positive assertions which have contributed but too greatly to mislead the opinion of Europe. My humble theory is this: the defeat of the South is *probable*, the return of the conquered South to the Union is *possible*.

If I have not arranged my propositions in this order, it has been to proceed at once to the great question; to that which disquiets earnest minds, to that which is worth the pains of debating. As to the chances of the struggle, I should have less trouble in showing the enormity of the errors which have been successfully propagated. It will suffice for me to take things as they stand at the moment of my writing, and compare them with the predictions which have been made us. The most decided and most untrue affirmations of the past will enlighten us on the value of the new affirmations which are produced without ceasing. We shall have neither to examine them in detail, nor still less to fling ourselves into the dangerous trade of political or military vaticination. I seek, it is known, to place myself on such ground that my observations will endure, whatever may be, moreover, the course of affairs in America. The study of principles should not resemble a book written for the occasion.

We are to distrust the news which is sent us from America. I know not where it is manufactured; but at critical moments, above all, and when it is in question to urge us to some folly, inaccurate accounts follow one after the other. I will only recall what happened in those weeks of anguish when the *Trent* affair was in process of negotiation, and when the peace of the world, as well as the fate of America, seemed to hang on a single thread.

The telegraph then informed us, again and again, first, that the city of New York had illuminated in honor of Captain Wilkes; next, that all the principal cities of the North had accorded to him the freedom of citizenship; lastly, which was more serious, that Mr. Lincoln had addressed to the new Swedish minister, Count Piper, an official address almost announcing a rupture with England. The precise language was given us: "It is our destiny to encounter, for the third time, the open hostility, hereditary jealousy and prejudices of Great Britain. . . . Well; be it so! we will sustain the shock of battle like freemen." What did it matter to the authors of this imaginary harangue that it would come to us later from Stockholm, just as it had been delivered; that is, as pacific and inoffensive as possible? Later would be too late; the North would be attacked and the South recognized.

The illuminations, of course, had existed nowhere but in the imagination of newspaper correspondents. And as to the diplomas, conferring the freedom of the cities, so far from having been delivered, freedom of cities does not exist in the United States.

I might cite many other examples; were we not informed that Kentucky and Missouri, the two principal Border States, had forsaken the Union, and voted their adhesion to the South? Now, the votes in question were those cast in a few villages by some wandering members of dissolved legislatures. At the same time, the statement of the genuine votes was published, and the result was, as far as Kentucky was concerned, that, of the one hundred and ninety-two thousand six hundred and fifty-six voters comprised in this State, one hundred and seventy-six thousand one hundred and thirty-one had voted in favor of the Union, and but sixteen thousand five hundred and twenty-five against it.

Later, when it was in question to prove to Europe that great military operations were impossible, it was gravely published in our journals that the armies "were going into winter quarters." There was some chance in this wise of exciting the impatience of the manufacturing centres, and deciding Europe to break the blockade. But I should be ashamed to dwell further on the subject.

If it be unjustifiable to invent false news, is it quite justifiable to propagate ill-founded predictions? Who may not be mistaken? Less than any, would I contest this right to err sometimes, but to err always, is somewhat less innocent, perhaps. Now, here are a few of the predictions which have made a great noise among us, which have been admitted as equal to truth, and which have been since replaced by others, no less cordially welcomed.

The South, being ready and armed, was in a few days to cross the Potomac, occupy the Border States, rally together all the slave States, and dictate peace in the walls of the capital.—We know how much of this it has done.

Missouri, Kentucky, and Maryland were about to make common cause with the South.—They have ranged themselves on the side of the Union.

After Bull Run the North, terrified, was about to lay down its arms; after Lexington, the gates of St. Louis were about to open; after the removal of General Fremont, and the discouraging reports of Adjutant-General Thomas, the West was about to witness the rapid triumph of the insurrection. Events have so fully reversed these prophecies that we may be pardoned for not being dismayed beyond measure on hearing the new prophecies—it is possible that the South may be foiled in its attacks, but it is itself inassailable; it will not be pursued home, the Federal army cannot depart from its base of operations; money is about to fail; an amicable separation is about to be signed.

"Near" recognition has been announced more than twenty times, with circumstantial details which should leave room for no doubt. The negotiations which were about to effect the contestation of the blockade by Europe have been reported in no less precise a manner.—The danger has been real, I am aware; it is nevertheless certain that the makers of prognostics have hitherto been unlucky in their predictions.

The North was without enthusiam, incapable of impulse and sacrifice; divided, moreover, drawn in different directions by the abolitionists, republicans, and democrats, comprising a great number of men devoted to the South, appealed to by its interests, it was about to force Mr. Lincoln to dictate peace and to impose compromises.—The unanimity has been complete; the idea of buying peace by concessions made to slavery has lost ground from the beginning, and has ended by becoming entirely effaced.

New York was to detach itself from the North, and declare itself a free city; the great Western States, through other motives, could not be long in doing the same; as to California, it was a matter of course.—New York, the West, and California are more than ever attached to the Union.

Riots were about to break out in large cities; socialism was already lifting its head; the numerous working men of New England, reduced to the most extreme misery by the scarcity of cotton, were preparing direful embarrassments for the Government at Washington.—The domestic peace has not been disturbed for a single instant.

Congress, irritated with Mr. Lincoln, had decided on deposing him; revolutionary measures would not be long in being adopted.—The conduct of Congress, from the beginning to the end, has been as calm as patriotic.

The reaction of great defeats could not be supported by the democratic populations of the North, the cry of treason was about to make itself heard, the Government was about to find itself drawn on to adopt extreme measures, to decree the penalty of death against rebels, to let loose negro insurrections.—Great disasters have been supported with the calmness inspired by strength, the Government has not shed a drop of blood, and has applied itself to prevent slave insurrections.

The *Trent* affair was premeditated; it was infallibly to bring about war; in default of the cabinet, the populace would take it upon itself to hurl the nation against England; the impulse would be irresistible.—The Government had premeditated nothing, the populace has exacted nothing, the nation and its leaders have preserved a most worthy attitude.

The enlistments of volunteers were to become impossible; States were cited where not a single man consented to rejoin the standard.—Six or seven hundred thousand men have rejoined it; every State has exceeded its contingent; and one State, Ohio, has offered by itself alone more volunteers than were at first demanded of the entire Union.

There could be none but three months' volunteers; an undisciplined and ridiculous crowd, unceasingly decimated by desertion, mutinying against its officers.—Volunteers for a year, volunteers for the war are alone accepted, discipline is making vast progress, there is no longer either mutiny or desertion.

Loans were to find no takers, taxes were to provoke insurrections, commercial and industrial sufferings were to bring the North to a composition. Loans have been taken, taxes have been paid, sufferings have been supported.

Probably we are not at the end. The paper currency is about to furnish a text for declamations; men will not content themselves with regretting the use of this means, but will see in it a symptom of dissolution; they will announce to us for to-morrow the forced cessation of the war, or for the day after, bankruptcy. It is evident of itself, besides, that the South, on its part, is neither exhausted nor miserable, that its loans are taken without difficulty, that its treasury is full, that its armies have abundance, that it can raise as many soldiers as it pleases, that it does not accept volunteers for three or six months, that its government is popular, that opposition and divisions are unknown among it, that, in a word, it possesses (I recall the language which was lately held to us) all the conditions of certain and rapid success.

Why then does it not succeed? Things went much better with it a year ago than to-day. In the beginning, it had every thing on its side; thanks to treason, it found itself in a position to attack, and the North did not seem to be in a position to defend. Notwithstanding, at the first cannon ball that it fired, the whole North arose, hastened forward, and raised an invincible barrier between the capital and Charleston. The South then lost its first illusion.

The battle of Bull Run made it lose the second. It lacked nothing, it seemed, but a great success, to demoralize the North and draw in Europe. It had its great success; yet the North was found firmer after it than ever, while Europe had not advanced a step. A conqueror, but terrified, as it were, at its own victory, it dared not risk itself outside its studied and leisurely fortified positions. Not to have marched at this moment upon Washington was to have retrograded, and greatly.

The third illusion of the South took flight the day its commissioners reëmbarked on board an English steamer. It had believed itself this time very near the end, recognition was within its grasp, and aid from outside was about to arrive. Bitter deception! Neither recognition nor aid; far from that, liberal and Christian opinion, the great enemy of the South, awakens from its torpor.

How the respective positions have become modified within the year! In the beginning, the South alone was armed, alone prepared, alone officered; it was three months in advance; the Federal army had been dispersed and sent to a distance with so much care, that at the moment of the greatest anxiety, the commander-in-chief had difficulty to assemble a few soldiers in the menaced capital; the fleet had been so adroitly dismantled that, on the 4th of March, 1861, when the new administration took the power, there were no vessels to secure the execution of the laws and protect the national property; of seventy-two vessels-of-war which the nation then possessed, the steamer *Brooklyn* of twenty-five guns, and the transport *Relief* of two guns, alone remained within reach of Mr. Lincoln; on the whole extent of the Southern coasts, the Federal fortresses had been abandoned to such a point that the greater part were seized at the first moment by the insurgents, as well as at least a thousand pieces of artillery; arms had been conveyed to the Southern arsenals, and this on a large scale; more than one hundred and fifteen thousand muskets of the best patterns had been sent into the slave States, and two hundred and fifty thousand percussion muskets had been sold to them beside, at a price representing less than one-fourth their value; the treasury, lately still so rich, had been outrageously pillaged; treason continued to surround the new government, not one of whose military measures was not communicated on the spot to the insurrectional generals; it succeeded Mr. Buchanan, who, in a solemn message, had just stammered out excuses, and rendered as doubtful as in him lay, the right of defending Fort Sumter against the assailants. Such was the starting-point; the Southern army, and I comprehend it, expected to encamp before long in Washington. How many weeks, days perhaps, would it need to bring to reason this handful of men, this novice of a president, this divided country, this population of farmers and merchants, strangers to the vocation of arms?

We have no longer to ask, as was then done, whether the regiments charged with protecting the capital could succeed in doing so, and could open a way through the hostile streets of Baltimore. To-day, in spite of several grave reverses, Bull Run, Springfield, and Lexington, the United States have everywhere resumed the offensive. They have an army, they have a fleet; they occupy the principal Border States; they have not permitted the war to go beyond the enemy's country; they have set foot on the territory of the insurgent States, while the South has not even succeeded in holding in Eastern Virginia the ground conquered after the battle of Bull Run, while it has lost two counties and a population of fifteen thousand souls; it has fallen back also in Western Virginia, it has fallen back in Missouri, it has fallen back in Kentucky; it has seen invaded under its eyes and without daring oppose it, the very suburbs of Charleston and Savannah. Port Royal in South Carolina, Tybee Island in Georgia, Fort Pickens in Florida, Ship Island in Mississippi; such are a few of the points occupied. Redoubtable preface of the more serious attacks in the course of preparation! The national flag, so rudely thrown down, now floats from one end to the other of the South. The South has not ceased to retrograde, the North has not ceased to advance.

The punishment of Charleston was not long in coming. A year had hardly elapsed, when already the fortress of Beaufort was retaken from the South Carolinians, already the principal outlets of the harbor of Charleston were closed by a barricade destined to last as long as the war. I do not speak of the sinister conflagration which vessels in the offing contemplated with terror a few months ago.

The impotence of the South has just been demonstrated by the year that has passed away. The rebellion began in pride, it runs the risk of ending quite differently. Whilst it has not succeeded in occupying a single inch of free soil, the North has created a navy and patiently disciplined an army; it is doing many things declared impossible—it has remained united, it has escaped disturbances from the mob, it has raised as many volunteers as it has wished, it has not sought the support which might have been lent it by slave insurrections.

Europe has known little of the spirit of patriotism and sacrifice of which the North has just given proof.

I remember the derision that found utterance among us, when Mr. Lincoln talked of raising four hundred thousand men. It was much worse when Congress increased the number to five hundred thousand. Half a million of men to be raised thus from one day to the next! Armies of this sort to be improvised! I do not know whether this is contrary to rule; but it cannot be now contested that five hundred thousand, I am mistaken, six hundred thousand men, and more, have offered themselves with eagerness—that the transformation of these volunteers into soldiers has been effected in some measure in spite of prodigious difficulties; history records few facts so extraordinary. There are some States, Pennsylvania for instance, which have furnished a hundred thousand men, greatly exceeding the amount of the quota required of them.

The impulse which followed the attack on Fort Sumter was truly magnificent; stores were deserted, farms remained untilled, manufactories interrupted their work—was it not necessary to hasten at the call of a menaced country? In a single day, New England found herself in the field; the West did not remain behind; far from the theatre of action, on the lakes, in the solitudes, men made ready for the combat. I add, that the battle of

Bull Run, instead of arresting this impulse, only gave it more ardor.

And the North has not only furnished soldiers, it has also furnished sailors. The fishermen of Maine and Massachusetts have hastened by thousands to the support of the government. The principal force of the North, the navy, has been thus re-created with marvellous rapidity.

The North—that country of the dollar! has been no less prodigal of its money than its men. In a few weeks, the patriotic donations reached the sum of one hundred and fifty million francs. The merchant princes of New York distinguished themselves by their liberality; at the same time that they sent their clerks to the armies, saying to them, "We will take care of your families," they sent to the State offerings of ten thousand, twenty thousand, fifty thousand dollars. And societies acted as largely as individuals; the Pacific Steamship Company made a donation of one of its best ships, and offered all the rest at a price to be fixed by three naval officers, two of whom should be appointed by the government. Note, that the citizens who acted thus in New York, Pennsylvania, Massachusetts, Illinois, Ohio, and elsewhere, had just lost a thousand millions by the repudiation of Southern debts, and were about to lose double the sum by the effect of the commercial crisis. The individualism with which men affect to reproach America, does not seem to prevent the national unity from manifesting itself there with energy.

This enthusiasm could not come forth in the Border States—each of them, in proportion to the influence exercised over it by the interests of slavery, has shown itself disposed to practice between the North and the South a policy of isolation. This has been one of the great dangers of the United States, and one of the best chances of the rebellion. If the thought which for a moment took form in Kentucky had attained its realization, if the neutrality of the Border States had been accepted, a sort of intermediate confederation would have been thus formed, a veritable rampart destined to protect the South. The government at Washington would perhaps have been struck powerless on the day that it should have encountered before it a so-called friendly coalition, which would have permitted entrance into its territory to neither army, which would have naturally set itself up as an arbiter, and armed mediator, threatening to pass over entire from the side of those who should not welcome its overtures.

Mr. Lincoln did not tolerate for a moment this equivocal attitude, for which justice should be rendered him. At the risk of transforming into adversaries those who still presented themselves as friends, he declared clearly that neutrals would be enemies in his sight. And firmness has borne here its usual fruits; to-day, the Border States, with Kentucky at their head, have declared themselves for the Union; their regiments are combating the South, the national vanguard against the insurrection is formed by Missouri, Kentucky, Delaware, Maryland, a part of Virginia, North Carolina, and Tennessee.

The territories also have remained faithful. As to the Indians, this miserable, too much extolled people, whose barbarous customs would not easily consent to dispense with slavery, have been tempted to range themselves on the side of the South, which may count perhaps on their scalping-knives. Nevertheless, as on the other side, the Indians cling to the pensions which are paid them from the treasury, it is probable that they will pause in time and wheel about, especially in case of the success of the North.

This success, it is said, depends on the army. Now,

the national army is inferior in all points to the insurrectional army; a dense crowd which is neither instructed nor organized, nor disciplined, nor commanded, is not an army, and will not go through a campaign!

It remains to be known whether the Northern troops still merit the jeers which men have so long persisted in lavishing upon them. Nothing is easier than to jeer, than to see the ridiculous side which is often presented by great things. But in full justice, is there reason to laugh so much at soldiers who, in equal numbers, have almost always beaten those of the South?

It is true that they have often found themselves inferior in numbers. The unskilfulness of the leaders seems to have resolved the problem of always having the most troops at their disposal, and always bringing the least into the field.

Herein was displayed for a time the military inferiority of the North. Taken individually, the soldiers were worth something; the officers were worth nothing in the beginning. The officers of the regular army belonged for the most part to the South, and had proffered it their services. There were in the South neither companies formed by contract, nor proprietor-colonels—poor colonels forced to ask pardon for their inexperience, and lacking authority over their troops. The social distinctions existing in the South in themselves facilitated command; rich planters enforce obedience more easily than merchants, lawyers, and members of Congress.

These were the calamities of the beginning. To-day, all is indeed changed. Incapable men have been thrown aside, the rest have learned their trade. The soldiers, on their side, bear no resemblance to those of a year ago. There is no more insubordination, as then, no more of those acts of lack of discipline which, two or three times, assumed alarming proportions. Obedience is perfect, the great army of the Potomac, removed from Washington, where it was becoming corrupted, and living in barracks, presents one of the most remarkable phenomena of our times. The three months' volunteers have disappeared, and volunteers in earnest have taken their place. Volunteers! Is it not already something to see immense armies in which not a single man figures contrary to his own will?

The armies are almost entirely American; the Irish element, the German element, most valuable, moreover, form therein but a comparatively small part. The sale of spirituous liquors has been forbidden, and this with the approbation of the soldiers themselves. The most of them send to their fathers, mothers, wives, brothers, and sisters from half to two-thirds of their pay. The letters addressed to relatives amount to an incredible number. We feel that the family ties preserve their full force. These armies resemble no others, and what finally characterizes them is that in every regiment, prayer meetings, presided over by the officers, indicate the forcible action of a motive power, the strength of which we Europeans can scarcely comprehend.*

These soldiers bear themselves valiantly on the field of battle. We are greatly mistaken if we suppose the Americans of the North unfit for the vocation of arms. Far from it, their temper is thoroughly warlike; they

* It is necessary here to render justice to the Germans; not only have they furnished admirable regiments and officers of the highest merit, but they have heroically accepted, in the service of the good cause, the calamities which have burst upon their families in Missouri and elsewhere. Their houses sacked, their little farms burned by secession neighbors, bear testimony to the sacrifices which they have made without hesitation.

have something of the ardor of the French and the solidity of the English. It is said that General McDowell has cavalry regiments which excite the admiration of foreign officers themselves.

The men who now make part of the army are strong, courageous, and intelligent; they have attended the public schools; they have a full knowledge of the principles at stake in the present struggle; they have enlisted through the feeling of duty. This is true, above all, of the soldiers from New England. Nevertheless, the enlistments, except perhaps those from a few large cities, have in general procured choice men.

Far from fearing that they will remain unfit for the vocation of arms, I fear much more that they will become soldiers in good earnest. I should pity America on the day that she should cease to merit our sarcasms. Happy citizens of the New World, who do not slaughter each other as gallantly as we, who do not know so well how to drill and charge in double-quick time! I desire, for my part, that there may remain some corner of the globe where there shall be neither great armies, nor great fleets, nor great budgets, where, to enter upon a war shall appear a difficult enterprise, where this enterprise shall be undertaken slowly and unskilfully, where bulletins, deploring the death of two hundred men, shall afford a subject of laughter.

As, moreover, the Americans do not fear danger, as their pioneers of the West run as many risks as our soldiers, it is not in question for them to give proof of it. Let them not give too much now, I entreat them! May they ere long unlearn what they are forced to learn today! If they do not unlearn it, it will be all over with the United States which we have known, and the day that the liberty of the blacks shall be proclaimed, the liberty of the whites will suffer a cruel diminution.

Resolved as I am to maintain my position in the region of general considerations, without entering upon the recital of facts, I leave military events aside. I cannot refrain, however, from saying a few words of the passage at arms which served so long, and still serves, to demonstrate in Europe that the definitive victory of the North is impossible.

Its first reverses astonished no one who gave them the least reflection. Inexperienced soldiers, commanded by no less inexperienced officers, acting in the enemy's country, marching at random through wooded solitudes where bodies could with difficulty keep up communication, attacking a studied and fortified position on which Beauregard had fallen back in all haste, and where it had been his constant desire to make himself attacked, the urging, contrary to the laws of war, and the advice of General Scott, the insane point exacted by the passions of certain journals, the men of the North could not but be foiled.

Every thing contributed to their defeat—Patterson did not come up, while Johnson, on the contrary, brought decisive aid to Beauregard; a panic broke out after a prolonged combat. There is nothing in all this to surprise us. Entered upon in such conditions, the battle was lost in advance. Far from accusing, as some have dared to do, the *cowardice* of the soldiers of General McDowell, we should on the contrary admire the tenacity with which these raw recruits struggled a whole day against batteries, against a ready prepared position, against superior numbers of the enemy. The number of their dead and wounded, a considerable number (for an American battle, be it understood, and for the effective force engaged), proves that they fought, and fought well. The panic occurred when it was learned that Beauregard had received an immense reënforcement, and that the reënforcement expected by McDowell had failed. Then, as usual, the drivers of the baggage-wagons gave the alarm, and the flight took place.* Beauregard dared not follow in pursuit; which was perhaps the most salient and most significant fact of the day.

If Bull Run had no military consequences, it had potical ones. In the first place, it taught the North that the war was a thing in earnest, and that the journey to Richmond was not a matter of mere sport. It next taught it, that the plans of a campaign should be made in the closet of the commander-in-chief, and not in the offices of influential journals. Mr. Lincoln has learned what a fault he committed in yielding to the cry of public opinion, and forcing the action of General Scott. Lastly, the United States have also learned one thing—that they were proof against defeat, which, far from staggering them, raised their patriotism anew.

Their attitude after Bull Run has never been sufficiently remarked. There was a firmness in it which was worth more than victory, and which must bring it sooner or later. Congress was in session at the time; it neither humiliated itself, nor gave way to agitation; it lent its ear to no dishonorable proposition; thoughts of negotiation or compromise were put aside more resolutely than ever.

It is much less in the hour of triumph than of reverses, that energetic peoples are recognized. The United States accepted their defeat openly, manfully, in the English manner. Instead of losing their time in disguising or explaining, they occupied themselves at once with repairing it. They went back to the causes, recognized the error committed, felt the necessity of *forming an army*,

* Since Bull Run, the Northern armies have many times given proof of heroic bravery, and the Southern armies have had their panics.

and set about the work without delay. Never had volunteers poured in more eagerly and in greater numbers; McClellan was charged with converting them into soldiers, and it was admitted that this would need time. Thenceforth commenced that period of systematic immobility, which has been derided among us, for want of having wished to comprehend it. The great army was set apart, the staff offices were purged, habits of discipline were created, camp manners appeared, they waited on the Potomac until Beauregard should take the resolution to make an attack in turn.

He took care not to come in collision with a chosen and fortified position; this would have been to furnish in his turn a Bull Run to the Northern soldiers. Beauregard therefore remained at home, in his position, constantly hoping that the North would be guilty a second time of the folly of seeking him there.

But the lesson has been a good one. The original plan has reappeared. To act with patience, to wait, to make ready, to leave the blockade to take effect; then, by degrees, to tighten the meshes of the net, to launch the great Mississippi expedition, to reach Virginia through Tennessee and by water, to throw down, perhaps, by menacing them in the rear, the renowned lines of Manassas; perhaps also to deal elsewhere than in Virginia, in the regions of the West, decisive blows which must crush the insurrection.

We may speak of this plan, for its general features are a secret to no one, while it may be infinitely modified in application. Even now, the Mississippi gunboats are ready. The battle of Somerset, the impression which these events have made upon Beauregard, forced to watch over the defence of his left flank, the expedition of General Burnside, arriving on the other flank of the great

Southern army, all announce that nothing has been lost by waiting. It was necessary to have an army; this is now ready, and it is probable that we shall not be long in hearing great news.

The intervention of the navy was necessary, moreover, to the execution of the plan of General Scott, faithfully maintained by his successor. Now, the North had no more navy than army. The point in question was, to improvise a fleet; this has been done, and it is not the least merit of the Government at Washington. The fleet will be called on to play a much more important part in the struggle than has seemed to be hitherto believed. This is doubtless the side on which the superiority of the North will be manifested.

If the materiel of the navy was lacking last year, the personnel was likewise deteriorated by the withdrawal of a great number of officers, natives of the South. As to the sailors, it is a fact worthy of remark that they all remained at their post.

The South endeavored to make up for the weakness of its naval resources by issuing letters of marque. Thanks to it, we have again seen privateers. This odious custom of private war, war as a speculation, justly abolished by the treaty of Paris, amid the applause of Europe, has been a moment resuscitated by the defenders of slavery. Bad causes call to each other and strike hands.

It is useless to add that the privateers have succumbed one by one before the American cruisers. The two last, the *Sumter* and the *Nashville*, no longer daring to navigate the waters of the New World, have come to fill our shores with consternation by their facile and lamentable exploits. A cry is now arising against this maritime brigandage; our ports are asking with anxiety how much longer the privilege will be maintained for the benefit of the South of stopping ships, without bringing them before any tribunal, and burning them on the high seas.

The question would have been long since resolved, had Europe, less ingenious in creating belligerents, accepted Mr. Lincoln's assent to the stipulations of the treaty of Paris. I recall this fact for the honor of principles; for the privateers will have no appreciable influence over the solution of the struggle in which the United States are engaged.

Once more, I predict nothing, I am sure of nothing; it may be that the North will still have disasters and great disasters to endure; it may be that the plan of its generals will fail, or be considerably modified. The perils of a Southern campaign are greater perhaps than is supposed at first sight; the heat, the difficulty of communication, the imperfection of the commissariat, are all obstacles which will not be easily surmounted. On the other side, I am tempted to believe that the attacks by sea, and those of the Mississipi flotilla, offer serious chances of success. Therein will be displayed those still unknown resources of the modern mind which, above all in an inventive country like America, may produce important results. But these things have nothing to do with this study, designed to evolve on all points the permanent and in some sort philosophic side of the struggle. Whatever may happen, I shall not have been less right in establishing that, in announcing to Europe the probable triumph of the South, there has been propagated among us a gross and very dangerous error.

I have sought to prove nothing beside. I know moreover wherein lies the great difficulty—it is in their finances. War at present is so costly (above all, war as they make it) that exhaustion quickly takes place. There is therefore, outside all European intervention, a power which will impose peace within a given time, unless the reduction of the South be promptly completed.

Although I admit this, I must protest, notwithstanding, against the inconceivable exaggerations which have found means of going forth on this point. The United States are not at present a ruined country, feeling the approach of bankruptcy and about to cease paying its soldiers. The attitude of American funds has not been bad since the beginning of the conflict. Considerable loans are made with facility; the banks of New York, Philadelphia, and Boston have taken up the first issues, and a large part has gone into the hands of private individuals.*

Official reports prove that from 1860 to 1861, the diminution of the importation of merchandise was sixty-six million dollars, while the diminution of the exportation amounted to a hundred and thirty-eight millions; but this diminution is explained by the absence of cotton; there has been in this single article at least a difference reaching a hundred and fifty-seven millions. The other exports, therefore, are far from having diminished. It is a remarkable fact that, with its sole productions, the North has been able to pay for all its imports, and thus be sufficient unto itself. In any case, it has suffered little hitherto; plenty reigns in its fields, and the ranks of agriculture are open to offer a refuge to the laborers whom manufactures leave without employ.

The position is by no means very unfavorable. The activity of the American ports, sustained until the winter by

* At the time of Mr. Lincoln's inauguration, the United States six per cents stood at 92½; they are now at 92. The last advices from London prove that confidence is reviving in England.

the enormous exportation of grain, has since given place, it cannot be denied, to a state of comparative stagnation. The clearances, and, above all, the arrivals of vessels have greatly diminished, immigration has fallen off; nevertheless, this falling off has been less than had been supposed in advance, and the sales of public lands have not sensibly decreased. In 1860, forty thousand new farms, averaging forty acres, were set off: for the year of a crisis, this was not bad. With the exception of the cotton mills, which are closed, or have reduced their hours of labor, the greater part of the manufactories are in activity; the shops are full, and business does not stand still; the bustle of the railroads has not abated; the funds of the Savings Banks are intact; lastly, as I have said, the agricultural prosperity remains complete, and we cannot discover in the North any sign of that discontent, discomfort, and disorder, which announces that a country will succumb ere long in its task.

The only alarming symptom which appears is the bill which, it is said, is about to authorize the issue of treasury bonds, which will not be redeemable in specie until after the war. Leaving aside the exaggerations which have gone forth on the subject, persuaded that Congress will take care to prescribe the payment of the interest of the debt in coin, and that it will regard it as a duty at once to establish new taxes designed to provide for this interest, I shall not go so far as to say that a plank for *assignats* has been just manufactured at Washington. Notwithstanding, while recognizing the facilities which the forced circulation of treasury bonds will give to commercial relations, while recognizing that the suspension of payments announced by individual banks may call for the introduction of a uniform national currency, I must point out how baleful in itself is the *principle* of the forced circulation of notes.

This principle is baleful, because it is too convenient of application. In the presence of great public needs, the temptation of multiplying the creation of treasury bonds becomes difficult to surmount. With the suspension of specie payments, we quickly succeed in forming all sorts of illusions; we always begin by resolving to limit the quantity; we imagine that we will make energetic efforts by-and-by to effect their redemption; then, recoiling before the increased prodigiousness of the enterprise, we end by stammering the too common words: "Necessity has no law." On that day we renounce the fulfilment of our engagements, we become guilty of robbery.

God forbid the supposition that America will come to this! But, in order that she may not come to it, she must pause at the first step in the dangerous road which she has just entered. Now that she is no longer subject to the yoke of the South and its theories of repudiation, she is bound to show the respect which she has for herself, and the determination which she has taken, under no pretext, to violate the laws of justice. By imposing on herself new taxes, and thus securing, by an honest and courageous effort, the payment of her war loans, she will win universal esteem. Let her leave to Jefferson Davis, accustomed of old to these proceedings, the monopoly of irredeemable paper currency.

It is a financial axiom that the representative value of money represents in reality just as much as it will bring in exchange. I am well aware that between the paper currency of the North and that of the South, there is always this difference, that the final redemption of the latter is as improbable as its success;* but this is not

* The Southern bonds have already fallen to less than half their

enough. A great country like America cannot be allowed to descend, even for a moment, to the rank of those debtors who live by expedients, and pay their creditors with mere promises. The first duty, the strict duty, always consists in securing by taxation the effective payment of expenses and the interest of the debt. Now, wherever this effective payment is secured by taxation, paper currency not redeemable by specie cannot long seem indispensable.

And let it not be said: "France and England have done the same!" If one wished to imitate all our follies, he would go a great way. We, Frenchmen, after our *assignats* have had our *tiers consolidé*, I recall it with a blush of shame. England has not gone so far as bankruptcy; her specie payments, suspended for twenty years, from 1797 to 1817, have been resumed without imposing the slightest loss on her creditors. But who would dare count on a like success?

Nothing is so tempting and dangerous as a violation of principles which has involved no visible catastrophe in its train; it is a bad example which continues to act for centuries. Since the forced circulation of *one pound notes* aided to overthrow Napoleon, irredeemable paper currency has been dreamed of everywhere. Let America beware! Although the measure may succeed, although it may be far from resembling an immediate bankruptcy, or bringing about a future bankruptcy, although very brief crises like this may seem peculiarly appropriate to an experiment of the kind, nevertheless, the peril is real. It would be a great misfortune to be able to incur heavy expenses, without having to suffer for them on the spot.

nominal value, even in exchange for the greatly depreciated paper currency of the insurgent government.

This correspondence between the direct weight of the taxes and the expenses of the war constitutes the sole guarantee against certain extravagances. Now I am forced to say that the present expenditure of the war of the United States, this expenditure of two million dollars a day, almost resembles an extravagance. I do not pretend that the United States, should they soon reach the end of their crisis, must find themselves crushed beneath a debt disproportioned to their resources. No more do I pretend that there may not be some good reasons for establishing the pay of American volunteers on the expensive footing which we cannot succeed in comprehending in Europe, so far distant is it from our habits. Notwithstanding, it must be granted that too little regard has been had for the financial equilibrium.

I recognize but one superiority in the South, but that is a real one—a portion of its troops serve without pay. It does honor to the soldiers who fight in this manner, without exacting any thing but their support. It constitutes, besides, an enormous saving.

The North, being much richer, has acted rightly in paying its volunteers, and even in taking account, in fixing their pay, of the national habits and the needs of families, to whom the pay in general is sent. Nevertheless, there are bounds which, it seems to me, should not be overstepped. I will not mention the twenty-five millions devoted, it is said, to the support of an army of musicians; this sum will be doubtless reduced. But to give thirteen dollars a month to soldiers maintained luxuriously, and to whom premiums and lands are promised besides when the war is over, is really too much. All of our European states would become bankrupt, if they were forced to pay their armies at this rate. Note, moreover, that Switzerland, which also has none but citizens, heads of families, snatched from their occupations, in the ranks of her militia, pays them barely a few pence a day, which has always been enough for them.

This would not be enough in America; granted. The prolonged service of soldiers cannot be compared to the momentary service of militia; that is true. I will even admit readily that the excessively small pay of soldiers has the deplorable result of rendering possible the creation of large armies. In this respect, the American system has its uses; so long as it is maintained, it will throw an obstacle in the way of standing armies and long wars. In the present struggle, this war, which appears to us extravagant, is perhaps destined to fulfil a providential mission. Who knows whether it will not be the means of abridging the struggle? It is impossible to continue long at the rate of ten million francs a day. It is impossible, on one condition, notwithstanding, and this brings me back to the principal subject of my remarks, on condition that the ten millions per day be really levied on the American people, or at least that the interest of the loans contracted for it be furnished by taxes. The suspension of specie payments often ends in suppressing or weakening this condition, it permits one to spend largely and pay little; it is for this, for this above all, that I denounce it to the patriotism of the Americans.

There is still another argument employed by those who wish to prove to us that the North cannot win. They oppose to the superiority of the eminent men placed at the head of the rebellion, the pretended mediocrity of Mr. Lincoln and his ministers. Mr. Davis and the members of the Richmond cabinet, after having passed their lives in counseling or dictating the follies of which Europe has unceasingly complained, have suddenly become personages of the highest distinction. As to the leaders of the American Government, there are not disdainful expressions enough to paint their insufficiency.

Pardon me for being of an entirely different opinion. I shall wait for better proofs of the incapacity of Mr. Lincoln, before permitting myself to treat with slight respect the man who personifies in himself so great a cause.

Opposition and criticism are natural to the heart of man, democracies in particular are not sparing of them; let Americans, notwithstanding, take care—if they cease to respect their government, they will furnish weapons with their own hands to their enemies.

I do not see, besides, that Mr. Lincoln has hitherto fallen short in his task, assuredly one of the hardest that could be encountered here below. He is not skilful in drawing up messages, I admit; he is somewhat devoid of that personal ascendancy, that *authoritativeness* which facilitates the action of the government; he has made a few mistakes; he might have more vividly depicted the principle of which he was the representative, and, without renouncing a legitimate prudence, have adopted an attitude better suited to rally the sympathies of Europe. But how many good qualities by the side of these trifling faults! If he has been lacking in brilliancy, what a compensation has he found in his good sense and integrity!

It is already something, yes, a great deal, to have a president who is an honest man; an honest man is a power as times go.

It is something also to have a president who knows what he wants, who has known it from the beginning, and who has had the merit of maintaining, through incidents, the unity of his policy. What he begun at the first moment, he has not since ceased to pursue—he has not ceased to purpose the suppression of the rebellion, he has protested against the title of belligerent, he has refused to welcome any idea of amicable separation. With a sang-froid which has never been contradicted, he has defended his programme, his ministers* and his generals. His firmness, which is not devoid of acuteness, has triumphed over the difficulties, as enormous as unexpected, which have come to him from Europe; and has none the less triumphed over difficulties from within. Through him, unanimity has been maintained, the ordeal of defeats has been surmounted, good order has been preserved, revolutionary measures have been turned aside from the struggle. The surety of his judgment will strike attentive minds in the end. The man who has succeeded during the past year in conjuring down, without ever abasing himself, the dangers of a foreign war, the man who, putting aside with a conciliatory hand the exactions of extreme parties, and postponing irritating questions, has nevertheless insured the onward march of abolition—this man is not as commonplace as some would have us believe.

If I speak before all of Mr. Lincoln, it is not that I

* A fact very honorable to Mr. Seward, dating back to last December, should be recorded here. A club having been formed in Philadelphia, with the design of paving the way for his election to the next Presidency, Mr. Seward wrote to them that he had taken the immovable resolution to decline to become a candidate. "I have entered into the government," said he, "to aid in saving the Constitution and the Union, or to perish with them. It has seemed to me, therefore, that I ought to renounce all chance of personal advantage, in order that the counsels which I may give the president during this crisis, may not only be disinterested, loyal, and patriotic, but may also seem so."—A great deal is said of the political corruption of American statesmen; I wish that the statesmen of Europe might never be more *corrupt* than Mr. Seward.

forget those by whom he has been seconded, particularly Mr. Seward. Their administration has obtained the result that, even at the moment when the military superiority went over to the South, the political superiority remained with the North. The *Trent* affair will not be useless to its renown in Europe. The diplomatic correspondence of Mr. Seward announces something else than incapacity. The government which, before having any suspicion of the English menaces, wrote the despatch of November 30, and suppressed even the mention of the *Trent* affair in the President's Message, could prove later, with a just sentiment of pride, that, in yielding to the reclamations of England, it secured the triumph of American principles.

This sometimes painful collision with Europe, these external difficulties of the crisis have evidently formed the statesmen at Washington. Their progress is visible. There is a rare comprehension of his position in the courteous liberality of which Mr. Seward has given proof for some time past. He no longer gives offence, he replies to remarks by loyal explanations, he unhesitatingly gives a favorable solution to all secondary questions, he speaks of England in affectionate terms, he spontaneously opens to the English troops a passage through the State of Maine.

This is what I call good policy. Let the American cabinet join to it a more energetic watchfulness over the finances, and we shall no longer have for it any thing but praise. Independently of excessive expenses and the dangerous principle of the forced circulation of paper, there is shameful waste which calls for unsparing suppression. Whoever is capable of despoiling the country in circumstances like these, ought to expect no indulgence. Disorder at this time is treason. Such as has been just pointed out by honorable members of Congress, Messrs.

Hall, Davies, and others, would arouse a sentiment of indignation in any country. To put an end to prodigality is to-day the first duty of Mr. Lincoln and his ministers.

. .

The bearing of the nation has been no less remarkable than that of the government. Great cities, full of unemployed workmen, have had neither coalitions nor riots. Mob violence has figured as yet only in the prophecies of the friends of the South. The *Trent* affair has brought out the energetic qualities of the American people; in spite of a few inevitable manifestations, the vast majority did not cease to preserve its calmness and follow Mr. Lincoln without hesitation. Who did not at that time admire old General Scott, who did not hesitate, despite his infirmities, to brave a new voyage in order to place his faithful sword at the service of his country? I acknowledge that Captain Wilkes himself appeared to me worthy of sympathy, when, recounting the conscientious perplexities through which he had passed, placing the interests of his country and justice before his own, he thus concludes his report: "Having acted upon my own responsibility, I am ready to endure the consequences."

The same patriotism has not ceased to animate both houses of Congress. I have followed their debates with some attention; and not only have I been struck with the talent for discussion which is displayed there, but I have admired the almost universal sentiment which has led all these men to divest themselves of the traditions of party spirit, and rally around the flag of the Union, which is also that of liberty.

It would be necessary now to place opposite this faithful portrait of the United States, a no less faithful representation of the position of the slave States. I shall not

13*

attempt it; I distrust the documents published by the Union journals. There are, notwithstanding, some points that I can verify, for my information will be borrowed from the Southern journals themselves.

Whoever has read the recent articles of the *Richmond Enquirer*, *Richmond Mercury*, and *Memphis Argus*, knows on what to rely concerning the pretended unanimity of the South. The discontent there goes on increasing, and without yet admitting that riots have occurred at the cry: "Hurrah for the Union!" it must be granted, in truth, that internal writhings have commenced. A distinction is beginning to be made between "the cause" and parties. Discouraging descriptions are given of the demoralization which is pervading the great army of Virginia; the recent abandonment of Europe is verified; lastly, it is exclaimed: "For a long time, we have heard it said that England would fight for us. . . . . We see the chances of peace receding through the miraculous increase of the Northern army and navy. Our armies and families are destitute of every thing. On regarding the future, we ask ourselves why every thing wears so dark an aspect."

What shall we add to this language of the *Argus?* Is it necessary to tell what are the paper moneys of the South, the loans of the South, the finances of the South? As to the state of agriculture and commerce in the South, I shall not proceed to prove, after so many others, that negroes have no longer but a nominal price, that the cotton crop is disappearing, that credit and labor are equally lacking; I shall content myself with quoting this significant sentence from the *New Orleans Picayune*, which certainly cannot be suspected of Unionism: "A mower might find wherewith to earn his livelihood from the grass that is growing in some of our streets."

I might have rendered infinitely more complete this study of the respective forces at the disposal of the North and South. The prosperity of the first reposes on bases which the war has not succeeded in shaking for a single instant. Whoever has taken the trouble to examine that mighty system of railroads and canals which goes inland more than two thousand miles to seek the inexhaustible harvests of the West, whoever knows the new works, pursued in spite of the crisis, which are to bring the Mississipi and its tributaries as it were to the harbor of New York, must have formed an idea of the resources of the North. The North has sufficed for itself during the war; it has not bent beneath the burden. Its commercial activity, for an instant slackened, seems ready to revive before long. Its irredeemable paper currency is only subjected to a discount of one, two, or at most four per cent. in exchange for silver; while we, in 1848, saw our irredeemable paper subjected to a discount of eight per cent.

Things are different in the South. At the first rumor of the defeats of the insurrection, it was proposed to burn the cotton and tobacco! Now, who does not remember that, on issuing its bonds, the Southern treasury gave this same cotton and tobacco as the guarantee of their value. It is, therefore, the very guarantee of these unlucky bonds that there is question now of destroying.

This, doubtless, will not be done; but the simple comparison which I have just indicated, permits us to lay our finger on the financial distress of the Richmond government. These, in reality are "paper rags." and nothing else.

Let us remark besides, that the time for planting has come. What shall be planted in the South? It is a formidable, distressing question which is passionately discussed from one end to the other of the slave States. If the war is to last, it will be necessary to sow wheat, to give up cotton, and to accept a system of culture which will shake slavery to its foundation, since it will secure to the negroes long months of idleness. If, on the contrary, cotton be sown, then this will be to say, in passably clear terms, that there is no longer thought of continuing the war.

Many other signs beside have shown already that the continuance of the war will not be easy. The demoralization of the Southern armies has taken the most alarming character; the habits of drunkenness there have acquired such proportions, that both the government and the press are forced now to undertake a campaign against whiskey. It is affirmed that Virginia is covered with distilleries by the mere fact of the presence of Beauregard's troops upon its soil; the same scourge has appeared in the train of Southern regiments in Kentucky and Tennessee.

Such is the position. The reader himself will resolve the question which of the two adversaries is better prepared for decisive struggles, which is more in a condition to wait.

And I do not need to anticipatate events, to suppose the rapid increase of the victories of the North, the rapid development of discontent and disorganization in the South. No, taking things as they are at the moment when these pages are traced, it is from this time certain that Jefferson Davis, despite his rare assurance, will have difficulty in long maintaining the fabulous assertions of his last Message. Of the two documents published at the same time by Mr. Lincoln and Davis, at the moment of the breaking out of the *Trent* affair, Europe will fully comprehend which expressed the truth.

If I had to seek a new proof in support of a demonstration which I believe complete, I would show the persevering patience with which the North puts aside the use of a violent means which it has at its disposal. It is no small honor for it to have rejected the aid of slave insurrections.

That these insurrections are possible, alas! cannot be doubted, and I can scarcely conceive how the South, which ought to remember what has passed within its borders, can carry folly and injustice so far as to provoke the North to this point. But the North, I hope, will maintain its noble attitude, despite provocations. We are no longer in 1812; General Jackson could then call to arms the colored men of New Orleans without propounding a formidable problem; to-day, it would be quite different, and if ever the negroes be armed, it must be admitted that nothing can limit the consequences of this act.

Better a slow than a polluted victory! Slowness, I know, is the great reproach which is cast upon the United States. We live in an age of steam; and when a crisis, however colossal it may be, is not terminated in a few months, our patience becomes exhausted. It is something, notwithstanding, to raise to six hundred and sixty thousand men an army that numbered sixteen thousand in the beginning, and to raise to two thousand six hundred guns a fleet that at first numbered five hundred and fifty. It was necessary to create armament, service, and administration; it was necessary to form staff officers and to introduce discipline. To dissipate the chaos which was found after Bull Run, to make a great army in a country where one had never been seen, and of which trained officers themselves knew nothing except by books—this is a work for which a few months might be well accorded to General McClellan. As to the naval improvisation, it has been prodigious in all points; of these vessels, of these gunboats, not a keel had been laid on the stocks at the advent of Mr. Lincoln; now, the most difficult blockade that has ever existed is maintained with an efficiency which Europe has ceased to dispute, and a formidable flotilla is preparing to descend the Mississipi.

The slowness of the North has been its greatest progress; it is a lasting triumph won over the impatience which has once already forced the action of the president, and procured to the country the defeat of Bull Run. To endure epigrams is no easy task. I have read pointed articles, each paragraph ending with, "Spend two million dollars a day, and do nothing." More courage has been needed to do nothing, than would have been needed to commit a new folly. Happily, General McClellan, to whom all in America do not render sufficient justice, and whom an ultra party implacably pursues, has been found capable of that patriotic temporization which the Americans have styled, with irony, perhaps, *a masterly inactivity.*

Be sure of it, Beauregard would have rather the service of an attack had been rendered him; in his own mind, he has appreciated at their true value the calculated delays of his adversary. Now the North, which has chosen its time, will also choose its place and manner; if the decisive action, of which I know nothing, take place in Virginia, it is probable at least that it will take place in new conditions. Morally, politically, militarily, the North has henceforth a decided superiority; the time of surprises is past, and the chances of the insurgents have become almost as bad as their cause.

This is the conclusion to which we are brought by the impartial study of the elements which compose the North and South. A more decisive conclusion would perhaps have greater success; but I am resolved to remain what I have sought to be from the beginning—very firm in my principles, very circumspect in my previsions.

It is not improbable that the fate of the war will be fixed before long, and that, notwithstanding, the war itself will be prolonged. The sultry season is approaching, and the campaign in the South will be less easy. This vast country, thinly peopled, intersected by morasses, is but too well suited to a guerilla warfare.

On the other hand, Europe is still ruled, and much more than is imagined, by the prejudices which I have just combated. If the awaking of liberal and Christian public opinion among Englishmen, an awaking which preceded, let it be said to their honor, the news of the Northern successes, oppose a powerful obstacle to the return of the egotistical policy, this policy is not therefore wholly dead. Doubtless, at the present moment, there is no longer question of developing the consequences which the term belligerent comprised within itself,* or of protesting against the stone blockade of Southern ports;† nevertheless, men have not in the least renounced the desire, the hope of a final separation. The creation of two Americas remains the ideal of many, and who

* Matters have been carried so far as to sound the Government at Richmond to know whether it would be disposed to assent to the Treaty of Paris. The despatches of its Commissioners have been printed for Parliament, precisely like those of the American minister, Mr. Adams.

† There is a sandbank near Savannah, for the removal of which Congress voted at Washington, in 1853, a sum of forty thousand dollars, on the report of a committe of engineers. Whence came this sandbank? From ships sunk during the Revolutionary War, by order of the commander of the English troops, to block up the entrance to the river. If the sinking of ships constitute an enormity without parallel, it must be confessed that it is not without precedent.

knows whether, under certain given circumstances, they might not be tempted to give it a little aid?

Let us not hasten, therefore, beyond measure to proclaim the triumph of the Union. According to all appearances, we have still before us grave difficulties to surmount on both shores of the Atlantic.

We will surmount them, with the help of God. It seems to me that, after having gone through the preceding, the reader must arrive with me at a two-fold conviction—first, that the work is far from being finished; secondly, that the most difficult part is accomplished, and that what America has just done is a guarantee of what she will do.

PART FOURTH.

THE INTERESTS OF EUROPE IN AMERICA.

CHAPTER I.

EUROPE IN AMERICA.

Arrived at this point of our study, a question presents itself to us, or rather forces itself upon our notice; that of the general interests of Europe in America. It is not my intention to dwell upon it long, but I do not wish to shun it. It seems to me easy to tell without many words what is our natural policy in the New World; little is needed for it, except to draw the logical deductions of the principles which we have just established.

The whole problem of our policy in America is bound up in the problem of our policy in regard to the United States. Every thing is connected to such a degree with the United States, that their power barely shaken, there is not a single American country, we may say, that does not appear to be open to European intervention.

I know some who conclude from this, that the weakening of the United States is desirable. "See how troublesome this immense republic is becoming," they say, "which has not ceased to increase for the last eighty years, whose annexations have been perpetual, which would not have been long in swallowing up Mexico, which attracts to itself a current of continual immigration. Beginning with three or four million inhabitants, it has already reached more than thirty million, and this population, which doubles regularly every twenty years, may attain proportions threatening to our repose. It closes the New World to us; it will not be long in mixing in the affairs of the Old. Is it not time to check this prodigious aggrandizement? What we ought to wish is that, instead of the United States, there may be two rival confederacies to watch over each other, and produce a balance of power."

Suppose that this end be attained without going further, that the separation of the South brings no other in its train, that this be not the beginning of veritable dissolution; suppose, also, that the South become an independent State, and not the dependent, the protegé of such or such a power, the gate by which Europe will enter without ceasing into the internal broils of America; yes, supposing this, let us ask ourselves whether, even in this hypothesis, most difficult to realize, the lasting interests of Europe will have been served or injured by the cause which it is recommended us to pursue.

One thing at least must be admitted—as far as France in particular is concerned, the weakening of the United States is by no means in conformity with her traditions. France aided in the foundation of the United States. By the cession of Louisiana, which at that time comprised a considerable part of the valley of the Mississippi, and from which several States have been carved out, France contributed to the greatness of the United States. And she did not do these things at random; she desired them by virtue of serious motives which, hitherto, have not seemed contestable.

The United States know this so well, that they count so far on France as sometimes, I fear, to delude themselves in this respect. I, myself, have had the pleasure of seeing my book become an occasion for Americans to render homage to the persevering sympathies of my country.

Why have these sympathies disappeared? Is this country no longer the same where French swords have always been drawn for a cause of liberty? Have not Rochambeau, Matthieu Dumas, and La Fayette, fought there with glory? Has this country ever figured in any of the coalitions directed against us? Has not its neutral flag, the only one which England was interested in respecting, rendered us signal service? Doubtless, the North, though separated from the South, will know how to maintain the honor of its flag; nevertheless, will there not be an epoch of transition, during which the guarantees of our commerce in the East will be found diminished?

As to the inconveniencies presented by the ulterior aggrandizement of the United States, they cannot succeed in alarming me. The policy of conquest has fallen with the preponderance of the South. Then, would it be such a great calamity, if, some day, when the United States shall have solved among themselves the problem of abolition, anarchical countries like Mexico should fall of their own accord into their strong hands? Would not this solution of the Mexican question be as good as any other?

Would it not comprise the progress of liberty, the Gospel, and civilization? Is it quite sure that governments founded by distant intervention would have as much solidity and hope for the future?

France, I think, would not have to grieve at such an event. Why should she grieve more at another event often announced with a feeling of dismay which I am incapable of comprehending? "The United States," it is exclaimed, "will some day pretend to meddle in the affairs of the Old World, and to figure in the concert of great powers!" Well, if this should be, what reason would we have to put on mourning? There is no such thing as distance to-day; and since Europe meddles with America, America may meddle with Europe. The solidarity of interests is real; is there a principle in opposition to that manifested by facts? Is it quite sure that the concert of great powers was completed in ten or twenty years, beyond the possibility of introducing the United States therein? Ought policy to live by fictions, or to seek realities?

If the greatness of the United States is not of a kind to trouble France, it can no more disquiet England.

I am well aware that I here encounter prejudices and traditions which contradict my theory. It seems, at first sight, that since the American navy may be useful to us, it may, by logical deduction, be injurious to the English.

I do not deny it; I even confess that, in the event of separation, the protectorate of the South will probably belong to Great Britain; according to all appearances, an agricultural republic will be formed there, wretched doubtless, and unceasingly menaced; but the products of which, whatever they may be, will be at the disposal of the English.

There was a time when considerations of this kind would have been contradicted by no one. At present, in England itself, the most enlightened men take a higher stand-point. Far from desiring new colonies and new protectorates, they urge the abandonment or progressive emancipation of the old ones. As to the marine, they have learned to comprehend that the conditions of naval rivalry are not at all what they were at the beginning of the present century. Henceforth, there will be several great navies; France, the United States, Russia, Italy, others perhaps, will have a part to play in those conflicts of which the sea may become the theatre. From this time, certain pretensions of absolute supremacy fall to the rank of old and superannuated theories; as it is natural that England should cling to maintaining a superiority which is her security, and propose to have twice as many vessels as any other nation, so is it impossible that she should dream of the absolute empire of the seas. A number of great navies always brings coalitions and alliances; it is no longer a question for the English to remain alone and annihilate all that does not belong to them; the question is to have friends.

Now, viewed from this stand-point, the greatness of the United States is far to-day from dismaying intelligent Englishmen. Lord Stanley, Mr. Gladstone, and many others with them, have not ceased for some time to declare that England is interested as much and more than any one in the prosperity of the United States; far from fearing it, she should consider it favorable to her own. Permit me to quote the expression of Mr. Gladstone: "I have no hesitation in saying, not only that England has nothing to dread from the elevation of the United States; but also that, if we have any selfish interest in the matter, it is that of seeing the American Union continue to subsist without disturbance."

This is the very truth; if the United States, in a certain measure, represent to France maritime equilibrium, they represent to England the equilibrium of the races. She cannot strike New York without striking Liverpool. Any weakening of the United States would be the weakening of the Anglo-Saxons, and the principle which they represent here below. Mr. Seward lately wrote a sentence of great meaning: "What is to the advantage of America is always to the advantage of England."

But it is necessary here that our point of view be enlarged. Let us leave France and England, and consider the interests of the human race. Shall we drag ourselves to the end in the miry and narrow paths of national selfishness, artificial equilibriums and antagonisms, or enter, instead, the royal road of harmony?

Among the discoveries of modern policy, none strikes us so much as this—the prosperity of all is of importance to all; it is not true that one profits by the misfortunes of his neighbors; no people is interested in the abasement of another people; there is on earth a solidarity of suffering and a solidarity of progress.

The new equilibrium no longer results from the opposition of contrary forces which neutralize each other by their antagonistic efforts, but from the harmony of friendly forces, which serve each other mutually. Now, among the forces which should thus contribute to the common advantage, there are few whose preservation is more essential than that of the free and individual genius of the Anglo-Saxons.

The United States have fulfilled, from the close of the last century, a providential mission, the importance of which it would be difficult to exaggerate, and which will some day form a chapter by itself in the history of the migration of peoples. At the north of that America which is covered in great part by nations without consistency or true liberty, God has placed a strong and liberal people. Over the vast territory which it occupies, the waves of immigration have unceasingly rolled, all taking the stamp of the Anglo-Saxon race.

Belonging myself to the Latin race, I do not mean in any way to dispute the services which it has rendered, and which it will still render to civilization. It personifies certain things in itself, also great and important; unity, order, administration, military power, tradition, lastly, that refined brilliancy of literature and art which belongs to a classic origin. But, what is the use of disguising it?—our tendency, if counterbalanced by nothing here below, would lead to excessive centralization, to the suppression of the individual. We need, for our own good, to encounter in our path that altogether different tendency represented by Germany, England, and the United States. The Germanic races are necessary to the Latin races.

These races, I hope, are not destined to combat, but to assist and complete each other. Woe to those whom a no less odious than blind policy urges on to a fearful conflict! I have seen with horror, in surveying Italy, men whose ideal appeared to be the future formation of a league of the Latin peoples, to be some day precipitated upon the Germanic peoples. Thank God! such fancies will never be welcomed by enlightened minds and generous hearts. The broad policy, the broad equilibrium, will always have the more partisans. For the safety of the modern world, the extension of the individualizing race will be maintained in opposition to the powerful organizations of the centralizing race.

CHAPTER II.

ATTEMPT TO REVIVE OUR OLD COLONIAL POLICY.

It is natural that the old policy should struggle against the new. We had reason to expect, therefore, the reappearance among us of the colonial traditions of another age; the crisis of the United States was too favorable an occasion for them not to attempt to profit by it.

What were these ancient traditions? America does not exist by itself and for itself; Europe should exercise over it a sort of paramount power; she should play the part of the mother-country, directing dependent colonies from afar, and patronizing minor peoples.

These traditions have their root in history; after the discovery of America, came its conquest. Each European state had a sort of transoceanic prolongation—there was an American France, an American England, an American Spain, an American Portugal.

This was a provisory and unnatural position, destined to cease on the day that a national spirit should appear in America. The English America was first ripe for independence; this was quite natural—it had been founded by free men. In detaching itself from its mother-country, it set an example which could not fail to be followed sooner or later by the other colonies. We know what happened toward the end of the wars of the empire; declarations of independence ran like a train of powder from the table-lands of Mexico to the furthest cape of Patagonia.

Since then, the colonial system has been maintained only at a few isolated points, in Canada and the West India islands. How long these last colonies will endure, I know not. I will only say that they are daily becoming more independent—Canada is endowed with a free government; the emancipation of slaves and the emancipation of commerce have broken the heavy chain which bound the islands to the mother-country, except Spain, which remains behind according to custom. Europe shows itself favorable to such progress. Metropolitan patronage is therefore disappearing, and the hand of the Old World is withdrawn from the New.

All was thus going on well, and the colonial mania seemed near becoming extinct when the crisis of the United States unhappily came to give it new life. We witnessed at that moment a recrudescence of old passions and covetousness. In the present weakening and possible dismemberment of the United States, we are in danger of seeing before all an opportunity to resuscitate the things of former times, to bring back Europe in America, to react against declarations of independence and foundations of republics.

Among a few (I mean this neither for the French nor the English), covetousness has been awakened, the signal of a quarry seems to have been heard.—Make haste! there may be but an hour: we must make the most of it at least! Reactions, counter revolutions, restorations—all these must be tried!

Certainly, in point of restoration, I can imagine nothing more gigantic than that retaliation for Bolivar which, for a moment at least, has been dreamed by Spain. Here are Mexico, Columbia, Peru, Chili, for aught I know! To re-create a European, and in some sort colonial America would be no small task. Let no one deceive himself, moreover; the complete destruction of the United States is the condition *sine quâ non* of this work; so long as there shall be a genuine American Government, it will not endure with a tranquil heart the denationalization of the New World. It may bow its head, through necessity, for a moment; but it will await its time and find it.

I am not the one to approve, without restriction, of that exclusive Americanism by virtue of which all contact with Europe should be avoided. As I have already said, the modern facility of communication has rendered isolation impossible. Our age does not allow it to Japan; it will not allow it to the Americans. There will henceforth be a general policy in a sense of which our fathers knew nothing; Americans will do wrong to be offended if we meddle to a certain point in their affairs, as we should do wrong to be terrified if they should meddle in ours. There will be alliances concluded, combinations arranged, influences exercised across the Atlantic; let every one make up his mind to it.

But aside from this excess, which I condemn, it is impossible for me not to render homage to the American spirit. The celebrated doctrine in which it has found its formula, the Monroe doctrine, is only the expression of a simple truth—Leave America to Americans! Why may not America have its own system of civilization, having a right to its place under the sun? Why deny this nationality? If America does not belong to herself; if we again apply ourselves (I hope that nothing of the sort will be done) to cutting her up into colonies, protected countries, second-hand governments; if our European intrigues introduce themselves there through the fissures that may be made by her internal troubles and civil wars, it will be a great misfortune to her, and a still greater one perhaps to us. The two solemn recognitions, that of 1783 and of 1824, proclaimed the accomplishment of progress, the emancipation of a continent; it would be strange, we must admit, if, to retrace such progress, we should choose the precise epoch, whose chief political dogma appears to be the principle of nationalities.

CHAPTER III.

INFLUENCE OF SPAIN.

I HAVE named the government which lately urged this reaction. The initiative of Spain has been visible from the beginning. Willing or unwilling, with a hesitation which does them honor, France and England have participated in the movement, with the hope, perhaps, of moderating it. A purely Spanish restoration in Mexico is what they had no wish to allow.

Spain has for some time given signs of vitality which I will not affect to disregard. Although it may be still far from that undisputed position, which classes a people among the great powers, it cannot be denied that its recent expeditions to Morocco and Cochin China, have given it a certain prestige.

How does it happen that, far from rejoicing, the general instinct of Europe takes alarm at this? Because Europe observes and remembers. She remembers what Spain has been in history—a violent, oppressive nation, hostile to all progress, as to all liberty, a baleful nation in a word, in the full force of the expression; she observes what is passing in modern Europe, without succeeding as yet in discovering the slightest trace of that liberalism which is remarked among so many other nations, whether Catholic or Protestant. The possible greatness of Spain has therefore appeared to us hitherto as a calamity, or at least a menace.

It is not that elevated qualities are lacking to the Spanish people; but it seems to have been slumbering in the Middle Ages, and now that it has awakened, it is still in the Middle Ages; its habits, its sentiments, its ambitions, are three or four centuries behind the times. One might be dismayed for less cause.

I seek something youthful, something modern in Spain. I do not discover it, unless this modern thing be revolution. Ah! in point of revolutions, Spain need envy no one; but, to us, who do not confound revolutions with liberties, this malady, supposing it modern, is an indifferent recommendation. We are struck with consternation to see that through these repeated revolutions, she has not found the means of inscribing a single generous principle upon her banner. Within her borders, political liberty is but an idle word, the liberty of conscience is openly denied, the liberty of negroes has not yet found a defender.

There are two courts at Madrid; how is it possible that no one has yet denounced there the infamies of slavery, and the still greater infamies of the slave trade? To start up indignantly, and make high-sounding patriotic speeches when Lord Palmerston denounced the Spanish slave trade, was very well; to suppress it would be better. Brazil suppressed it when it really wished to do so. In Cuba even, a captain-general conscientiously opposed to the slave trave has sufficed at once to reduce its proportions. But General Valdès has not instituted a school; the Cuban slave trade has troubled no consciences either at

Havana or Madrid. Thus it has increased: in 1858, it imported seventeen thousand negroes; in 1859, it imported thirty thousand; in 1860, fifty thousand. And all this, in the face of two treaties; that of 1817, in which the King of Spain pledged himself to abolish the traffic from 1820; and of 1835, in which the King of Spain accepted for this object four hundred thousand pounds.

What took place but the other day on the West Coast of Africa? A small ship, the *Quail*, bearing the flag of a new State, Liberia, stopped a slave trader off Cape Gallinos, bearing the old flag of Spain—it was necessary to avenge such an insult! A Spanish ship-of-war entered the port of Monrovia, the capital of the republic of free negroes, and attacked the *Quail;* but met with so warm a reception that it was soon compelled to return to Fernando Po, in order to repair its damages. The affair would have had direful results, had not England intervened.

I have mentioned Fernando Po. It is there, in a deadly climate, in a colony where troops can remain but a short time, lodged in pontoons, that the courts-martial, sentencing beyond power of appeal, have sent the unhappy peasants of Loja. After the crushing speeches of M. Olozaga and Marshal Narvaez, it is not necessary, doubtless, to show what has been the nature of this pitiless oppression.

Another fact has filled the conscience of Europe with consternation. Humble Christians, strangers (it has been admitted) to all political intrigue, for the sole crime of having adopted and professed the Protestant faith, have been condemned to the punishment of the galleys. Who has not read the touching letter of Matamoras? "My delicate health makes my penalty one of death to me; nevertheless, had I not one, but a thousand lives, I would sacrifice them all with Christian tranquillity upon the altars of the holy cause of Jesus, our Divine Redeemer." An appeal has been made to the Queen. I cannot for an instant doubt her decision. But how long will Spaniards be reduced to implore as a grace, the first of all rights, the right of adoring God according to their conscience?

We may say this, we, French Protestants, who have not ceased to denounce the Protestant intolerance of Sweden, and who will pursue its last remains until a Christian faith shall be no longer insulted by protection.

CHAPTER IV.

ST. DOMINGO AND MEXICO.

It has cost me much to write the preceding pages; in recalling the present conduct of Spain, I have been forced to reassure myself by the thought that the noble qualities of its people will not be long in prevailing; that political liberty, the liberty of slaves, and the liberty of conscience will find generous champions in its bosom; that it will turn at length from the Middle Ages to enter into the modern world.

In the mean time, we need to know the chief instigator of the colonial restoration, to appreciate it justly. Spain has already taken two steps toward restoration in America—she has regained possession of the Spanish portion of St. Domingo; and has obtained that Mexican expedition which she would have gladly undertaken alone, and which she will cease perhaps to desire, now that she cannot undertake it by herself and for her exclusive interests.

The first act is already judged. So long as the United States were to be feared, we saw no desire manifested in St. Domingo to overthrow the Dominican Government and recall the former rulers; from the very moment when it was believed possible to offend without risk a power transiently enfeebled, the affection for Spain reawakened with sudden unanimity.

It is true that, behind this pretended unanimity, we gain a glimpse of something quite different. Scarcely had the Dominicans surrendered themselves to Spain, when a national resistance was manifested, which it became necessary to suppress at the point of the bayonet. After the battle, came the executions. General Sanchez, and nineteen patriots were shot the same day in the city of San Juan.

The legitimate government being thus reëstablished, it was fitting to make the negro and republican government of Geffrard feel that, henceforth, its days were numbered. A fleet was despatched to impose on it, within the space of twenty-four hours, the signature of the following conditions—an indemnity of a hundred thousand piastres for the armed resistance to which President Geffrard had remained a stranger; the expulsion of all the Dominican refugees; and the prohibition of any discussion of the Dominican question in the newspapers of Hayti.

If the Haytian newspapers are condemned to silence, it has been impossible to force the same system on those of Jamaica. Immense meetings have been held in this island to denounce the act of violence accomplished at St. Domingo. Parliament has formally stated its reservations, and the English minister has held a language on which Spain will do well to reflect. I advise it no more to lose sight of the solemn protest which the United States have taken care to address to it.

In order to tranquillize English opinion, Marshal O'Donnel has given a pledge in behalf of his country, not to reëstablish slavery in St. Domingo. Will this pledge be better kept than that given with respect to the slave trade? I should doubt it strongly, did I not look in the direction of the United States. There, the question of slavery is being resolved at this moment, not only for them, but for Spain and Brazil. As soon as the principle of abolition shall have been decidedly laid down by the government at Washington, it must necessarily make its way at Havana and Porto Rico.

It is thus that St. Domingo will be preserved. As to the grandiloquent phrases which are inserted in the preamble and not in the articles of the decree relative to St. Domingo, I do not imagine that they will oppose an insurmountable barrier, should certain *necessities* (such is the recognized expression) ever arise, should the slavery party ever become turbulent at Cuba or St. Domingo, should planters from Cuba or Porto Rico come to St. Domingo with their slaves. The president of the council could well write to Madrid: "The inhabitants are free; slavery, that indispensable plague spot of the other colonies, is in no wise necessary to the working and culture of this fertile country, and your Majesty's government can never think of reëstablishing it here." What, however, would prevent another policy from being adopted, provided that the *indispensable plague spot* of the other colonies should some day appear no less indispensable in this?

I distrust promises of liberty founded upon reasons of utility. I distrust, because I remember. Seizures are always accompanied with liberal programmes; the Leclerc expedition, which went to reëstablish slavery in this very St. Domingo, announced its determination to do nothing of the sort. When the rich valleys (so badly cultivated) of this great island demand the introduction of blacks, when the inhabitants of the other Spanish colonies come thither accompanied by their slaves, I doubt whether zeal will be carried so far as to emancipate the latter. My scepticism on this point equals that of which Lord Brougham gave proof in the House of Lords.

The Mexican expedition has surprised no one who comprehended the expedition to St. Domingo. It was in question to profit by the embarrassment of the United States, and as speedily as possible to put into execution the general plan of American restorations.

I say, "it was in question," because affairs have changed greatly during a few weeks. Our good sense which, in the face of results, has quickly seized the scope of a question, indifferent in a military point of view, of vast importance in a political point of view; the growing repugnance of public opinion in England; the sudden coolness of Spain herself, who hoped for a restoration, almost a conquest, and finds herself in the presence of very different prospects; the protests of the United States, the better listened to inasmuch as their recent successes may bring a speedy reëstablishment of their power, all seem combined to oblige us to render the expedition much more inoffensive than it was near being for a moment. I am ignorant whether my previsions will be confirmed by the event; but, whether they be or not, we are bound to account for the principle by virtue of which we have been tempted to act. We do not fully renounce errors, until we know why we renounce them. This feeble desire to return to our colonial traditions, and to monarchical restorations in the New World, is a symptom so serious, that we should fail in our duty, did we neglect to study it, whatever may be, moreover, the fate of our present enterprise.

Admitting that it return this time without having effected any thing else than a treaty with President Juarez, or perhaps a rapid dash on Mexico, what is there to prevent it from being some day again undertaken? Will not Spain be on the watch for a better opportunity? Will its dreams of counter-revolution in Mexico suddenly cease? Provided that the embarrassment of the United States be prolonged, will not the captains-general of Cuba endeavor to obtain in the ancient American vice-royalties, the same kind of success which they have obtained at St. Domingo?

I contest in no manner our right to chastise an unworthy government, and to exact the reparation due our fellow-countrymen; what terrifies me, and what we should keep in sight, is that Spain, in the illusion of her first hopes, may impel us to replace reparation by intervention, which is quite another thing.

Remark that, however detestable the existing anarchy of Mexico may be, it is perhaps superior in more than one point to the infamous system which Spain imposed during three centuries on these magnificent colonies. Without even speaking of the bloody period which followed the conquest, taking the Spanish administration in Mexico at its mildest and best time, what a spectacle does it present to us? The Indians (that is to say, almost the entire population) penned up in their villages as in so many ghettos, the mixed breeds held as vile, and classed as it were among beings devoid of reason, the creoles systematically excluded from offices reserved solely for Spaniards born in Spain, slavery in full vigor, the inquisition flourishing, the torture applied with cold cruelty, the power of printing, selling, or reading books not existing in any degree. Not only was the circulation of ideas interdicted, but the circulation of merchandise was subjected to the most incredible regulations; the working of a colony for the benefit of the mother country had rarely been carried so far. As to the security of strangers, as to the complaints which European countries, particularly France, would have had a right to make at that time, those who know how the government set to work to combat the insurrection at its birth, will have no difficulty in forming an opinion. It was a trifling consolation to see, from this epoch, as many colonels and captains, as many plumes and gilded uniforms in the most obscure Mexican villages as may be seen there to-day.

Among the most shameful pages of history, there is nothing that can be compared to this long, bigoted tyranny. Indeed, when it was overthrown by the great American Revolution in the beginning of the present century, its downfall excited not a shadow of regret either in the New World or the Old. In fine, the present Mexico, to which Spain, if left to herself, would have gladly given a lesson in good government, is polluted neither by slavery, nor by the inequalities of race, nor by intolerance. It is fitting to render it some credit for this.

But who knows? religious liberty and civil marriage were not perhaps in the eyes of the Spaniards, the least trifling misdeeds to punish, and the most abominable acts to reform in Mexico. It can no longer be doubted that at the first moment they dreamed of the pure and simple establishment of the Spanish monarchy. It is for this reason, in great part, that France and England have been unwilling to let them go alone, which they would have greatly preferred to do. The triple expedition is no longer, thank God! either a reëstablishment of viceroys, or a reaction against the principles of civil and religious liberty, or a campaign in honor of Miramon and the clerical party.

It is no longer this; nevertheless, let us beware! in such a matter, it would be but too easy to do what was at first projected. Pretended political necessities rise up one after another. A government has been destroyed; it is absolutely necessary to replace it. And how? Upon what shall it be based? We are forced to accept parties as they are. Thus, we deviate insensibly; at first, it is only in question to demand reparation; later, the question is to accord indirect encouragement, and at length we find ourselves launched into intervention proper.

I call attention to this peril. Non-intervention should be the sovereign rule of a time so favorable to the principle of nationalities. I know all that may be said: "The republican system has been the ruin of Mexico; it is only in question to bring it back to its genuine traditions, transiently and involuntarily abandoned; monarchical Mexico will become another Brazil." Suppose this prospect to be most seductive, suppose institutions to have the power within themselves that is attributed to them, and form to prevail over matter, suppose it easy to withdraw after having aided in a political revolution, and intervention to bring no protectorate in its train, I nevertheless persist in confessing my distaste for the system which pretends to render men happy in spite of themselves. Were it in the service of the best constitution in the world, had it no other result than to secure the free manifestation of the national sentiment and the lasting satisfaction of the country's needs, the armed propaganda of a foreign power would always seem to me suspicious. It is no small thing, moreover, to overthrow for the first time a republic on the American continent; projects of monarchical restoration may appear one after another; Spain, it is said, has already spoken of Peru, and other tottering and ill-governed republics have been pointed out to the attention of Europe.

It is in vain that these things are effected through the hands of the natives; it remains, nevertheless, certain that the mere counsels, still less the presence of European regiments, constitute the most decisive of influences. Thus begin those interminable tutelages to which I should be unwilling to see us return. Monarchies implanted in this wise would never have any thing except a borrowed strength; national life can be developed neither in nor about them; far different in this from the Brazilian monarchy which we have just cited, and which was invented by no one. Born on the soil, it has not had to invoke the support of European protectorates.

I hope that we shall avoid entering too far into an enterprise strewn with embarrassment. The language of the English government and the English press, has proved for some time that public opinion is on its guard among our allies. I do not believe that the enthusiasm will be much greater among us. Spain, herself, much cooled since the personal chances of her dynasty have disappeared, is perhaps about to cease to urge a policy of intervention.

It remains to be known whether, in the sole aim of arresting the expansion of the Anglo-Saxon race, and replacing the Americans in Mexico by Spaniards and Austrians, we are willing to introduce, henceforth, a subject of inevitable and deadly conflict between the United States and Europe.

The overthrowal of the republican system in Mexico, would be the most sensible check that could be inflicted on the United States. It would also be a menace, the scope of which they would measure, and even exaggerate. They know that, had it not been for their present difficulties, no one would have ever entertained such a thought. They content themselves at present with complaining diplomatically, and making their reservations; with receiving at Washington plans of a treaty signed by Juarez; with verifying the profound emotion which the resurrection of the old colonial policy causes from one end to the other of the New World; by-and-by, they will be tempted to do more. Is it prudent to pave the way for such conflicts in a perhaps early future? Is a monarchy in Mexico worth, I do not say, a war with the United States, but a rupture of amicable relations? Are we to commence what we can neither finish nor sustain; what we cannot sustain in any case except at the price of formidable complications?

These questions propound themselves of their own accord. The wisdom of Europe will resolve them.

PART FIFTH.

TO AMERICANS.

CHAPTER I.

THE CRISIS OF THE UPRISING.

THE other day, on opening my letters, I found one beginning thus: "The downfall of a great people." My anonymous correspondent proposed this subject for my meditation, exulting over my credulity and absurd optimism.

I must confess that he is not alone. The idea of seizing on the moment when a great people is entering a painful crisis to celebrate its uprising, will always appear ridiculous in the eyes of unreflecting men. Pausing at appearances, what do we see? An enormous diminution of power, mistakes, reverses, doubtful or disputed successes, heavy taxes, loans, deficits, embarrassment within and without, a social fever enfeebling and over exciting by turns, a crowd of problems which propound themselves alone, but which do not resolve themselves alone; lastly, in the future, an obscure, uncertain issue, at which no one can as yet rejoice. To wish us to compliment this people on the position in which it is placed, on its divisions, its civil war, the contempt of strangers, the profit which they derive from its distress, is indeed to be very exacting. One is not, to this point, a lover of paradoxes.

This great subject of political paradoxes has been touched in passing by a generous and scholarly pen. "I do not wish to speak ill of statesmen," wrote M. Laboulaye, "but their policy often consists in shutting themselves up in the present moment, and seeing nothing beyond it; for this reason, the solution which they choose is old at its birth. Religionists and philosophers are generally very disdainful toward sages; nevertheless these men, who are not at all practical, are almost the only ones who are right in the end. Why? Because they believe in ideas. Passions wear themselves out, interests change place, whilst ideas germinate, grow, and become facts. We can foretell their victory, as, in the spring, when the wheat shoots from the ground, we can foretell the harvest. Who, for twenty years, have been exclaiming in every key, that the United States were hastening to ruin through injustice? Dreamers. Who have pointed to the statistics of population, tonnage and bales of cotton, to show that the prosperity of the United States was continually increasing? Practical men. The United States began its uprising on the day when the North and West broke with their own interests to defend the cause of justice. . . . Whether the North reëstablish the Union, enclosing slavery within a limited circle, or remain alone with her free institutions, she may again become what she was in former times, the admiration and envy of Europe."

I have not resisted the desire to quote these admirable words. If it be a paradox to believe in a moral uprising which costs something to material prosperity, there will still be a few of us who will sustain such a paradox. If struggles for humanity and right appear insane, there will be a few of us who will continue to applaud them. If it be told us that America "is now making a melancholy exhibition of herself," we will answer that this melancholy exhibition was made by her lately, before the crisis, before the wretchedness, before the pretended decay.

Before the recent successes which have somewhat changed the points of view, I met none but sorrowful, disappointed, and discouraged men, exclaiming that all was lost. This was told us in a country which has witnessed dragoonades, Louis XV., the Revolution, European coalitions; which has been lost, I know not how many times, and which is still existing. All was lost in England after the Stuarts; all is lost in Italy, to hear some men. The peoples appeal from these sentences.

Do you know what is fatal? To become accustomed to evil and resigned to iniquity. Where crises of uprising are lacking, crises of death supervene. And crises of uprising do not go forward without their train—disasters, reverses, transient weakening.

I have occasionally asked myself for some time past, on hearing so many lamentations, whether men had really believed in the possibility of a crisis without suffering; whether they had really been resigned to accept the continuation of the shameful system to which the election of Mr. Lincoln put an end. It is the one or the other: either the former condition was tolerable; or the colossal transformation which it is in question to effect, should have cost no one any thing. If they had adopted neither of these hypotheses, they would not have been thus dismayed; they would not have deplored so loudly the American crisis; they would not have clung with the eagerness of despair to any arrangement, good or bad, honorable or disgraceful, which seemed suited to end it.

Since the funeral oration commenced at the precise instant when the North rose against the policy of slavery, this policy was therefore the condition of the United States' existence! They were therefore to let the evil and crime increase! They were therefore to pile up dollars, to prosper, to make favorable treaties of commerce!

Ah! I know well that great reforms make noise, while ignoble decay makes none. One vanishes gently, gliding down miry slopes, and falling into the abyss, and this without disturbing human communities as do rude efforts and generous combats.

Before the election of Mr. Lincoln, the United States were rich; they were receiving great numbers of immigrants, they were advancing boldly into the deserts, they were exercising great influence, and England sent them no ultimatums. Well, then was the time when it was fitting to mourn. And we did mourn, indeed; we, who are blamed for our optimism, then incurred quite a different reproach. Under this false prosperity, the true ruin was being accomplished; this great country was sinking and debasing itself apace.

This was the time when President Taylor traded in slaves, when the slave trade was organized publicly in New York, when every census brought proof of the increase in the number of slaves: three million two hundred thousand in 1850; four million in 1860; when the extradition of fugitive slaves became the legitimate law of the whole country; when the whole country descended to this shame, and seemed to justify for a moment the sarcastic litany of Theodore Parker—St. Judas Iscariot.

To deplore the existing crisis is to regret that time. There was no longer either truth, or liberty of the press, or freedom of discussion; the imperious voice of the South dictated the acts of the Republic and prescribed the elections; the South exacted a violent outside policy; it wished Cuba, it wished Central America, it wished space and virgin lands to which to transport its slaves; the Supreme Court adopted its maxims, terrified liberty recoiled before triumphant slavery, an envious democracy levelled down all superiority and crushed all independence; public morals were corrupted, commercial improbity was approved, principles were blotted out before facts and conscience before numbers; the standard fell, fell continually, and to heighten the misfortune, the prosperity went on increasing. One of the most eminent magistrates of the United States exclaimed lately, on referring to this fearful time! "I despaired of my country."

He despaired of it, on his side; but we Europeans had but one voice to applaud it. America, to hear us, had reached the summit of prosperity. We, who sigh so much to-day, had then neither grief nor terror. After having blamed in passing a few acts "to be regretted," after having deplored as a matter of form "the necessities of policy," which force one sometimes to sacrifice justice and to maintain peace at the price of troublesome concessions, we consoled ourselves fully in thinking that, if America were invaded by slavery, if her institutions were perverted and her honor compromised, she had not ceased to increase and grow rich.

As to those who think that the uprising was necessary, but that it should have cost nothing, I ask whence they have derived an illusion of this nature. It has not been, at all events, from history. If there be a truth shown clearly in its pages, it is that every uprising is a crisis. To dream of roses without thorns and of progress without suffering, we must shut our eyes. Nothing is so disagreeable to witness as the uprising of a people; there are struggles, mistakes, reverses, and dangers; there is blood and ruin; prudent men stand aside, feeling hearts are roused to indignation, vulgar minds disparage and anathematize. Why not die decently, tranquilly, instead of troubling the world by these paroxysms of feverish agitation?

It is almost always at the epochs when the good resumes the lead that we behold the appearance of social sufferings. It does not enter into the designs of God for great iniquities to be blotted out before their chastisement has made itself felt. And here, the fact is remarkable, the chastisement falls at once upon all the guilty ones: upon the South, which sustained slavery; upon the North, the accomplice of the South; upon Europe, indifferent to the wrong and too long disposed to profit by it.

We must bow our heads and adore the hand that smites us. God has sent the wars, the commercial crises, the miseries of all kinds; they are the pains of travail, they will last until a new America, a free and just America, shall have come into the world.

We always pay more dearly for a progress than a fault; or rather, it is at the hour of a progress that the account of faults is settled. Struggles for the right then break out; and reparation is wrought through suffering. When our ancient French society, rotten to the core, crumbled away at the close of the last century; when its old, accumulated crimes, tyrannies, persecutions, and corruptions encountered other crimes in their way; when the terrible expiation of the past of France was wrought, wise men did not fail to write: "We are witnessing the ruin of a great people." Nevertheless, it was not ruin, but uprising, which was effected in this manner.

Since the cannon of Sebastopol slew the retrograde policy which was personified in Nicholas, Russia has entered into the way of reforms.* A new emperor has generously given the signal, and serfhood is beginning to die. Here is another country which is about to pass through a crisis, because it is about to accomplish a progress. Hasten, ye prophets of misfortune; announce anew the ruin of a great people! See, serfhood does not disappear alone, it draws along in its train the entire old organization. This is true; but where is the harm? Was there not need of transforming the entire organization? For a long time we have been striving here below to repair worm-eaten edifices, yet it always happens that, after having replastered again and again, we are forced to build anew. We will build anew then in Russia; the bureaucracy, the censorship, the police, will not long survive serfhood; the publicity of judicial debates, the discussion of budgets, the intervention of the country in its own affairs, will not be long in coming. Already, the assemblies of the representatives of the nobility at St. Petersburg, and above all, at Moscow, have cast votes which must have made the Emperor Nicholas rise in his tomb. Are we to grieve for it? Let us grieve that there are so many abuses to reform, that there is so much corruption to combat; this is well; but let us not grieve that life is to be more agitated, more turbulent than death.

* Do not those who obstinately persist in not comprehending the Crimean war, see what has sprung from it? It has in no wise resuscitated the Turks, for whom very little was cared; it has forced Russia to abdicate its absolutist patronage, and to undertake its own transformation. The liberal alliance of the West has borne fruits of liberty.

Crises of uprising mark the great epochs of history. What crisis, I limit myself to this, what crisis can be compared to that which dates from the coming of Jesus Christ? He said: "I do not come to bring peace, but a sword." The immensity of the benefit is measured by the immensity of the suffering. Behold the whole antique society succumbing; behold pagan serenity disappearing; behold the national religions perishing; behold divisions introducing themselves everywhere, in the State, in the family, in the very recesses of the human soul; atrocious persecutions, religious wars spring up unceasingly from their ashes; the refinements of cruelty and the excesses of hatred are about to have full sway; the blood of Christians will be shed; and Christians (or those that bear the name) will shed blood in their turn; it will flow in torrents; the world will be in anguish. But the world will be transfigured, rejuvenated, upraised. Above the mire of ancient society, a new society will have appeared, like unto the lands which, when our globe assumed its present form, rose at the voice of God from the bosom of the troubled waters.—The ignominies of Rome have disappeared, slavery has fallen back slowly before the gospel; the family has been formed, and woman has become the mother of the family; individual conscience has conquered its rights, direct relations have been established between the soul and God, light has been shed on life, death, and eternity: the mind has known needs, agitated questions, entered upon spaces of which antiquity knew nothing; modern liberties have made invasion, modern thought has been born. These are marvels, dazzling marvels, which we should better appreciate if we were more accustomed to them, if any one could make us feel but for a day the icy contact with human communities, such as they were before Jesus Christ.

And I speak of communities, I leave aside all that concerns the individual salvation. It will not be useless, however, to cast a glance into the depths of the soul, and to seek there, there also, the characteristics of this supreme crisis, which is the crisis of uprising. They know something of it, who have tasted the sufferings and the ravishing delights of faith. They know what rocky paths are travelled, what sufferings are passed through, what continual struggles are carried on within us from the moment that we begin to see ourselves as we are, and to feel the necessity of internal reform.

Ah! it is with nations as with individuals. The peoples who make progress are the peoples of suffering and combat. Noble sufferings, glorious combats, without which uprising is impossible! No, I will never consent to rank among disasters, the bloody victories of humanity; it would be to veil the moral side of history. In spite of all the weeping voices which lately joined in a concert of lamentations, I congratulate Americans on having willed the cure with its necessary conditions; on having recoiled neither before the bitterness of the remedies, nor the sharp pain of the operations, nor the transient despondency which precedes and paves the way for the reëstablishment of strength. I should doubt their uprising, I acknowledge, if they had not passed through weakening and the chances of ruin.

What an immense step America has just taken! Between the presidency of Mr. Buchanan and that of Mr. Lincoln, there is the distance of a social revolution. The sons of the Puritans are slow to move; but once set in motion, they go forward, and nothing stops them. Can there really be souls cold enough not to rejoice at the thought, that the time in which we live is that of the great triumph over slavery? Is it nothing to have seen it with our own eyes while we are on earth?

Slavery has received its death blow; doubtless, I have no longer to demonstrate it. What the last election commenced, the providential defeats of the North have completed, and now he would be mad, indeed, who should attempt to return backward. A man who can be believed on his word, for he has a right to be more fastidious than any one in the matter of abolition, Charles Sumner, exclaimed lately at Worcester: "The victory is *already gained*, the country is *already saved!*" And he added the animating words: "Others may despair, not I. Many others see the dark side, I cannot. . . . . However great the peril of our country may still appear, it was far greater when it was falling, year after year, under the yoke of slavery."

Slavery, indeed, is not a yoke for the slaves alone, it is a yoke for the governments themselves; it was the question first of all to emancipate the government of the United States. God has had pity on America in not permitting the South to be more adroit; that is, more moderate. If it had consented to return speedily to the Union, much would have been accorded it; it would have been left with a majority in the Senate, with the support of the democratic party in the whole North, lastly, with the always ready and still powerful menace: "We will secede on the day that you touch slavery."

I wish to cite on this subject, one of the most powerful orators of America, the Rev. Henry Ward Beecher: "I hear many exclaim—'It is horrible to think of brothers slaughtering each other.' But is it not just as horrible to think that, on the Southern plantations, so many men are yielding up the last sigh, torn by the whip of the overseer? . . . Ah, civil war is a fearful thing, but I know of something that would be still more fearful—to see the evil which reigns in the South invade the whole country. . . . Peace is not the first good for a nation, justice is still more precious. You have no right to wish for peace, until God has made justice to reign. Such is the teaching of the Gospel. When we shall have done with injustice, our peace will flow like a river. . . God forbid that peace be obtained until the reign of justice be established among us!"

This prayer has been granted. The reign of justice will be established; the true uprising, which great hearts place above prosperity as above peace, will be finally accomplished.

We shall not be long in perceiving it; American policy will regain the standard below which it had fallen. No more wars for slavery, no more Walker expeditions protected by Mr. Slidell and his friends, no more vetoes opposed by a new Jefferson Davis to the vote of a State desirous of paying its debts! Waste will be severely reprimanded, now that the passion for struggles on the subject of slavery is no longer at hand to cover every thing, now that direct taxation has come to make the knaveries of administrators weigh upon each citizen.

Not only has the government just received its letters of emancipation, but individuals themselves will breathe henceforth with a freedom which had ceased to be known in America. The emancipation of slaves will bring with it the emancipation of politics and of characters. Two questions have been treated and resolved at the same time—the question of slavery and that of democracy; it was time that the elasticity of individualism resumed its vigor, and ceased to be restrained by the despotism of numbers.

No despotism has surpassed this—thanks to the demagogic pressure let loose by the passions of the South, popular sovereignty had become a rude idol; it seemed as though morality were put to vote, and infamy became honest as soon as it obtained the majority! What do the ravages of such principles tell? Public and private morals corrupted at the same time; for there is, thank God, aunity in man, and the pretension to remain honest in certain acts while becoming a knave in certain others, has always received the contradictions of experience.

It will not be the least proof of the uprising which is being wrought, to see individuals rise up before the masses; lately crushed, ground down, confounded by force with the State, they will dare listen to their conscience and be of their own mind. There will no longer be unlimited power in America; that is, there will be liberty at last.

A last progress will have been accomplished; the United States needed to receive lessons of defeat and trial. A spoiled, infant people, they could, no more than other peoples, dispense with the harsh instructions of adversity. They had been accustomed to success and flatteries; they had conceived an unreasonable opinion of themselves. Thence came some presumption in language, and some arrogance in action. Now they have passed through the crucible in which we leave our scoriæ.

To renounce adulation is not to renounce, far from it, the esteem of others. Never, on the contrary, has the true power of America more fully broken forth. This uprising through justice will remain one of the great events of history. This people, fallen so low under Mr. Buchanan, and which succeeds in rising, this new Antæus, that regains strength on touching the soil of liberty and law, no one, believe me, will regard with disdain.

It might have been said formerly that the United States subsisted only through their privileged position—without neighbors, consequently without enemies, exempt from the efforts exacted by war, life had been easy to them; their vast political edifice had not been tried, for it had struggled against no tempest, and there was right to suppose that the first torrent which beat against the wall would overthrow or shake the foundations. To-day, the torrent has come, and the foundation remains. The impotent nationality which had been shown us submerged beneath the waves of immigration, has been found an energetic and long-lived nationality. In the face of the rebellious South as in the face of the menacing South, there is found an American nation. It has broken forever; yes, broken, even in the event of the effective separation of a portion of the South, the perfidious weapon of separation. It has passed through the triple ordeal which all governments must endure—the ordeal of foundation, of independence, of revolution. It has affranchised with one blow, its present and its future. At the hour of disasters, it has displayed the rarest quality of all—patience to repair the evil. It could at that time utter the confident speech: "The Americans of the North are only the better for having been beaten once or twice." Lastly, while engaged in a struggle with difficulties from without, the United States have known how to accept the consequences of their embarrassment, without ceasing to hold a language full of dignity; they have made their protestations and maintained their principles, while awaiting better days.

I shall not waste my time in demonstrating that, if the Union come out of the crisis victorious, it will come out aggrandized. The *uprising of a great people* will then have numerous partisans, and my paradox will become a commonplace. I have been anxious to establish another theory, no less true, but less popular—to-day, during the crisis, in the midst of difficulties and perils, whatever may be the issue of the struggle, the uprising is already accomplished. Already, America has said to slavery: "Thou shalt go no further." Already, it has said to the South: "I recoil neither before thy plans of disruption, nor before the sovereign influence which thy cotton must exert on the determinations of Europe." Already, it has resisted the terrible ordeal of treasons. Already, it has maintained its unity and avoided mob violence. Already, it has accepted heavy charges which will leave their traces on the American budget, like the noble scars which remain stamped on the countenance of conquerors.

The uprising is therefore already accomplished. It may be that the United States will still combat and suffer, but their cause will not perish; and their cause is their greatness.

CHAPTER II.

MAINTENANCE OF FREE INSTITUTIONS.

UPRISING is not revolution. It is even quite the contrary. Revolution is what the South has been striving to effect; the triumph over the South will consist in maintaining as they are the free institutions of the country.

Americans! it is necessary to give a contradiction to the prognostic, "The civil war will kill slavery in the South, and liberty in the North." Distrust those among you who turn to unity of power as to a refuge; do not listen to those sceptical minds which always expect something, because they believe nothing and hold to nothing. Remain yourselves, or rather, become yourselves again; aspire, as to the greatest progress, to the faithful preservation of your ancient Union, without religion of State, without budget of worships, without great armies, without centralized administration. Remain yourselves, remain America, this will be the greatest of originalities. It is important that there be something ancient on your soil, something which has passed through crises and survived battles. Your institutions will be this thing; henceforth tried and in some sort venerable, clothed with a character of which the fundamental law of a country cannot be divested with impunity, they will secure a more inviolable asylum to your liberties. Come out of the struggle with the programme which you had on entering it, with the political unity of the State, with the administrative independence of the States; do not make the common country bear the penalty of the crime of a few; above all, reject the counsels of those who urge you to ape Europe. As your flora and your fauna are not ours, so your social organization should not be that of the Old World. Is it better? Is it less good? Idle questions: it is *different*, and different it should remain.

The comparative examination of republic and monarchy is in place in *Cinna;* in the reality of human affairs, these great questions resolve themselves by virtue of necessities, which have no connection with the arguments of political philosophy. But, independently of forms of government, which are not here in question, there are principles which may be more or less applied under all forms of government. America has the privilege of having comprehended them better than any one; let her not abdicate this superiority.

She is also as little governed, above all as little administered as possible; an immense advantage, which might be weakened or disappear under the influence of existing events. The American budget rose to three hundred million francs in 1860, and the American debt did not exceed this amount; that is to say, the capital owed by the United States was only the equivalent of a year of their revenue. Well; this is the ideal toward which it is important ere long to return.

Ideal is indeed the word. History will have difficulty some day to believe that a great nation was able to live more than seventy years without establishing among it direct taxation. This was a golden age, which doubtless will never again be found; I do not delude myself on this point. Once having left the happy epoch when a few indirect taxes sufficed to defray their expenses, the United States will not return to it; the question is only to approach it as nearly as possible. Despite the permanent burden which will be imposed on them by the interest and liquidation of the enormous debts contracted during the war, despite the burden which I hope will result from progressive emancipation, and the indemnity allowed by the treasury, there will still be means of establishing at Washington, budgets bearing very little resemblance to those we vote in Europe. And this is essential; at an epoch when financial embarrassment is the plague of almost all the countries of the Old World, the New World would do very wrong to suffer itself to be seduced by the evil sophisms too well accepted among us. Superb theories have been made for us on the merits of taxation, on the natural increase of taxation, on the advantage of paying more and spending more. What the result has been for us, Frenchmen, every one knows. When our budget, to the general stupefaction, reached the amount of a thousand million francs, all exclaimed against it. M. Thiers made the speech in reply, which was, alas! a prophecy: " You complain of this budget of a thousand millions! Look at it well, for you will never again behold it." Let our example instruct the Americans; unless they energetically retrace their steps, they will speedily become accustomed, as well as we, to spending thousands of millions.

Europe has not only great budgets, she has great armies, which are still more dangerous. I shall not ask Americans to return to their army of sixteen thousand men; I am fully conscious that this is no more to be thought of; let them say to themselves, however, that all their energy is about to be needed to resist the temptations to which the condition of war will have given birth. Doubtless it will be pretended that it is fitting to profit by these numerous soldiers, disciplined and inured to war, that there are questions to regulate in Mexico and elsewhere, that there are conquests to make, that the opportunity is admirable for seizing Cuba, the Antilles, who knows? perhaps South America to Cape Horn, that, moreover, the South still needs to be watched over, that prudence does not permit radical measures. Now, there are cases in which radical measures alone succeed. Happily, the sentiment of the incompatibility between the American system and standing armies has not ceased to make its presence felt in the United States. While developing their defensive forces, the fortification of cities and frontiers, the organization of militia, the improvement of military schools, they have firmly maintained the provisional character of their armaments. They have wished, and I praise them for it, none but volunteers. They have rejected plans of conscription. Perhaps, at peace, they will keep up a tolerable large navy; they will not, if they are wise, keep up a large army.

These are friendly counsels. While comprehending that there will be changes, that in one sense, it is impossible that a new America should not come forth from such a furnace, I would wish the new one greatly to resemble the old, and above all to take care not to reject its best features.

The modifications, which may be easily foreseen, will be designed to give a little more strength to the central power. Without imperilling the principle of self-government, which is the very essence of liberty, the Americans will doubtless realize in a more precise manner, the fundamental unity of the nation. The idea of confederation, already so weak, will become still more obliterated. This is precisely what happened in Switzerland, after the rising in arms of the Sonderbund.

It is probable that the banking system will be subjected to alteration, and that the unconditional emission of paper currency in every part of the country will be prohibited. The independence of judges needs to be guaranteed; there are States in which they are elected but for one year; and others where the quota of their salary is unceasingly called in question. The impotence of the law in the presence of great popular disorders will demand preservative measures, the adoption of which has become possible since the passions of slavery have ceased to rule the country. Lastly, and without speaking of the principal change, of that which will determine the conditions of the complete abolition of slavery, I should not be astonished if it should be wished to give a little more prestige to the position of the Chief Magistrate of the Republic. Without returning to the etiquette established in the time of Washington, when he held great levees, when he invited none to his table but foreign envoys holding the rank of Ambassadors, when his carriage, drawn by six horses, was escorted by two aides-de-camp, when the managers of theatres received him at the bottom of the steps, and all the spectators rose at his entrance, it may be that the simplicity of the White House will be judged too great. I give no opinion on the question, but I confess that this president, so powerful in fact, and surrounded by so little paraphernalia, this chief of a great people, with his civil list costing one hundred and twenty thousand francs, does not appear to me lacking in greatness.

What is more important is that he should be checked

in the path of dictatorship which he has entered for a moment. On separating in August, Congress voted him veritable full powers. Mr. Lincoln has not abused them; the impetuosity which existed for a month or two has given place to a more reserved attitude; he seems to have called to mind the speech of our old publicist Jean Bodin; "The power to do every thing does not give the right to do it."

Nothing is so tempting and so convenient, but also so dangerous, as full powers. It is reasonable, doubtless, to take some exceptional measures when the position itself is exceptional; the necessities of war are incontestable; a government, surrounded by spies, and whose plans are regularly communicated to the enemy, has a right to defend itself. Notwithstanding, let us not hasten to believe that we shall be much stronger, because we are at liberty to trample the laws under foot; there is much more strength, upon the whole, in that respect for the laws which goes so far as to accept difficulties and extreme restraint, rather than have recourse to arbitrary measures.

Coups d'état have never strengthened any one; it is by avoiding *coups d'état* that the *coup d'état* of the rebellion will be better suppressed. The law is the great strength of the North; let it not quit it, or let it hasten to return to it! Mr. Lincoln, I doubt not, has had very strong reasons for suspending *habeas corpus*, for ordering arrests, and for suppressing newspapers. There has been great exaggeration in saying that the law of the suspected has been put in force, that Mr. Seward has issued *lettres de cachet*, and that Fort Lafayette, (what an irony of fate!) has been transformed into a Bastile. At all events, the Government at Washington comprehended its true interests on the day that it restricted the extent of this exceptional system. At the present time, it has nearly disappeared—the prisoners of state have been set at liberty, and the passport system, a moment adopted, has been already abolished.

There are energetic acts from which the president has been a thousand times right in not shrinking. The arrest of those members of the Maryland Legislature who were preparing to vote for secession, and had extended the hand to Beauregard, will never be brought as a reproach against General Banks. But other acts would be less easy to justify.

It will be, above all, at the hour of decisive success, which will strike ere long, I hope, that we shall be able to judge American policy. Then will be propounded the problems of pacification, more important and more difficult perhaps than the problems of the struggle. Then the question will be to give a contradiction to those who announce that the North, incapable of adopting the glorious solution furnished it by liberty, can only enter that wretched path of punishment, reprisal and distrust which leads straight to military despotism. Already, it is urged in this direction; it is put on its guard against the sentiments of "false generosity and false pity" which would spare the principal leaders of the rebellion; it is insisted that there shall be, at the end of the struggle, a certain number of exemplary punishments. If it were proposed to render those men interesting who are far from being so at present, and to preserve the germ of new insurrections, this would be marvellously well adapted to the purpose. In the sequel of civil wars, we never lack good reasons for erecting the scaffold, and publishing amnesties studded with exceptions. Beware! these amnesties, the public conscience calls lists of proscription. It does not like courts of justice to be convoked on the morrow of the battle; in its opinion, the decrees rendered there by the conqueror always resemble vengeance more than justice. How glorious it would be to conquer one's self after having conquered the South! Pardon for all, liberty for all, equality of right for all, this is the vengeance of the North. It seems as though the greatness of the part were fitted to tempt it.

As to the proceedings which have hitherto accompanied the war, it must be recognized in full justice that they do honor to America. I except the Confiscation Bills. That of the North is only a reprisal, I am aware; the South, not content with confiscation, has decreed the non-payment of debts. But if the South adopt odious measures, is it a reason for the North to do *as much?*

I hasten to add, that it has not done *as much.* The South has gone so far as to prescribe the general confiscation of property possessed in its territory by Northern citizens. Numerous deputations having insisted with Mr. Lincoln that the North, in turn, should confiscate all property within its limits belonging to Southern citizens, the President opposed the measure. " But they do it on their side," it was objected.—" If they think themselves free to commit an act of injustice," the president replied, " I have neither the right nor the wish to do so."

The war, whatever may have been said of it, has not for a moment borne the character of cruelty. In spite of the principles which seemed opposed to it, the United States have not once treated as rebels, prisoners taken with arms in their hands; the privateers themselves have been spared.

Upon the whole, there has been fighting, but the horrors which have hitherto polluted civil wars, have been avoided with care. Exchanges of prisoners are made daily; many obtain their liberty on parole. The progressive invasion of the States is marked neither by devastation nor pillage. Mildness has been carried so far as to commute the death penalty pronounced in Missouri against the wretches who, by burning railroad bridges, had caused the death of numerous men, women, and children. Lastly, since the commencement of hostilities, the scaffold —mark well this fact—has not yet been erected a single time by the North. After the taking of Fort Sumter, when treason was everywhere; after Bull Run, when the enemy was marching on Washington, the United States had no days of September.

The South is far from having shown the same moderation. The terror which has reigned in its bosom for years has become still more violent. The vigilance committees there have done their well-known work; we know from the letters of Mr. Russell, that battalions proceeding toward the North, bear before them a coffin on which "Abraham Lincoln" is inscribed in large letters. As to the war, that of the extreme West, pursued with the aid of Indians and pillagers, has shrunk neither from conflagration nor more detestable atrocities.

It is important to us all that the American institutions come out intact from the trial. The solidarity which today unites all peoples is so great, that nowhere can any question be agitated to which we may say that we are strangers. It is our own business that is in question; it is the house of our neighbor that is burning, *paries proximus ardet.*

Republic and monarchy aside, the whole world is interested in the issue of the debate. The success of America would be a decisive argument in favor of liberty. If liberal institutions come out victorious from a tempest where many hoped to see them perish, if it happen for the first time that a civil war ends without establishing an exceptional system and an excessive concentration of power, will this be nothing? Not only is the abolition of slavery a prodigious deed, made to honor our century, and the influence of which will make itself felt afar, but other problems propounded in the New World will now be happily resolved without profit to Europe. We are drifting toward democracy; is it indifferent to us to know (what is not yet demonstrated) whether it accords with liberty? We are struggling under the embarrassment of the Roman question; that is, of establishing relations between the churches and the state; shall we learn nothing on the day that we see how much the victory of the American Government has been facilitated by the fact that it has not had to trouble itself about the churches, and that the political conflict could not become complicated with a religious one?

CHAPTER III.

ABOLITION OF SLAVERY.

I do not wish to repeat what I have said elsewhere, but to sum up in a few words the results of our study on this essential point.

What is henceforth important is, not that abolition may be effected—this, no one can prevent; but, that it may be by the desire of the American Government. To know one's duty is sometimes more difficult than to do it; now, the duty of the United States is not perhaps as yet sufficiently known to them. They have comprehended and accepted the necessity of arresting the extension of slavery; it remains for them to comprehend and accept the necessity of abolishing it; that is, of taking measures immediately for this end. Without in any manner making an abolition war, without arming the negroes, without making a change of front which would divide the North and alarm the Border States, the American Government may fully pave the way for the decisive struggle which alone can give to the present crisis the character of a crisis of uprising. Slavery, as the great enemy and obstacle to reconciliation, should receive its death blow.

Let its slow and progressive extinction be proclaimed—this is natural; let an indemnity be accorded—this is excellent policy; but let no half-way measures be adopted. Half-way measures embitter; thorough measures have in themselves a tranquillizing power. The South itself seems to have been willing to prepare the way for this great reform—in causing offers of progressive emancipation, more or less in earnest, to be presented to Europe, the South has taken away from the most timorous minds and the most dismayed interests of the Free, or the Border States, the right to be scandalized, when Mr. Lincoln shall accomplish against the rebellion what Mr. Davis proposed to accomplish for it.

Honest men will not be lacking, when the hour of great successes shall have struck, to entreat Mr. Lincoln to do nothing. To abstain, seems always the height of wisdom; it is sometimes the height of folly. To abstain, in certain cases, is to act. If, contrary to all appearances, Congress and the President should put an end to the rebellion without putting an end to slavery; if the cause of the evil should survive, America would not be long in paying dearly for such an error.

Until now, I have comprehended all the circumspection used; I shall still comprehend it in the future. Reserve action for time, put aside abrupt and violent systems, but, in Heaven's name, be resolved, and do not leave the enemy in possession of the field.

This enemy will be no longer what it has been, that is certain; slavery can no longer set itself up as master; it will remain on the defensive. Is this a reason, however, for not demanding that the Southern States, in due form of law, shall give their assent, without delay, to abolition? Otherwise, what fatal agitation will ensue both in the South and the Border States! What an obstacle to true union, the tranquillizing of minds and the fusion of interests!

It would be to keep up irritation, to maintain antagonism, to necessitate military occupation, lastingly to prevent American institutions, and to secure before long the renewal of the rebellion, to set to work in any other way. There will be in the South neither the immigration of free labor, nor the formation of a middle class, nor the definitive fall of the violent party, until the principle of abolition shall be laid down in terms that will permit of no return. Then, only, the aspect of things will change; the *raising* of negroes will have an end; deprived at once of the domestic and foreign slave trade, slavery will vanish, the problem will be resolved. Then, too, will be produced the so much contested unity and homogeneousness of the American people.

What has been the question during the past year? To know whether slavery will kill the Union, or whether the Union will kill slavery. That Mr. Lincoln may be convinced of it, God will hold closed all the avenues that lead to peace, until justice shall be satisfied. Durable peace, peace worthy of the name, peace which a second time will found the United States, this peace the American people cannot taste until it has first nobly and absolutely done its duty.

This will take place, whether the Union be established, or the separation of a few States be accepted. Yes, even in assuming this last, painful hypothesis, we shall not have to doubt the uprising of the United States.

America will remain one of the most powerful nations of earth. Resolutely resigning itself, and turning its gaze within, it will consecrate itself to a glorious work. To complete the abolition of slavery within its own borders, to suppress all traces of dictatorship, to reëstablish the free workings of its institutions, to return to material prosperity, to a prosperity better than the former—this would be no insignificant enterprise.

Many men less confident than myself, are obstinate in believing that so long as separation does not take place, the amalgamation of principles will subsist. They wish the North to constitute a purely abolition State. They think this the only means of dissolving the democratic party, and destroying the thought of compromise. It seems to them, that, slavery being concentrated on one side and liberty on the other, it would be to the advantage of every one. The constitutional transformation which abolition supposes, might be accomplished with the majorities required by the compact; every thing would go on, therefore, in a more regular and surer manner.

I comprehend this point of view, which is not my own. Once more, if the question were to choose between Union without abolition, and abolition without Union, I would vote for the latter, certain that it alone could accord with the honor and greatness of the United States. The miserable Union which would be purchased by an act of cowardice, would not be worth the trouble of picking up; it would tarnish the cause of America, and compromise its future.

To decrease materially and increase morally is not to decrease. This people would uprise—this people, which would no longer represent any thing but liberty, this people, which would have affranchised its institutions and policy, and which, surrounded by universal esteem, would advance with the Divine blessing toward its noble destinies. It would consecrate itself to the fruitful work of abolition in the Border States, it would give to the Border States that unexampled prosperity which they will enjoy, the day that they shall be penetrated by free labor; it would give to the prosperity of the Border States the enduring lesson of the wretched and fallen South.

Its first duty is its first interest. It finds itself in one of those privileged positions, where the apparent discords of politics and morality become effaced, one after the other. It is about to be judged by its acts, not its words. Now, let us confess it, if its acts have often been good, they have not always been so. Abolition will be effected. Of that I have no doubt, but the conduct of the North toward the free colored race is as yet little modified; it remains as a cruel contradiction, which the North gives in person to its speeches against slavery. These five hundred thousand men, who endure there the iniquities and outrages of which every one is cognizant, seem to accuse of hypocrisy the nevertheless sincere declarations of the orators of liberty.

At the door of the meetings where Mr. Sumner is applauded, at the door of the churches where Mr. Beecher eloquently stigmatizes slavery, at the door of the journals where the crime of the South is denounced, the crime of the North remains standing. This is sad—it should change. Do you remember, citizens of America, do you remember the bitter speech? "They wish to be free, and they do not know how to be just." Be just, become just, I entreat you! Compromise yourselves sacredly for justice! Do precisely the thing which costs you the most, it will be the best in the eyes of men as in the eyes of God! I have sought in your public newspapers for symptoms of an indispensable change, and, I grieve to say, I have not found them. Where are the churches that have set the example? If there be those which accept both blacks and whites as members, which open their pews without distinction of color to blacks and whites, which take disciplinary measures against whoever has been wanting in respect to a negro—if there be such churches, why do we not know of them? We are bound to rise to the level of our cause. The cause of the Americans of the North is great; they will grow, it is inevitable. In demanding of the South a colossal sacrifice in the name of the law and the gospel, they will feel that the law and the gospel cannot remain long disregarded by themselves.

The law and the gospel are still disregarded, and to a point of which we can with difficulty form an idea. Who would believe that, in the present year of 1862, the convention charged with revising the constitution of Illinois, entertained a proposition designed to banish all negroes from the State? This infamous proceeding was of course rejected; but, I scarcely dare say it, twenty-one votes were found in its support. Twenty-one citizens of a free State, in spite of the law, Christianity, and the commonest rules of humanity, wished this, supported this! I knew well that the prejudice of color reigned above all in the West, I was not ignorant of the geographical, political, and social reasons which served as its basis,—nevertheless, I would have never imagined that it could go so far as this, at the very hour in which it was combating the cotton States, which had rebelled in the name of slavery, at the very hour when it laid claim, with reason, to the sympathies of Europe.

There is a whole past of infamy to repudiate in the North, and I consider it a duty to say something respecting it.—We will lay aside every thing exceptional, the sale of lots in certain cemeteries, with this condition, publicly expressed: "No colored persons will be buried here;" the violent and unpunished demolition of an establishment for higher instruction, founded in New Hampshire,—an establishment sanctioned by the legislature, and which proposed to receive, without distinction, youths of the white and the colored race. We will content ourselves with once more recalling the fact (such things cannot be too often denounced) that in the greater part of the churches white men alone are admitted, that, if a small space be reserved near the door for colored persons, they cannot occupy any other place without being immediately expelled, and that it is taken very ill if they approach the communion—yes, the communion—before the whites have partaken of the sacrament. Let a colored woman go to a watering place on account of her health; as soon as she approaches the spring, the cup is snatched from her hand, and she is threatened with ill treatment if she dare return. Let another enter a public vehicle; she will find wretches there to take her by the throat and forcibly eject her; and, what is most serious,—for there are cowards every where—the courts will refuse to receive her complaint, on the ground that her presence has shocked the public sentiment. It is said that there is a vehicle to be seen to-day in the streets of New York, bearing the significant inscription, "Colored persons allowed in this car."

What is to be said of the decisions taken in Ohio and Illinois, sometimes to hamper the settling of colored men on the territory of the State, sometimes to expel the greater number, sometimes to dispute to them even the exercise of the right of petition? I will not dwell on these acts, which are already of ancient date, and which doubtless would not be renewed to-day. Still less would I wish to expatiate on the monstrous doctrines which, several times, have authorized all colored men, condemned to a fine which they were unable to pay, to be *put up for sale.* This belongs to ancient history, not so ancient, however, that it may not be useful to meditate on at the present time. The proposition which was discussed the other day in Illinois proves that progress on this point is effected with lamentable slowness.

A number of Northern States might be cited which refuse to colored men the quality of citizens, which refuse them in fact the exercise of political rights, which do not even accept their testimony in law. The example given by New York, which, in 1857, constitutionally proclaimed complete equality, has not been generally followed. Other States, I will cite Pennsylvania, seem rather to retrograde.

Such is the crime of the North. And let no one seek to extenuate it by saying that the South carries much further the violation of the rights of the free colored race. The champions of liberty have different obligations and different responsibilities, I presume, from the defenders of slavery. Yes, the South refuses, much more than the North, to accept the testimony of men of color. Yes, the South, not content with debarring them the entrance to the common schools, does not usually permit them to have schools of their own. Yes, the South goes so far as to reduce free negroes to slavery; here, because they have married persons of the white race, there, because they have given refuge to a fugitive, in another place, for the sole fact that they have taken the liberty to remain in the State after their emancipation, or because they have passed through it. But, once more, the enormities of the South do not excuse those of the North.

I have hastened to place by the side of these detestable facts, other facts which show that the North is beginning to be disquieted at its crime, and that, if its progress be slow, much too slow, notwithstanding, it is not absolutely void.

The proposition made in the last Message will be first

remembered—two black republics for the first time, will have representatives at Washington!*

It is known, next, that a colored man, the Rev. Mr. Garnett, has received a formal passport from the Secretary of State, which recognizes him as an American citizen, contrary to the usage established hitherto, contrary to the opinion expressed by the Supreme Court under the presidency of Mr. Buchanan.

A colored lawyer has been recently admitted as a member of the bar in Boston. He is the third, moreover, who pleads thus, on a footing of equality with the whites, in the courts of this city.

If the West in general is still ruled by the unworthy prejudice of color, New England, accustomed to generous initiatives, applies more and more the principle of human equality; usually, she has no black schools; her colored children are not set apart. Let us add, that they distinguish themselves by their progress, and that it often happens that they are the first in their class. The Rev. Mr. Fisch,† of whom I borrow this detail with several others, relates that he questioned these children on the geography of France. "They pointed out to me the course of our rivers," says he, "better than is ordinarily done in our own schools. There are not many Parisian children who know much about the Susquehanna, Delaware, and Chesapeake. I have heard young negresses explain the laws of gravitation, and point out the diameter, gravity and distance from the earth of the different planets. In the colored Academy at Philadelphia, founded

* Let us hope that Hayti will not entertain the strange idea of permitting herself to be represented by *a white man*. This has been pretended, but I will not believe it.

† See the series of articles which he published in the *Revue Chrétienne* after his visit to the United States.

by the Quakers, I have asked young girls to construe for me at sight a portion of the Æneid.' I have done the same with the Greek Testament."

The country which has opened the mixed schools of New England, the country which, in a less liberal thought, has founded the colored schools of Pennsylvania and New York,—this country will learn ere long the respect due to man, whatever may be the color of his skin. It is not the future that disquiets me, but the present; I am jealous of the honor of the United States, and I wish that they themselves, on the spot, by a generous impulse, might place the reform of the North by the side of the denunciation of the crime of the South.

Never was a moment more serious. After the political crisis, after the military crisis, after the commercial crisis, the crisis of success may suddenly supervene. Then will be the time when men will intrigue and embroil questions to their hearts' content; then will be the time when evil counsels will crowd in, from within and without, from America and Europe. Therefore I am far from saying, like some persons, that it is henceforth useless to lay down principles, to examine the line of conduct to be held, and to study problems. Material triumph, supposing it complete, will resolve nothing by itself. The internal and external dangers will all subsist, to appear again to-morrow, next year, who knows? if the true solutions be not immediately applied. Yes, to-day it is necessary to look backward, to-day it is necessary to collect one's thoughts, to-day, it is necessary to take account of the real nature of the conflict, to-day it is necessary to tell the truth to the whole world, the truth which alone raises anew and cures.

After so many hopes fallen one by one, the friends of

the South still preserve two, to which they cling in despair for their cause. They would like, in case that the Union be reëstablished, at least to maintain slavery; that is to say, the cause of discord, that is to say, the chance of a new rebellion, attempted under better auspices; they would like, above all, to persuade Europe that the Union will not be reëstablished.

Have they not dared announce to us even now that amicable separation was about to be accomplished? Have not several members of the English Parliament, Earl Russell himself, declared that before two months, we may, perhaps, see the North admit the independence of the South?—Every thing is possible, I grant; but this is the least possible thing that could be imagined. It is difficult to believe that the victories of the North will result in the complete victory of the pretensions of the South. This rumor is, doubtless, but a last consolation which those give themselves who, for a year, have not ceased to build all their plans on the definitive character of Southern secession.

As to compromises, as to the political weakness which, in order to win back the South, would avoid touching the question of slavery, I have already said what were the reasons for fearing as well as for being reassured. Certain so-called moderate counsels always make themselves easily welcomed; but, on the other side, the American opinion is formed, and the great enemy is henceforth known. It is now almost impossible to spare it.

The peril would be especially grave, if the idea of calling a convention, and thus, with the South, reconstructing the general Constitution, should succeed in gaining admission. I like to believe that Mr. Lincoln will put aside with a firm hand these revolutionary proceedings. He has struggled for the Constitution, why not maintain the Constitution? Would it not be glorious to arrive at the end of this formidable career without having modified the programmes of the beginning? Here is the Constitution; it is reëstablished, or rather, it continues to impose its laws in spite of every thing, and to the advantage of every one. No extraordinary power, convention or any other, has been put in action; the independence of the States, self-government remains standing.

A plan is recommended at this moment, in the name of some of the principal leaders of the abolition party, which would overthrow the Constitution, destroy the independence of the States, and pave the way for central despotism. To suppress the States which have taken part in the rebellion, to organize and govern them like territories, such is the means which it is sought to adopt in order more rapidly to abolish slavery.

I do not believe that abolition would gain much by being effected too quickly. The essential point is that it be effected, and that the principle be laid down irrevocably. It would be easy to attain this end by scrupulously remaining within the limits of constitutional orthodoxy, by using only the right which the preceding sessions of Congress have used themselves, by respecting (this comprises every thing) the boundary which separates the political and general action of the nation from the local and administrative action of the States. Independently of the acts which may be accomplished during the war according to the terms of the doctrine of John Quincy Adams, important measures can and should be voted.

For this decisive act, there will be a single hour, the value of which will be beyond appreciation, and by which the United States will doubtless know how to profit—it is the hour that will complete their victories. A little sooner or a little later, it will come, I hope; I have faith in the final triumph. Then, the States who have taken part in the rebellion, will be still in a state of anarchy; they will not yet have elected representatives to the Congress at Washington. Their absence, for which they can accuse none but themselves, will secure to Mr. Lincoln the needful majority.

What is there to prevent the adoption, at this moment, of a series of resolutions designed definitively to settle the fate of slavery? To abrogate the Fugitive Slave Law, to suppress slavery in the District of Columbia, to interdict domestic slave trade; to decide that no new slave State shall be henceforth admitted, and that all the territories shall belong to freedom, to offer lastly an indemnity to such States as, within a given time, shall decree progressive abolition,* all this is strictly constitutional. This is not to say that it would excite no opposition; such there would be, perhaps, even in the Border States; the passions of slavery are not accustomed to yield easily. But it is precisely because it may be opposed and refused, that the right of States will be seriously respected. To stop at this series of measures, is to put aside all violent intrusion into the internal affairs of the South.

Yet, notwithstanding, it is to decide the question as well, or rather a hundred times better than would be done by exceptional measures. The oppositions will fall one after the other before the irresistible power of the movement which is being wrought. America will thus obtain the triple result of maintaining intact the

* If the indemnity be fixed, as was done in France and England, at about \$200, it will be a total expense of \$800,000,000, which, apportioned over twenty years, will impose on each year a burden of \$20,000,000. Never will expense more glorious or more productive have been entered in any budget!

institutions in the name of which it has combated, of securing the at once prudent and certain extinction of slavery, and of solidly founding the Union.

I do not pretend, of course, to draw up such a project; such audacity would ill befit me. I have been only desirous to show that the United States are not reduced to choose between the subversive plan projected by an extreme party, and the complete letting alone of another party no less extreme, composed of old democrats and the citizens of the Border States.

These last go on repeating that slavery will fall *if no one meddles with it.* This is true to a certain point, but it is essential to meddle with it. Do not be too sure that the war has resolved the question, that the party conquered with arms in hand will be also conquered politically, that the country now will be governed in the interest of liberty, that things will go on as it were of themselves, that detestable laws will be no longer executed, that the institutions of the South, without protection and without future, will die a natural death. I recognize all this, I know that it is given to no one henceforth to prevent, whether by attempts at ignoble negotiation or by a culpable letting alone, the great progress which is about to be accomplished. Yet, notwithstanding, how scandalous, should there be negotiation or letting alone!

It is of importance to the honor of America that she should herself draw the moral conclusion of this formidable conflict. She will have peace only at this price; she will have Union only at this price; she will have the sympathies of the world only at this price. And the sympathies of the world, let her not forget, have been, are, and will be her chief strength.

At the present time, facts are needed, decisive facts, which will shut the mouth of the enemies of America.

To hear them, the reëstablishment of the Union would have no other effect "than to replace slavery under the ægis of the Federal Constitution." They always return to the point of separation; when the United States shall have thus accorded to the rebellion all that it pretended to obtain, it will be readily admitted that they have cast out of their bosom the leprosy of slavery, that they form at length a true republic; sympathies will then be accorded them.

If Mr. Lincoln, as I think, is little disposed to accept separation, if he cares little to treat with rebels, if the idea of a treaty concluded through the mediation, and under the guarantee of Europe pleases him indifferently, he is bound to prove ere long that the reëstablishment of the Union will not take place without laying down in fact, and much more surely than all treaties, the principle of progressive abolition.

To attain this end, it would be fitting perhaps to address first the Border States. In aiding emancipation among them, a first very considerable result would be obtained, a few of the intermediate would be transformed into Northern States; they would be attached indissolubly to the national centre, and insurrection and slavery would be confined within constantly-narrowing limits.

This, moreover, could not suffice. As the Government at Washington does not propose to rectify the frontiers of the free States, but to reëstablish in the slave States the authority of the common Constitution, it should think also of these last. They may have to decide, in the plenitude of their independence, between the prudent abolition which would be facilitated to-day by the indemnity promised by the Union, and the formidable chances of a future in which the resurrection of the chances of the slavery party can in no event find place.

Thus conceived, the proposition of indemnity would answer to all the necessities of the position in America and in Europe. It is self-evident that other measures will follow in the train of the principal one; it is the essence of a moral conflict such as this to increase, do what one may, the moral power of the Government and of Congress Subtle interpretations of the Constitution will have small chance, henceforth, against the need of suppressing abominable infamies; no one will be persuaded that self-government implies the right to suppress marriage at one's pleasure, to destroy the family, to sell separately and carry away the father, mother, and children, any more than it implies the right of the Mormons also to attack the family in their way, by establishing polygamy.

The President and Congress may therefore lay down the principle of indemnity, and secure the approaching success of progressive abolition, without having recourse, I trust, to those extreme acts of general emancipation, proclaimed through military power, which the prolongation and exasperation of the struggle might bring about. The independence of the States will be protected with jealous care. It will be doubtless indispensable to provide for certain necessities which will result from the armed struggle. If the United States win, they should appoint provisional governors, and secure the working of some sort of an administration, while waiting till the regular order be reëstablished. The essential point is that this period of transition be as brief as possible. The provisional governors will have no other mission than to reorganize the insurgent States, to put again in force the national constitution, to administer the oath of allegiance, and to reinstate all liberties, including the liberty of opposition. It is during this time, which will separate the state of war from the state of completed reorganization, that Congress, composed as yet almost exclusively of Northern representatives, will pass, I suppose, all the acts destined to regulate the new position of slavery, to resume the healthy tradition of the fathers of the Republic,—of those illustrious men, all enemies of servile institutions,—to exhaust, lastly, in this end the rights of the national government, without doing violence to the rights of the local governments.

Perhaps I should enter here upon the study of the social problem which will some day succeed the problem of abolition; but I have made it a rule unto myself not to repeat in this volume what I have said in my preceding work.

We are told that emancipation will bring grave difficulties in its train! Who doubts it? No one has yet discovered the means of effecting a colossal transformation without suffering. I add, however, that of all the forms which this inevitable crisis may put on, none is less alarming than that of a progressive abolition peaceably accomplished, with the powerful assistance of an indemnity, with the still more powerful assistance of Northern capital returning to give life to Southern cultures. Compare with this prospect, that of abolition violently accomplished by war, or, if you like better, that of abolition accomplished willingly or unwillingly by the Southern Confederacy under outside pressure. Here, all is constraint, all is misery;—a community subverted, ruined, menaced, impotent, forced unceasingly to guard its frontiers, having neither money nor hands to replace the slavery which it loses. I marvel at those who wish things to go on thus, who consider definitive separation as an ideal, and who fancy in this manner to serve the cause of abolition! It will be a bad recommendation to it for men to believe themselves authorized to say: "Abolition is effected, and the South has become a desert."

It will be quite otherwise with abolition wrought in those conditions of vigor, prosperity, and political health —pardon me the expression—which the South will secure by its return to the Union. A great people will be there, with unceasingly increasing resources, interested in resuscitating the cultures of the South. It will then become possible to render healthy the swamp lands, to introduce the improved machinery and processes which will facilitate the employment of European workmen. These will come by degrees, while slavery itself will fall back by degrees, furnishing still for a certain number of years the labor which could not be found immediately elsewhere, and permitting the transition to be managed with care.*

But let us not delude ourselves; it will be in vain that we surround affranchisement with all necessary precautions, if the prejudice of color is to subsist as it is. Affranchisement is only the end of the present solution; another question, still graver, and upon which I am anxious to dwell, will demand to be resolved in the United States. The question of race will subsist there when the question of slavery is settled; when America is no longer in error.

* I have refrained from taking into account here an element of success which might be disputed, but which I believe to be of the highest importance. The influence of the gospel among the slaves has created bonds which will be broken with difficulty. For the maintenance of order, for the preservation of labor, it is not a matter of indifference that souls have been moved by the Christian faith. The dispersion will also, perhaps, encounter an obstacle in the attachment inspired in the poor negro by the church.

To transform the slave into a Pariah would be small progress. The question is not to throw upon the side walks of great cities a multitude of unfortunates, repulsed from honest occupations, deprived of the rights belonging to every citizen, condemned, as it were, to wretchedness and degradation; the question is no more to undertake a gigantic deportation, hurling violently on Africa, St. Domingo, Florida, or some other corner of the earth reserved for them, and where they will be speedily subjected to an exceptional regime, these four millions of men, called to liberty.

Such a liberty, derisive and lying, would arouse feelings of universal reprobation against America. It is not allowable to be just by halves; those who do good are under the happy obligation of being unable to stop on the road, and of going further than they had at first projected. America is condemned, thank God! to go on to the end of her glorious enterprise.

Enterprises like this succeed only by going on to the end. There, there alone, are encountered beneficial solutions; there all becomes simple, because all has become just. The difficulties will fall one after the other from the day that Christian and liberal America accepts all the consequences of her principle; from the day that she consents to say: "We are about to apply henceforth, restricting it in nothing, the fundamental dogma of our constitution; the time must come when none but freemen shall be found among us, and when all free men shall be truly equal. We have not to trouble ourselves to know how the free negro race which will soon be affranchised will be distributed over our territory. Perhaps it will accumulate in certain regions, perhaps it will be gradually effaced before the waves of European immigration; in going where it suits it to go, in doing what it suits it to do, it will make use of its right. The respect of right will be now our policy."

There is but one saving policy; it is that which accomplishes the decrees of justice. It is in vain to cry: "On to Richmond!" unless you cry at the same time, "On to justice!" Supported by these three great measures, progressive abolition, voluntarily decreed, indemnity accorded to the masters, and equality secured to the affranchised negroes, America will confound its calumniators, and gain for all humanity the greatest liberal contest of our times.

Once laid down by it, the principle of abolition will make the tour of the globe. It will visit Brazil, Spain, Portugal, and Holland; it will go to Liberia, and Sierra Leone, to fortify these advance posts of liberty on African soil; it will penetrate that vast Africa which travellers, and above all, missionaries, are on the way to discover; it will drive back the wretches who are even now pursuing on the banks of the White Nile, their cruel chase of men, women, and little children; it will go unto Asia, unto the Mussulman world, to awaken questions torpid for centuries.

The American crisis is one of the events of which God makes use to move the world. No one can tell where its consequences will stop; but we can say from this time, that the United States, in effecting the abolition of slavery within their limits, will have done more than England herself for the cause of affranchisement; they will have given a signal which all, whether willing or unwilling, will be constrained to obey. However lofty may be the ambition of a great people, it seems to me that it ought to be content with this.

CHAPTER IV.

GREATNESS OF THE FUTURE.

I MIGHT have elaborated the preceding chapter. It has seemed to me more in conformity with the general character of this study, as also with the duties imposed on me by my position as a foreigner, not to present plans, properly called, for the solution of these two connected problems—the abolition of slavery, and the rules of conduct to be adopted toward the free colored race.

Of the two problems, the second is not the one presenting the less difficulties; it will need a heroic impulse of the Christian conscience. The prejudice of skin is so closely interwoven with American manners, that even colored men, they who suffer from it, are not the less eager to obey it. When free blacks form volunteer regiments in the South, they often observe the gradation of shades with significant scrupulousness; the first company is almost white, the second a little darker, and so on to the last, the soldiers of which are as black as jet; no man in the United States cares to mingle with those whose skin is less transparent than his own.

As to abolition, the reader will remark the care which I have taken, not to counsel any measure which would not be strictly constitutional. I should have grossly contradicted myself, if, after having advised Americans to preserve their institutions, and resemble at the end of the struggle as nearly as possible what they were in its beginning, I had urged them to violate these institutions themselves in their fundamental principle. The liberty of the States is no less important to maintain, than the sovereignty of the nation. A rebellion against the Constitution should not be combated by a rebellion in the opposite direction, and the two original features of the American organization should neither perish in the furnace of civil war. It would be glorious to see the United States come out of it with their local independence, as well as their civil unity, having left nothing but slavery in the battle, like the three young Jews of Babylon, who came out of the flames as they had been thrust into them, with the exception of their chains.

Let the fire devour the chains, but nothing more!*

* I entreat those who dispute the constitutional character of the measures pointed out in the preceding chapter, to examine them in this point of view.

The offer of abolition with indemnity leaves subsisting the independence of the States; I need not revert to it.

The abrogation of the bill of 1850 concerning fugitive slaves may legally take place, since Congress is at liberty to revoke what it was at liberty to pass. Until further orders, the act of February 12, 1793, will doubtless remain, which, by virtue of a stipulation of the Federal Constitution, authorizes the owners of slaves to seek those who have fled, to seize them wherever they may find them, and take them before the magistrate. But this act, as we know, does not command any public officer to second such pursuit. It remained without effect so long as the detestable bill of 1850 had not come to give it life and force by the creation of special commissioners, charged with effecting the seizure of fugitive slaves. Who will be made to believe, after what has just passed, that the South would have much reason to complain, if an advantage were

Thus will open before the Union that noble career, in which, through obstacles, through sacrifices, through victories over its enemies, and, above all, over itself, it will advance toward the greatness of the future. It belongs to the Americans to demonstrate by irrefutable proof, that they are a great people, and a people on the way to uprise.

withdrawn from it with which it very well dispensed for fifty-seven years, from 1793 to 1850?

The interdiction of the domestic slave-trade comes within the powers of Congress. If it has suppressed the African slave-trade, it has shown no more hesitation (as former deliberations prove) in regulating the conditions of the transportation of slaves in the interior. It has even abolished the domestic slave-trade, by an express act, in the District of Columbia. The matter belongs to the National authority, not to that of the local Governments.

As to the most important measure which would close the territories to slavery, its legality is clear; for, under the ancient Constitution of the United States, which exaggerated beyond measure the independence of the States, the celebrated ordinance of July 13, 1787, was decreed. It excluded slavery from all the Northwest territory; it was by virtue of this ordinance that Ohio, Michigan, Wisconsin, Indiana, and Illinois, were preserved (sometimes, indeed, despite themselves) from contact with the "peculiar institution." The present Constitution, adopted shortly after the ordinance of July 13, has not diminished these supreme attributes of Congress; Article IV. states explicitly that Congress shall have power to dispose of the territories, and of all other properties belonging to the United States, and to establish on the subject all the regulations and measures which it may deem fitting. The sole exception to the rule is encountered naturally in the territories which. detached from the States of Virginia, Georgia, and Carolina, were ceded by them only on the express condition that Congress, renouncing its normal right over these territories, should prohibit therein any measure opposed to slavery.

Finally, the action of Congress being sovereign in the District of Columbia, abolition can evidently be proclaimed there without in any wise violating the Constitution. This is so true, that this abolition has been many times discussed, especially in 1847, on the proposition of Mr. Lincoln.

A great people! it is said. Does it suffice to be great to occupy a great territory, to have great clearings, great plantations, great banks, and great warehouses? Do you not see how mediocre every thing is in America, and how far its hero, Washington, brave, courageous, and sensible as he was, is from equalling the stature of a Cæsar or Napoleon? Are we to admire those revolutionary Puritans, before whom the conservative elements of society have disappeared, one after the other, and who have almost erected into an idol the will of the greater number? Does this rabble of great cities, which burns now a convent and then a hospital, do these Vigilance Committees, which apply Lynch law, these Plug Uglies, who stain the elections with blood, to suit their needs, afford subject for panegyrics? Is levelling liberty? Does the systematic exclusion of higher classes and higher minds do honor to the democracy of the New World? Do we find consolation in meeting, here polygamous Mormons, there conventions presided over by women, in which the "rights of women" are expounded, everywhere men barbed with revolvers, and ready to do justice to themselves, as is done among the savages?

It is easy to frame an accusation, when we thus condense in a single picture, all the misdeeds of a nation; what is accidental and what is general, what happens only in a few corrupt cities, in which immigrants from our Europe flow unceasingly, and that which is met in the whole country; finally, what takes place in all democracies, and what characterizes that of the United States. Is this just? Are we to judge America by what it had become under the yoke of the slavery party, and refuse to see what it is to-day? Has not the history of America for the past year demonstrated to the blindest, that a great people is found there? Here is a democracy which restrains itself, which governs itself, which never forgets itself in the darkest days; it has massacred no one, it has not once disturbed the peace of the public streets, it has accepted, followed and respected its elected leaders, it has suffered under the most exciting circumstances, a policy of peace to be pursued toward Europe. Where we have unceasingly (even yesterday again) predicted excesses, acts of violence, disasters, lack of discipline, impotence, anarchy, and bankruptcy, it has known how to place order, firmness, the organization of armies, the creation of a fleet, confidence in the public funds. What it has done has been so completely, so radically in opposition to what had been foretold, that the reprinted correspondence of almost all our journals, relative to the story of events, would constitute at the present time the most piquant book that could possibly be published.

It seems to me that this is no indifferent matter; in proof of great things, we may quote at this time, whatever may be the result, the conduct of the United States since and including the election of Mr. Lincoln. Our Old World, always in commotion, unskilful to resolve, I know not how many questions, in Turkey, in Russia, in Poland, in Hungary, in Italy,—our Old World, rendered sleepless by the temporal power of the Pope, is a little too hasty, perhaps, in triumphing over the embarrassment of America. As I am correcting these last proof sheets, I receive letters depicting the material uprising, the more or less tardy, but, no less certain consequence of the moral uprising. Let me quote a few sentences: "It does one good to be here at this moment. You would enjoy it to the full, could you witness what is passing in the heart of this youthful and valiant nation. Tried, afflicted, battered by storms, *it is finally uprising.* The week that is closing has intoxicated us with its numerous victories, every hour brings some glorious news. Traitors are concealing themselves or taking flight; the air vibrates with joy as it waves the thousands and thousands of flags that float under our beautiful sky. Slavery is about to disappear; it is wounded unto death."

I know that vicissitudes of fortune are possible, the hour of reverses may yet arrive. Notwithstanding, to have reached the present point, manly virtues were needed.

The United States have neither the capacities nor the defects of old nations; they are great in their way and not in ours. This is what many men in Europe will neither understand nor pardon. America has the gift of exciting among us antipathies which resemble hatred.

I know of but one antipathy which may be compared to this—that with which we are inspired in general, and through analogous reasons, by the English Puritanism of the days of the Stuarts. There are men who fly into a passion at the mere thought of a Puritan. Tell them neither of his virtues, nor his austerity, nor his courage, nor of the thousands of men and women, who for long years, accepted the loss of their goods, gave their lives, and endured unheard of sacrifices; tell them no more of the indomitable firmness with which the English liberties were defended, or rather founded. They are determined to ignore all this; they must have cavaliers, refined and perverse courtiers, brave with the sword in hand, cruel and persecuting in all else. Charming debauchees, careless profligates, with a good mien and grace, please them a hundred times more than honest people, rigid, narrow, and sullen.

Let me be understood rightly. I am of those who think that honest people do wrong to be sullen; that rudeness is not a merit, and that disagreeable virtues are only half virtues. I do not praise the Roundheads, far from it, for having anathematized literature and art, narrowed the human mind, introduced formalities and jargons of command, answered intolerance by intolerance, and too often also, cruelty by cruelty; I certainly do not praise them for having ended at length in Cromwell. But under the rough and coarse bark, under the affected forms, the religious uniform, in spite of faults and crimes, beyond detestable leaders and hypocritical imitators, I gain a glimpse of a great thing—a moral protest against the infamy, iniquity, and servility, of which the fine Cavaliers of the Stuarts were usually the living personification.

A strong and free England has come forth from this. Again, a people which has the very real fault of not possessing all the amiable and chivalrous virtues; again, a people which belongs to the individual rather than the sympathetic races! One might regret it, and I regret it. Is this, notwithstanding, a reason for hating, for condemning and rejecting *in toto*, for shutting the eyes to its capacities?

I have been anxious thus to put the whole question on the subject of the United States. The Americans are not Englishmen, no more are they Puritans; yet, nevertheless, the motive of our extreme aversion, if we wish to go to the bottom, is really that which makes us often prefer Cavaliers to Roundheads, and Russians to Englishmen.

There is no point, perhaps, on which the division of the two classes of minds which coexist here below is produced more clearly. And this is from ancient history. I seem to hear the declamations at Versailles, in the time of him who has been so strangely styled *the Great King*. Change the names, put the Americans instead of the Dutch, and you have all our antipathies of to-day. We then detested with all our heart, that shop-keeping, republican, Protestant, arrogant, ill-taught people; that country of journals, discussions, and intestine divisions; those gross men, rebels but yesterday, without a past, without monuments without fine arts, except their grotesque figures of porcelain.* Yet it was found that Holland, nevertheless at the moment of perishing, arrested the fortunes of Louis XIV.; it was found that these shopkeepers, nevertheless ready to sell their country for a few crowns, sacrificed their property, opened the dykes, and buried all Holland under the sea, in order to save its independence.

Let us signal out the faults of the Americans, let us unsparingly condemn whatever is stiff, harsh, and austere in their manners; they have this vice and several beside. I am far, very far, from saying that all among them is perfect; but it seems to me that all is not perfect among us, and that, if it were wished to paint us, portraits might be made of us too, which would not be flattering. Is the cringing of graceful peoples of more value than the ungraceful stiffness of angular peoples? I need not resolve the question. I verify the fact that America is one of the most moral and enlightened nations on earth. I verify the fact that, if democratic levelling be detestable, America has at least known how to abstract from it what makes the man—conscience. If certain acts of violence have taken place, the electoral contest in America has almost always preserved complete liberty: these orators of the different parties arriving, like princes, to the sound of salutes of artillery; these assemblies of ten thousand, twenty thousand auditors; these vast questions

* I entreat the country which has produced Powers' statues, and Church's landscapes, to forgive me this comparison.

in which the fate of nations is involved, discussed from the shores of the Atlantic to the recesses of the desert—all this is a spectacle which does not lack majesty.

And the system of public instruction! Scarcely had the first pilgrims landed at Boston Bay, when schools were established. Twenty years after, a university, that of Cambridge, was opened. To-day, there is not a town, not a village, not a clearing which has not provided for the education of youth. The support of the schools swallows up one-third of the revenue of some of the States. The vocation of instructor is honored everywhere. In New England, the first families of the country devote their daughters to this career.

The Sunday schools, comprising three million pupils, are conducted by the voluntary and gratuitous care of four hundred thousand teachers of both sexes, belonging to all classes of society.

The family worship is celebrated everywhere. The gospel exercises an influence over the entire country, the scope of which it would be difficult for us to measure. To form an idea of it, one should visit that quarter of New York city known as the *Five Points*, the alleys of which remind one by their names. that it was once a den of assassins. Formerly, no one durst venture there in broad daylight! now schools are established in its heart—spacious halls, resounding with the songs of children snatched from crime and misery—and thousands of visitors of the highest classes go thither to carry aid and good advice to families.

The Christian liberality, which has given six hundred million francs to build churches, which every year devotes a hundred and twenty million francs to the support of worship, which furnishes countless millions to charitable and religious societies, which, even in this moment of crisis and suffering, sends to enterprises in distress princely offerings of ten, a hundred, two hundred thousand francs, such liberality does not appear to me a token of decaying and wretched life. At the present time, a profound transformation is being wrought; with the national sin, other vices will fall; the most sceptical will then comprehend that the American people is a great people.

There are those who compare the United States to Brazil—a community where every thing is in motion, to a community where every thing is asleep. When the political or moral character of Brazil has been shown me, its influence on earth, its literature, its scientific discoveries, especially when Brazil has been shown me, agitating the subject of her slavery, and laboring, at the cost of gigantic sacrifices, to repair the evil which it has done, then I will take this burlesque comparison in earnest.

Meanwhile, the United States are going onward; the two years, 1861 and 1862, will mark their progress; in two years, they will have lived a century. Whatever may happen, I think I have proved that their uprising is certain.

As regards the South in particular, the problem of its future lies still before it. Hitherto, it has seemed resolved to perish; the cotton production, already injured by the mere fact of the war, will finally disappear if the slave States refuse to suffer the liberating metamorphosis which offers itself to them.

A gigantic displacement is on the way to be wrought —the cotton culture, which has been the stay of slavery in America, is about to become in Asia and Africa an instrument of liberty. The providential work which is being accomplished in this manner is one of the most glorious that mankind has ever witnessed. To the uprising of the United States, the uprising of the Indies, of

Australia, of New Zealand and of the interior regions of Africa will, perhaps, respond in little time. England, which every year spins cotton enough to measure ten times the distance of the earth from the moon, is making prodigious efforts at this moment to break forever her former dependence, and to seek under other skies the raw material which the South has had the privilege of supplying it heretofore—India perhaps will lessen the sufferings of the cotton crisis for England, while through the cotton crisis, England will give new life to India; and the free negroes of Hayti and the Antilles will have their share in the prey which the South lets escape it.

Will it let it completely escape? I hope not. True superiority is long-lived, and American cotton, placed in conditions which are not elsewhere to be found, will keep its place, provided America consent. What she needs for this is firmly to establish the principle of abolition, and to call into the South that multitude of free laborers, that capital, that agricultural machinery which asks only to hasten thither. The experience of the Antilles proves that the emancipated blacks are not at all unfit for labor; the products have been maintained, and even increased among these populations transformed by liberty and regenerated by the gospel. And also, at the present time, is it not to the labor of free negroes alone that the Union intrusts the culture of the celebrated Sea Island cotton, the special product of the suburbs of Port Royal?

The transformation will be easier in the cotton States, inasmuch as considerable progress has been already accomplished there. Let us be just; a large number of masters have favored the moral development of their slaves. Since the foreign slave trade has ceased to bring rude Africans daily upon the plantations, the negro race of these States has been rising higher and higher. This is one of the miracles of the gospel, whose liberating virtue always displays itself, do what one may; it has accomplished, in fact, a vast preparatory work, and has rendered abolition easier in the heart of the Southern States, than it was in our colonies, or even in those of England. Under the influence of the churches, of which they are members, and to which they are in general passionately attached, many slaves have become pious and intelligent; their manners are polite, their conduct is good, their conscience is awakened, the sentiment of duty has a large share in their life; there is among them the germ of a laborious and peaceful class.

These things must be confessed; in the first place, in order not to calumniate the South; secondly, to prove to it that the prudent abolition of slavery, far from drawing in its train the perils and horrors with which it is charged, is on the contrary the only means of escaping danger, of avoiding ruin, of entering without too rude a shock into a new era of prosperity and peace.

I make no pretensions to know how things will happen. The prevailing opinion in Europe, and especially in England is that the separation of the South will be ere long accepted by the North, and that the victories of the latter, if it win, will have no other result than that of securing it better boundaries. I shall be greatly astonished, for my part, if this be true. After having carefully studied the events and discussions of these two years, I remain convinced that the United States have not ceased to pursue the integral reëstablishment of the Union. I remember the words of Mr. Lincoln: "Our popular government has been often considered a mere trial. Already, thanks to the nation, it has given proofs of its capacity on two points: it has succeeded in establishing itself and in ruling. It lacks still but one thing—it must succeed in maintaining itself against a formidable attempt to overthrow it. It is for the nation to demonstrate now to the world that those who can win an election can also suppress a rebellion, that ballots are the lawful and peaceful successors of bullets."

The question thus laid down at the first moment, has remained the same ever since. Unless constrained thereto by the ill success of their arms, or the intervention of Europe, the United States will be little disposed, in my opinion, to admit that bullets should prevail over ballots. This problem of a revolution in the heart of a free country touches the inmost recesses of their political faith and national life.

However it may be, we have just seen that two results are from this time secured—the decline of slavery and the uprising of a great people. If, contrary to my present conviction, the separation should make itself accepted, the North may confine itself to taking measures to preserve the Border States by aiding them to pass as speedily as possible from the rank of slave States to that of free States. If the North should justify my prevision and persist in not pausing until it has conquered, it is probable that more general measures will compel all the slave States to decide between the maintenance of their institutions, thenceforth struck with death, and the acceptance of an indemnity designed to facilitate progressive abolition.*

* Let us say once more that this indemnity will not be an overwhelming burden on the American finances. It will not involve ten or fourteen thousand million of francs, as some have had the audacity to pretend, doubtless estimating the slaves, men, women, and children, at an average value six or seven times greater than that paid by France and England. But four thousand million francs are needed, distributed over

Will the South, though conquered, continue to resist? Will it, on the contrary, comprehend its true interests? Will it again become an integral part of the Union? Will the American people, reconstructed thus in its elements, at once recover the regular working of its institutions, its small armies, and its insignificant budgets? I hope so, without disguising from myself, however, that neither the armies nor the budgets can again descend to the standard of two years ago. Nevertheless, should a few of the Gulf States insist on self-destruction, should they condemn themselves to suffer through separation instead of prospering through union, the suffering will then accomplish its work and impart its instruction. Drawn in contrary directions, divided and subdivided to infinity by their new principle, the right of separation, forced to maintain troops on their frontiers, in constant struggle and frequent war with the United States, these unhappy States will come to regret their isolation; they will end where they ought to have begun, the Union will reappear. Do what one may, indeed, the power of absorption which the United States possess will continue to act; and where will it act with more force than toward this kindred people, bound to them by so many ties?

twenty years; that is, two hundred million francs a year. And again, this is supposing all the slave States to have accepted the conditions in the required time and to be entitled to indemnity, which is scarcely probable.

PART SIXTH.

TO CHRISTIANS.

CHAPTER I.

ATTITUDE OF CHRISTIANS IN AMERICA.

I HAVE a word more to say before laying down the pen, and this word I shall address to Christians.* The work of the emancipation of slaves and the uprising of the United States should be theirs; it imposes upon them a special responsibility, of which they have not had sufficient consciousness hitherto.

Slavery and the gospel—two adversaries—are here. They landed almost at the same time on the shores of America; the one with the Puritans of New England, the other with the colonists of Virginia. Since then, they have been constantly engaged in a struggle; and even when the churches have imperfectly comprehended their exalted mission, it has not been in them to suppress

* Thanks to the progress which the truth of positions has made in our terms, I can employ this term instead of having recourse to paraphrases. We need no longer pretend that every man is a Christian; he who professes Jesus Christ and he who considers Christianity as a mere national custom.

it. Christianity is a decree of emancipation, and he who preaches the Gospel, paves the way for emancipation, whether he knows it or not, whether he wills it or not. "Christianity," wrote M. de Tocqueville, "is a religion of freemen; neither its detractors nor its false friends can take from it this truly divine character." By the side of, or rather above abolitionism considered as a party, there is profound abolitionism, that which acts within the abolitionism of Jesus Christ. Open the books of an illustrious honest man, such as Tacitus, and compare the sentiments found expressed there with those which are now prevailing; measure the distance between our time and that when slaves, tortured to death for having thrown light on a question concerning their masters, moved no soul, however generous; make this comparison, and tell us what has been the work of the Gospel. To abolish the servitude of negroes, the heart of the white man must be changed, and who can do this miracle, except Him who loves both white and black, who has died for both white and black, who opens wide the doors of the same paternal mansion alike to white and black. Moral force will always be stronger than brute force.

> "A thousand prisons, crumbling 'mid the flames,
> Equal not, in the freeing of the soul,
> The drop of blood that trickles from the cross."

These beautiful lines of M. Arnould express a truth which is written on every page of history.

"It was religion that really emancipated the blacks in the English colonies," said the Duc de Broglie in the report which we all have read. "It was religion that emancipated the blacks in the United States," is what the annals of America should proclaim in turn.*

* This preparatory work of the Gospel is more advanced than is believed. The slaves pray for their liberty, they expect their liberty, they

Have the American churches been unfaithful to their mission? We would be disposed to think so, should we pause at appearances.

I do not pretend to deny the evil. It is very great; were it not so, my work would not contain this sixth part. There are those who pass their time in invoking the holy Scriptures against the poor slave; those who, according to the eloquent expression of Mrs. Stowe, drown the lamb in its mother's milk.

The preachings of the South are, in this respect, one of the scandals of our times. The South has its bishop, Leonidas Polk, who is at the same time a general, and who, followed by several members of his clergy, has taken the field in Tennessee. The South has its consecrations of banners, its prayers in behalf of slavery, its passionate appeals to the protection which the God of love should accord to slavery.

If I recall these things, it is not that I wish to give myself the easy advantage of refuting such monstrous doctrines. No, my thought is directed toward the North rather than the South. The faults of the Northern churches should call our attention to-day. The Christians of the South are subject to an impulse which we never take sufficiently into account. Indulgence is the more in place here, that we all have been accomplices in the crime with which we reproach them. All Europe contributed to introduce slavery into America; England in

await it piously from the hands of their Saviour. There is a *jubilee song* which is sung secretly in the South, 1862 being the year of jubilee. The following is the chorus:

> "In eighteen hundred and sixty-two,
> My people must be free;
> It is the year of jubilee,
> My people must be free."

particular protected the slave trade during the last century with so much earnestness, that it made one of the grievances at the insurrection of the colonies; these colonies themselves, moreover, all participated during long years in the traffic in negroes from Africa, and on this point we have not the right to except the Puritans; lastly, but the other day, who equipped more than twenty slave ships every year, if not New York? No one is therefore authorized to cast the stone at the Southern planters; they have simply continued a little longer, under the influence of exceptional circumstances, what we have practised as well as they. Is it certain that, placed in their surroundings, we should have shown better conduct, and held better language? Might we not have succeeded, as well as they, in perverting in good faith the meaning of the Gospel, and displaying enthusiasm for slavery?

This enthusiasm exists in the South. The South contains a large number of pious, excellent, charitable men, morally equal to the best Christians of any other country, who really see nothing else in slavery than a beneficent tutelage, designed to bring up a minor race, which will be some day restored to its providential destinies. These men are friends of the Colonization Society for emancipated negroes and the negro colony founded by it in Africa. These men have come (how, I know not, but national passions work these miracles) to see about them neither families sold at retail, nor marriages broken, nor young maidens surrendered to the first comer. The crimes which spring up in emulation of the first crime, man sold to man, public crimes, honored, and satisfied with themselves, crimes sanctioned by the law and recognized by the courts, they assimilate to those troublesome but inevitable crimes which are born of all communities.

Well; the more I reflect, the more I am astonished, the less also I feel the right irrevocably to condemn the intentions of any.

I address myself to the Christians of the North, because I have the hope, still better, the certainty of being understood. We will quickly agree, as well on the faults of the past as the duties of the present and the prospects of the future.

The faults of the past have been grave, but I do not design to dwell on them. While recalling them, it is necessary that I apply here my principle, to believe in the good. It is by sympathy, by confidence, and not by incessant recriminations, that those can be encouraged who are leaving an evil course, and adopting a better. I can never understand why we should choose the precise moment when an effort takes place, when, despite many obstacles, and at the price of many sacrifices, the old errors have been abandoned, to institute inexorable investigations. Under the pretext of justice, we risk being neither very able, nor very charitable, nor even very just.

It is unhappily true that many churches and religious societies have seemed to shrink too long from the austere duties imposed on them by the question of slavery. Two examples will suffice to characterize this period of deplorable hesitation. The Tract Society refused writings condemning the crime of slavery; the American Board of Missions, restrained by the fear of provoking a crisis in its work among the Choctaw and Cherokee Indians, miserably tacked about among the rocks, sometimes passing resolutions against the principle of slavery, then refusing their application, managing the position of its missionaries and the prejudices of the Indians, until the moment when the most extreme consequences of its conduct broke forth to its terrified gaze—a slave* had been burned alive by his mistress, a member of the Choctaw Church, and this mistress, as well as her accomplices, had continued to belong to the Church, and devoutly to partake of the communion, while the missionaries had not deemed it possible to oppose it!

Since then, the American Board has broken with them, as a matter of course. But where find a fact which better points out the indefinite fruitfulness of evil in an ambiguous position? We think that we can limit the consequences of our principles; we will never succeed. Some day, we will find ourselves on the brink of an abyss, as happened to the American Board.

Plausible arguments had not been lacking it. It had said to itself that missionaries were called to preach the Gospel, not to meddle in social or political questions; that the Gospel would end by destroying slavery without needing to attack it directly; that the Scripture contained no positive commands with regard to it; that the liberty of action of the missionaries should be respected; that slaveholders could not, from the mere fact of being such, be cut off from the Church.

Once launched upon this declivity, one goes fast and far. The committee of the Society reassured itself by praying for the abolition of slavery, or inserting a few

* I am no longer obliged to refute the gross literalism which, discovering the mention of slavery in the Gospel, thence concludes that the Gospel approves slavery. The apostles who, doubtless, personally believed in its lawfulness, and who, moreover, were charged with no revelation relative to political laws, had received a higher mission; they had to lay down the bases of that Christian morality before which many social crimes, which had never been denounced by the Gospel, were to fall in turn. Cruel tortures have disappeared, slavery is about to disappear, and we certainly are not at the end.

inoffensive wishes in its reports. Then, when terrible questions propounded themselves: "Are we to constrain our missionaries to cut off from the Church Indians who separate families, selling the daughter without the mother, or the husband without the wife? Are we to provoke the anger of the Indians and the expulsion of the missionaries? Are we to destroy the work of half a century? Are we to do this, against the advice of the missionaries themselves?"—the committee dared not come to a decision; it closed its eyes, sighing; it took shelter behind those general maxims of prudence and patience, so convenient and so dangerous in such a case.

Thus have acted respectable men, whom I do not intend to judge. I shall rather judge us all. We are leaning toward utilitarianism; utilitarianism is perhaps the greatest vice of the Christians of our times. To sacrifice principles to utility, to accept errors which serve or seem to serve the cause of the Gospel, to reject or at least postpone truths which would stir up obstacles, to deplore progress which resembles trial, to be dismayed at crises of uprising, such is the tendency which prevails among us. Every moment, you hear—"This is not perhaps quite in conformity with the Gospel, but it will be productive of good; let us beware how we put any obstacle in its way."

The Saviour commanded us to cut off a hand or pluck out an eye, rather than suffer ourselves to be persuaded by those who condemned His word. These painful amputations are not to our taste; to cut off the Indian mission rather than compound with the infamies of Indian slavery, would have appeared to us blamable. Nothing less was needed than the tragedy of which I have just spoken to modify the points of view.

The utilitarian instinct, which to-day is everywhere,

exercises in particular a marked influence in the United States. It alone explains the equivocal attitude which so many churches have preserved for so many years toward the problem of slavery. If they had energetically made use of the influence which belonged to them, we should not now see even several Northern States, Iowa, Illinois, Indiana, Pennsylvania perhaps, preparing infamous bills designed to close their territory to free negroes, and to render necessary (they will not succeed in it, thank God!) the transportation of the masses of slaves whose emancipation is foreseen. It must be said that the idea of breaking with the Southern churches, and bringing about a formidable crisis in all their works, had rendered Christians timid and circumspect beyond measure. They persuaded themselves—as is often enough the custom in such cases—that their action would be the more *spiritual*, (let us distrust the word,) the more it remained a stranger to the discussion of social problems.

Thence those prayer meetings, excellent and touching, but in which the cessation of slavery rarely obtained a fleeting mention. Thence those lamentations which come to us from America regarding the inevitable consequences of the crisis—brothers who labored together are now separated! The Christian pulpit, on both sides, has become an instrument of civil war! The enormous expenses of the country restrict donations for the advancement of the Gospel! Religious societies are passing through a time of trial!

I comprehend these sufferings; they are legitimate. No one can contemplate without affliction, those excellent American missions in Asia Minor and Syria, now deprived in part of the resources by which they were maintained. But I have this confidence, first, that the suffering will be short, next, that missions liberally founded on the development of indigenous elements, missions which ere long become churches conducted by the pastors of the country, will uprise better than others which long preserve the character of an exotic importation.

However it may be, Christians should know that God demands of them fidelity more than success, and that He reserves to Himself some day to proportion success to fidelity. It would be sad to be more grieved on the subject of churches rent in twain and receipts endangered, than we were formerly on the subject of the monstrous iniquities of slavery.

I have told of the evil, I will now tell of the good. And first, vast progress is being accomplished by the very ruptures which the different churches have just endured. The Baptists, Methodists, and Episcopalians of the South have broken with those of the North. The Presbyterian synods of the South have just adopted a similar measure.*

Thus by a dispensation of God, which may appear grievous, but is above all salutary, the churches of the North are snatched from the utilitarian anxieties which they had laid upon themselves. They have become free, and their action, their attitude have manifested it on the spot. I have recent resolutions before my eyes which announce that slavery is at length judged by all as it was

* This is their *Address to all the churches which are upon the earth:* "The antagonism between the North and South on the subject of slavery, is at the root of all the difficulties which have resulted in the rupture of the Federal Union, and the horrors of an unnatural war. It is certain that the North cherishes a profound antipathy for slavery itself, while the South is animated with an equal zeal in behalf of this institution. The events of the day necessarily confirm and strengthen this antipathy on one side, and this zeal for slavery on the other."—This is speaking clearly.

formerly by a few. The report presented in 1861 by the Trustees of the American Congregational Union is worthy these devoted sons of the Puritans, old champions of civil and religious liberty. The Baptists have not shown themselves less firm; their church in Virginia has just had the honor to suffer the consequences of the hatred with which it had inspired the slaveholders. It is known that the Baptist and Methodist are the two favorite denominations of the negroes; the greatest obstacle to their insurrection would be found, perhaps, were we to search closely, in the very great influence which the Gospel thus exercises over them.

Several American missions, that of the Sandwich Islands among others, have declared themselves with earnestness. The American Missionary Association has an openly abolition position. Lastly, the progress has for some time been such, that at the last GeneralAssembly of the Evangelical Alliance, the representatives which America numbered in her midst joined in the unanimous vote which it cast against slavery.

And I say nothing here of the churches, infinitely numerous, in which the patriotic impulse of the North has been strikingly manifested. Without speaking of such pastors as the Rev. Mr. Brownlow, who has taken the musket and faced the troops in Tennessee commanded by Bishop Polk, churches are not lacking which are busied in sending the flower of their youth to the banners of the Union. Mr. Beecher alone has furnished a hundred and twenty-five of these young soldiers; a member of his church has taken it upon himself to furnish revolvers to all who go; the church maintains the absent and their families, and sewing circles are constantly occupied in the manufacture of military equipments.

The influence of the Gospel is immense in America.

Since the churches and religious societies have declared themselves in its favor, the cause of abolition is won. The South has never been deceived; after the Nat Turner insurrection, its first thought was to close the Sunday schools and arrest the religious movement. In spite of the grave faults which I have recalled before, the Christians of the United States have been unable to suppress even for a single day the fundamental antagonism which will always exist, thank God! between the Gospel and slavery. It was Christianity that in former times produced the abolition proclaimed by the Northern States; it is again Christianity which will now produce abolition in the Southern States. The remarkable revival which agitated the whole North, and which, save at a point in Baltimore, stopped short at the frontiers of the South, has been the great providential means against slavery. Christians have formed everywhere the nucleus of the Republican party which has elected Mr. Lincoln.

To-day, the heart of the nation beats in the army; it is found again in the camp; now, what is the spirit of the army? I have already described it; things happen there which our old Europe is perhaps incapable to comprehend. These young men, who, with Bible in knapsack, have gone to fight for the country, these prayer-meetings held in all the regiments, these millions of tracts, distributed by the hand of the officers themselves, these New Testaments printed for the army, at the rate of several a minute, and which have found so many earnest readers in the ranks, these religious libraries founded, these orders of the day stamped with an openly religious character, this proscription of spirituous liquors, accepted with eagerness by the soldiers,—all this forms a sum total which carries the mind back to the old Huguenot bands or the camps of Gustavus Adolphus.

The Puritan element makes its presence felt. There are numerous officers who set the example of vital piety. Was not General McClellan himself, before taking command of the army, impressed with the need of praying on bended knees with a clergyman, one of his friends? "I had given myself to my country, now I have given myself to God," were the last words, it is said, of this interview.

Other generals have published decidedly Christian proclamations. Colonels care like fathers of families for the moral conduct of their regiments. Who does not remember the young and handsome Ellsworth, the first victim of the civil war? His soldiers had all taken a pledge of good conduct before quitting Chicago; we will add, that almost all have done honor to their word.

Colonel Anderson, illustrious through his defence of Fort Sumter, is also a decided Christian. On being entreated lately to say a few words to a Sunday school, he declared in words as simple as touching, that his rule of conduct had been: "Do nothing without placing yourself under the eye of God!"

I might cite a score of regiments where Sunday schools are held by the colonels, or other officers. I might point out the works of evangelization pursued by the Christian soldiers of one of these regiments, under the name of the *Havelock Society*. I might add that the navy presents the same spectacle as the army. Under the influence of leaders, such as Commodores Dupont, Mackean, and Foote, the ships often resound with the singing of psalms.*

* One of the signs of this spirit is the movement that has been manifested against *Sunday battles*. It has been remarked, that whenever the North made the attack on this day, it was always beaten, witness Bull Run, Big Bethel, and Ball's Bluff. Since the order of General MClellan, the South has made the Sunday attacks, and been beaten.

These are great things. A country in which such sentiments exercise so much influence, in which the habit of looking higher than the earth has been contracted by so many souls, is not a country of which we need despair. It will go forward, it will not succumb beneath its task, however heavy it may be; it will finish, in the name of the Gospel, and by the strength given by God, the colossal work of abolition. The example is set in high places. The ministers of the State publicly invoke the blessings of God on themselves, and the direction of public affairs! There are prayers at the White House; Mr. Lincoln is not only an honest man, surrounded by universal esteem, and whose family anxieties with respect to his children's health are the anxieties of the whole country; he is also a Christian. Those who have read his proclamation designed to set apart a day for fasting and prayer, know the distance that separates this manifestation of a vital and personal faith, from so many documents in which official piety is accustomed to display its cold formulas, known and granted in advance. I have also gone over the proclamations published by the governors of the States in answer to the invitation of the President, and I have been struck with the deep seriousness, at once Christian and patriotic, with which the faults of the people are therein confessed. This entire nation seems to place itself under the eye of God, according to the counsel of Colonel Anderson.*

* Religion exercises so decisive, and in some sort universal an influence in the United States, that the same demonstrations of piety take place in the South. The Messages of Jefferson Davis end sometimes with prayers.

CHAPTER II.

ATTITUDE OF CHRISTIANS IN ENGLAND.

During this glorious crisis, which they are passing through in the name of the gospel, and for the holy cause of justice, the United States counted on the support of England, above all of Christian England. England is their mother, she has furnished them almost all their original population, she has absorbed into the Anglo-Saxon nationality the later immigrations. They are bone of her bone, and flesh of her flesh. Furthermore, a religious tie, stronger than that of blood, unites the two nations which show themselves devoted above all others to the propagation of the gospel on earth.

We know to what point the frigid attitude of English Christians has for long months disappointed the hopes founded upon them. I speak of it the more freely, inasmuch as this fault is already almost a thing of the past—and sympathy is on the way to awaken.

Yes, for long months, English Christians have not had, as it were, a single word of encouragement to place at the service of those who were combating (as I have proved) and suffering for a noble cause. Not a meeting, not an address; the journals which serve as organs to the principal churches have almost all made it their study to discredit the movement, to point out with an accent of triumph the mortifications of the republic, to exaggerate the successes of the South, and depreciate those of the North, to deny that slavery was in question, to legitimatize the separation, to present as a desirable ideal the definitive maintenance of a Southern Confederacy.

This was sad, very sad. Christian England has not forgotten the moment when the eloquent cry of betrayed affection crossed the seas, "Oh, Englishmen, Englishmen, could you not have watched with us one hour?" It will be remembered that Mirabeau once proposed the resolution in the National Assembly: "The silence of Sieyès is a public misfortune." With stronger reason, the resolution might be adopted by all of us, continental Christians, dismayed by the attitude of England: "The silence of English Christians is a universal calamity."

They have sent us invitations to prayer, but among the subjects pointed out, we have never perceived that which preoccupied all our thoughts. The great moral and religious interest of our age was systematically omitted; the word slavery seemed to have become as suspicious in England as it had been in America. One would have said that, desirous of justifying the prejudices of their enemies, they wished to prove to the whole world that English interests passed with them before everything, that their abolition zeal was extinct, that questions of principle were incapable of moving them. During this time, blood was flowing; that blood, the effusion of which would have been prevented or promptly checked by the energetic intervention of European sympathies, that blood of which we are guilty, all we who have been unwilling to discourage the monstrous insurrection of the South.

One of the problems that has most tormented my

mind has been to explain the conduct of English Christians in certain affairs, and at certain moments. I know of no men more energetic or devoted; at the present time, a very large portion of the good which is accomplished on our globe is accomplished through their powerful initiative; yet there are inexplicable breaks in their action. One would say at times that political England alone remained, while Christian England had disappeared. Did we not hear it said but the other day, and with a show of reason, that in the extreme East, in China, France had sustained the moral and religious interests, whilst England represented there nothing but the interests of her commerce? If such things are thought, if they appear plausible, and are generally received, whose is the fault?

English Christians have succeeded in persuading themselves that slavery is not in question in the United States. How? Truly, I cannot yet succeed in comprehending. The fact is certain, notwithstanding, and it alone explains the attitude which has grieved us so deeply. By virtue of a marvellous transformation, the same men whom English opinion formerly condemned with just severity, have become almost interesting since, by treason and perjury, by pillaging public property, and repudiating private debts; taking care, moreover, to proclaim the sanctity of slavery, they have endeavored to overthrow their free constitution, and have supplicated foreign powers to aid in the destruction of their country.

Whence comes such a metamorphosis? Whence comes it that the question of slavery, which formerly figured alone in the debates of the North and South,* and

* This care for slavery had been carried so far as to propose expressly, that a free State could not be admitted unless a slave State were

which also figured alone in the ordinance of secession,* fades away all at once, and passes in the eyes of English Christians as preserving only a secondary part? I need not again inquire how. I limit myself to affirming, and no one will contradict me, that if, before the too well received sophisms of these last years, it had been announced to Europe that a President opposed to the extension of slavery was about to be elected, the English Christians would have manifested the liveliest joy. And if it had then been added, that the South would break the Union on account of such an election, it would have been thence concluded that slavery was alone in question, since the mere threat of arresting its extension sufficed to precipitate the South into an armed revolt.

Then too, those to whom a Free Soil President would not have been sufficient, would not have thought of discouraging the movement, but of encouraging it, on the contrary.—The President and his friends do not go far enough; well, we will endeavor to make them go further; we will sign addresses, we will stir up abolition agitation, we will show ourselves ready for every thing else in fine, than to accord to the champions of slavery the support of our abstinence, and to refuse to its adversaries, the vainly solicited aid of our cordial sympathies.

admitted at the same time. Another plan, proposed first by Mr. Calhoun, and taken up again in 1860, by Senator Hunter of Virginia, proposed that henceforth two Presidents should be elected, the one from the free, and the other from the slave States, and that without the signature of both Presidents, no act of Congress should have the force of law.

* In the ordinance of secession passed by South Carolina, a single argument is presented "before heaven and earth,"—that slavery is in danger. After thirty years of agitation against slavery, a man had just been elected President, "whose opinions and designs were hostile to slavery."

I have pointed out elsewhere the causes of a misunderstanding, for which I shall never succeed, I think, in accounting sufficiently. Perhaps, in fine, it cannot be better explained than by recalling to what point the United States, under the domination of the slavery party, were really on the way to become an odious government, without liberty within, without equity without, without scruples in public and private affairs. However it may be, light is now dawning, the organs of independent churches, in particular, are holding a language which will be understood. It is heard already; in the very heart of the manufacturing countries, among the populations that have suffered from the American crisis, the impulse of generous sympathy has burst forth; it is extending, it is becoming consolidated, it has already forced back before it the sad policy of last year; it will force it back anew, should it endeavor to reappear; it does not hold to observing moral neutrality; it holds to proclaiming loudly that the wishes of the English people are on the side of the North; it prepares the broad and solid bases on which the friendship of the two countries will henceforth repose. The party of the Bible has risen; Christian England, for her honor and for the good of America, is about to make reparation, and more, for the evil she has done.

CHAPTER III.

SOCIAL MISSION OF CHRISTIANS.

The Christians of England have made a bad campaign. What are we to conclude from this? What is now to be done to make a better one? Remember the speech of the general: "The battle is lost, but we have time to gain another."

We have time. Only let us remember that battles are not gained by folding the hands. We perish by the inertia of those honest men who bewail themselves, sigh, see inconveniences everywhere, hesitate to act, and discourage those who do act.

Christian selfishness, pardon me this conjunction of words, does not cease to impede the good and to chill generous impulses. Under the pretext of thinking only of the Gospel, it succeeds in cutting off one by one the finest fruits of the Gospel. This it is, which pretends to occupy itself with the conversion of slaves, and not their emancipation. This it is which, calculating the chances, and gaining a glimpse of the real inconveniences which every energetic initiative entails in its train, asks with anguish whether such or such a progress will not cost too dear, whether it will not endanger the prosperity of existing works. These works then become idols to which to offer up sacrifices; provided that the works suffer in the sequel of a generous movement (and they will suffer infallibly), the movement itself is blamed, it excites more ill humor than it attracts sympathy.

How often for some time have I heard the complaint: "Ah! if there were a Christian party, what mission would it now fulfil?" God does not twice in an age lend his servants striking occasions to manifest by social benefits the excellence of the Gospel. Christians might have seconded in America the greatest progress of the times, and they did not do it; Christians might have arrested at its beginning the insurrection for slavery, and they did not do it; Christians might, perhaps, have prevented civil war, and they did not do it; Christians might have conjured down the chances of a horrible war between England and America, and they did not do it.

It is because we have not sufficiently comprehended the social mission of the Gospel. The Gospel! we imprison it in its sphere, and in some sort in its specialty. We too often draw a difference between the sacred and the profane. Now, one of the great benefits of the Gospel has consisted precisely in abolishing this distinction, in reëstablishing unity between the human soul and life. To upraise everything, to sanctify everything, to *preserve* everything, to put the sacred everywhere and leave the profane nowhere, such is the marvellous work which it accomplishes. Great things and small, affections and interests, duties as fathers of families and as citizens—we have the right to declare nothing profane; that is, to abstract nothing from our God.

Have we two principles of life, as well as two kinds of morality, the one for the church and the other for the world; the one for private relations and the other for politics? Ah! I would weep my eyes dry, should the enemies of the Gospel deem themselves authorized by our fault to dispute its social mission.—"See these renowned Christians!" they murmur already in our ears, "they know very well how to compound with vices, profits, or national prejudices. Opium has imposed silence on them; now they will be hushed by the presence of cotton."

Our Christianity has the air sometimes of having *gone outside the age*. All that is not the direct work of preaching or of charity seems to awaken its scruples. As if any thing human could remain a stranger to us, as if the Gospel, which surrounded the earth and sky, did not comprehend political communities; as if it proceeded by mutilations instead of transformations; as if, like false religions and petty morals, it sanctified man by diminishing him, taking away the affections, taking away the external duties, taking away the arts, taking away literature, taking away, in fine, always and everywhere, and making the world believe that one loves God, only on condition of loving nothing else.

The world is but too much disposed to admit this doctrine. Every Christian, in its eyes, is a man who has entered a convent, an incomplete man, who will pray, but will no longer act, who glories henceforth in interesting himself in nothing here below, in calling the affections idols, in having no heart either for *creatures*, (as it is said,) or civilization, or liberty.

I feel no embarrassment in saying these things, for, of all Christians, perhaps, those of England have best seen and best practised the principle which I have just cited. Their history is the most substantial demonstration of the social mission of the Gospel, of which I know. What would have become of the renowned English liberties, if the Puritans had not been found in the way of the Stuarts? These snuffling Presbyterians (and it is not for this quality that I praise them) moved consciences and accomplished a moral revolution, and the progress of events was changed; they were drifting towards despotism, great armies were about forming, as on the continent; all this became impossible.

Even in considering only the things of our times, see the *agitations* by which the churches of England have paved the way for so much progress and effected the abolition of slavery. Herein is found the proof of the fact that they did not fear to secularize the Gospel. Precisely because the Anglo-Saxon race separates the Church and State, and considers the profession of faith as a personal act not at all connected with the hereditary capacity of citizen, it is not condemned to those conditions of sacred and profane by which others endeavor to limit the fatal confusion which gives to the State a religious power and to the Church a civil power. When the enemy is in place, it is necessary, indeed, to erect barricades; when the ramparts of the human conscience are intact, why obstruct the circulation?

The English know this, and because they know it, their abstinence during the first year of the American conflict has had the strange character which we have felt it incumbent on us to point out. The European demonstrations of sympathy, in favor of the North, have come from Christians of the continent; England has scarcely taken part in them. I recall here the address signed in France and Switzerland; the society of a penny a week for slaves, founded in the Canton de Vaud by the Rev. Mr. Bichet; the numerous churches in which prayers are put up for America; the still more numerous houses where family worship is scarcely ever celebrated without entreating of God the peaceful abolition of American slavery; the proposition made by myself, and so generally welcomed, for the Christians of Europe to participate in the celebration of the fast appointed by Mr. Lincoln; lastly, and above all, the solemn and unanimous vote (cordially joined in by the English Christians) which the General Assembly of the Alliance cast at Geneva, in spite of its programmes and regulations. The president of the Alliance, M. Adrien Naville, set the example in his fine opening address: "You are," said he to the representatives of the United States, "at this moment tried even unto blood, but it is in order that the wound from which you have so long been suffering, may be, by degrees, but finally cured. How many thanksgivings the Christians of Europe, like those of America, will render to the Lord on the day when your noble country shall number none but freemen!"

The resolution adopted by the members of the Alliance, was no less firm and precise: "The Conference of the Evangelical Christians of all countries, assembled at Geneva in 1861, testifies to its brethren of the United States the lively sympathy which it experiences for them in the terrible crisis which is desolating their country. . . . Convinced that it is to the existence of slavery that the cause of this war must be traced, the Conference entreats the Lord to incline the hearts of His children in America to provide, by wise and Christian ways, for the suppression of this institution, as contrary to the spirit of the Gospel, as it is to the peace, prosperity, and progress, of this great nation. . . . ." *

Christianity is fighting its last battle against slavery,

* Against slavery and the slave trade, agreements on this subject will be certainly negotiated before long. The new American government

and, what is admirable, in doing a work of liberty, it is about to do a work of peace. All kinds of progress cling together, and what is of service to one, is of service to another; the powerful unity which I pointed out a moment ago between the human soul and life, may be also pointed out in the heart of communities.

Since the tocsin of alarm which the *Trent* affair sounded among us, the interests of peace have resumed their place among the anxieties of pious men. This is seen now in a vote of the English Bible Society, offering to come to the aid of the American Bible Society during the crisis, now in a speech of Mr. Newman Hall, electrifying thousands of London auditors. Who, better than Christians, can strengthen between England and America, not only external and official peace, but cordial affection? When sympathies shall have resumed their sway among the one, prejudices will fall among the other, and the strong currents of mutual affection will begin again to flow.

This is, certainly, a glorious mission for the Christians of both countries to accomplish.

owes it to itself to show that it does not confound the liberty of the seas with the liberty of slavers.

GENERAL CONCLUSION.

I do not wish to conclude without once more recalling the essential idea, which is, as it were, the soul of this study. This idea is faith in principles. Principles are interests, principles are success; and if success keep us waiting, no matter, principles remain: we are to love them for themselves.

I know of no other position that is sure. He who believes in principles and admits the rights of truth, is sheltered behind an impregnable rampart. Happen what may, he has done his duty, and, furthermore, has practised great policy. Miserable policy lives on expedients, interrogates the winds and stars, and, incapable of the victorious tenacity which gives confidence to good, dares hazard nothing, but goes on from day to day, modifying its maxims to suit circumstances or the chances of success.

The chances of success appear to me great in the United States, but I ask the reader to render me this justice, that I have not waited to see them, in order to believe in them. I believed in them because I believed in principles. I greeted from the first moment the uprising of a great people, because I saw from the first moment that this great people was undertaking a great thing, that it was fighting for justice and liberty. One always uprises in this vocation.

Others, I know, have propounded the problem differently. Will they succeed? Such has been, such is, such will still be doubtless the principal question. I am not ignorant what the United States lack to be approved and applauded. A good cause? to be evidently in the right against the secessionists? No. They lack *full success.* Let them but triumph over the South, and I shall have no anxiety about their renown on earth; there will be crowds of people everywhere eager to celebrate their virtues and greatness.

Is this to say, that it is a waste of time to seek to establish unrecognized truths, to demonstrate, for instance, that slavery is the true cause of the American conflict? I have been so far from thinking it that I have written this large volume. Another proof of my faith in principles.

They are, in reality, so powerful, that we succeed in weakening them only when we begin to veil them. The worshippers of success know this, for they pervert ideas in order to succeed in corrupting actions. Every political error has commenced by a moral error; if the Southerners had not for a moment persuaded Europe that slavery was not in question, they would never have extorted the title of belligerent.

What force there is in justice! To be rich, to be powerful, to be able, is to be small; to be great, is to be the servant of justice. Principles prevail as surely in social struggles, as in the operations of physics and chemistry. It may take long, but it surely happens at the end of the reckoning.

What has elected Mr. Lincoln? What has created the patriotic impulse of the North? What has weakened the South? What has checked Europe? What yesterday prevented an impious war? What will perhaps to-morrow constrain the South itself to proclaim or to suffer abolition? What has opposed an insuperable barrier to interests, intrigues and malevolence? What has given to the Lancashire operatives this resignation worthy of respect? What has, in so short a time, caused such great progress in public opinion? What provides it with weapons in advance against the possible return of the policy of intervention? What throws obstacles in the way of the desire, unceasingly springing up on our side the Atlantic, to cut the United States in two? What? Justice.

A just cause has something so triumphant in itself, that men dare not attack it boldly face to face. They turn round it, they deny it, they affirm that it is not itself; for if it were, who would dare sustain the shock?

I speak, the reader will comprehend, of just causes which have made their place on earth, of those which are such in the eyes of the world. History is full of just causes which have waited, which have suffered, which have been perfidiously trodden under foot, which have been defeated times without number. These will also have their turn; it has not yet come. They manifest their superiority alone in the inmost recesses of the souls by whom they are believed, they win only internal triumphs. But let the day come when, by force of internal triumphs and external defeats, they will have constrained the public conscience to give them recognition, and woe to those who shall wish thenceforth to check their onward movement!

Abolition is one of these just causes, whose advent is accomplished. The champions of slavery are lost in advance; they feel that the world goes against them.

This is why I am certain of success; this is why, having proved that the great American people has taken sides against slavery, I call it a great people uprising. The difficulties are great! Who doubts it? Principles take time to pass from the domain of ideas to that of facts! Who denies it? Military operations may fail! Who disputes it? My confidence would be weak indeed if it rested on the skill of McClellan, on that great army, marvellously created in a few months, and stretching farther than the distance from Madrid to Moscow, on the prosperity of the North, on the ruin of the South, on the discredit of its notes, which already are at a discount of forty-five per cent for gold, on the need which it will soon perhaps experience of exporting its two cotton crops, and of profiting, to offer it to our famishing manufactures, on the ports which the Union fleet will doubtless occupy and open within its limits. The reasons of my confidence are different. I reflect that a just cause is in question, a cause which has gained its suit; I look at the unanimous convictions of the nineteenth century; I remember, above all, that there is a God.

Yes, you will be the stronger, generous defenders of justice; you will be the stronger, if you ally yourselves to justice and to God. Hope! God himself has implanted the need of encouragement in the inmost depths of our soul. Hope! Cling to hope, preserve a serene and impregnable faith in the triumphs of eternal right.

Danton said: "Audacity, audacity, and again audacity!" I say willingly: "Hope, hope, and again hope!" This crisis, despite the suffering that it includes, will be the honor and consolation of our times. Never, perhaps, were matter and spirit so directly at strife; the question is a moral one; it is for America to know whether the Puritan element will win—for the whole world to know whether liberty and justice will finally prevail.

The whole world, I have just said, is engaged in the contest. The uprising of this people upraises us also; this spectacle of sufferings nobly accepted, does us good. We feel that one of those storms which purify the atmosphere is passing at this moment over our globe.

Those over whom it passes have to suffer; but after the tempest comes fine weather, and, like that fleet which, after having been dispersed by the storm, found itself again entire in the smooth waters of Port Royal, America will seem, perhaps, almost to sink beneath the violence of the winds, until it attain the end. This end is peace.

Having once succeeded in suppressing the fearful evil which was devouring them, the United States will not feel that their present sacrifices are disproportioned to the progress accomplished. Acquired at this price, the abolition of slavery will not have been bought too dear.

The question in the end is a second creation of the United States. This is carried on by the American method, that of Washington, that of the war of 1812, that which begins in weakness and ends in grandeur.

No, the sixteenth President of the United States will not be the last; no, the eighty-fifth year of this people will not be the last; their flag will come out of battle pierced with bullets and blackened with powder, but more glorious than ever, without having let fall, as I hope, in the mêlée a single one of its thirty-four stars.

DOCUMENTARY EVIDENCE.

I borrow from the collections of official documents published by the American and English Governments, a few extracts which seem to me suited to cast much light on the questions so imperfectly known in Europe, to which I have devoted the first part of this work.

NOTE FIRST.

[*See Part First, Chap. IV.*]

THE QUALIFICATION OF BELLIGERENTS ACCORDED TO THE SOUTH.

[*Mr. Seward to Mr. Adams.*]

DEPARTMENT OF STATE,
WASHINGTON, June 19, 1861.

SIR: On the 15th day of June instant, Lord Lyons, the British Minister, and Mr. Mercier, the French Minister, residing here, had an appointed interview with me. Each of those representatives proposed to read to me an instruction which he had received from his Government, and to deliver me a copy if I should desire it. I answered that, in the present state of the correspondence between their respective Governments and that of the United States, I deemed it my duty to know the characters and effects of the instructions, respectively, before I could consent that they should be officially communicated to this Department. The ministers, therefore, confidentially and very frankly sub-

18*

mitted the papers to me for preliminary inspection. After having examined them so far as to understand their purport, I declined to hear them read, or to receive official notice of them.

. . . . . That paper (that of Lord Lyons) purports to contain a decision at which the British Government has arrived, to the effect that this country is divided into two belligerent parties, of which this Government represents one, and that Great Britain assumes the attitude of a neutral between them.

This Government could not, consistently with a just regard for the sovereignty of the United States, permit itself to debate these novel and extraordinary positions with the Government of her Britannic Majesty; much less can we consent that that Government shall announce to us a decision derogating from that sovereignty, at which it has arrived without previously conferring with us upon the question. The United States are still solely and exclusively sovereign within the territories they have lawfully acquired and long possessed.

What is now seen in this country is the occurrence, by no means peculiar but frequent in all countries, more frequent even in Great Britain than here, of an armed insurrection, engaged in attempting to overthrow the regularly constituted and established Government. There is, of course, the employment of force by the Government to suppress the insurrection, as every other Government necessarily employs force in such cases. But these incidents by no means constitute a state of war impairing the sovereignty of the Government, creating belligerent sections, and entitling foreign States to intervene or to act as neutrals between them, or in any way to cast off their lawful obligations to the nation thus, for the moment, disturbed. Any other principle than this would be to resolve government everywhere into a thing of accident and caprice. . . . .

It is, we take leave to think, the common misfortune of the two countries that Great Britain was not content to wait before despatching the instructions in question, until you had been received by her Majesty's Government, and had submitted the entirely just, friendly, and liberal overtures with which you were charged. . . . . . .

One point remains. The British Government, while declining, out of regard to our natural sensibility, to propose mediation for the settlement of the differences which now unhappily divide the American people, has nevertheless expressed, in a very proper manner, its willingness to undertake the kindly duty of mediation, if we should desire it. The President expects you to say on this point to the British Government, that we appreciate this generous and friendly demonstration, but that we cannot solicit or accept mediation from any, even the most friendly quarter. The conditions of society here, the character of our Government, the exigencies of the country, forbid that any dispute arising among us should ever be referred to foreign arbitration. We are a republican and American people. The Constitution of our Government furnishes all needful means for the correction or removal of any possible political evil. Adhering strictly, as we do, to its directions, we shall surmount all our present complications, and preserve the Government complete, perfect, and sound, for the benefit of future generations. But the integrity of any nation is lost, and its fate becomes doubtful, whenever strange hands, and instruments unknown to the Constitution, are employed to perform the proper functions of the people, established by the organic laws of the State.

Hoping to have no occasion hereafter to speak for the hearing of friendly nations upon the topics which I have now discussed, I add a single remark, by way of satisfying the British Government, that it will do wisely by leaving us to manage and settle this domestic controversy in our own way. . . . .

CHARLES F. ADAMS, &c., &c.

[*Papers Relating to Foreign Affairs*, p. 91.]

[*Mr. Seward to Mr. Dayton.*]

DEPARTMENT OF STATE,
WASHINGTON, June 17, 1861.

SIR: Every instruction which this Government has given to its representatives abroad, since the recent change of administration took place, has expressed our profound anxiety lest the disloyal citizens who are engaged in an attempt to overthrow the Union should obtain aid and assistance from foreign nations either in the form of a recognition of their pretended sovereignty, or in some other and more qualified or guarded manner. Every instruction has expressed our full belief that, without such aid or assistance, the insurrection would speedily come to an end, while any advantage that it could derive from such aid or assistance could serve no other purpose than to protract the existing struggle, and aggravate the evils it is inflicting on our own country and on foreign and friendly nations.

We have intended not to leave it doubtful that a concession of sovereignty to the insurgents, though it should be indirect or unofficial, or though it should be qualified so as to concede only belligerent or other partial rights, would be regarded as inconsistent with the relations due to us by friendly nations.

That paper (the paper which Mr. Seward had refused to hear read) does not expressly deny the sovereignty of the United States of America; but it does assume, inconsistently with that sovereignty, that the United States are not altogether and for all purposes one sovereign power, but that this nation consists of two parties, of which this Government is one. France proposes to take cognizance of both parties as belligerents.

This Government insists that the United States are one, whole, undivided nation, especially so far as foreign nations are concerned, and that France is, by the law of nations and by treaties, not a neutral power between two imaginary parties here, but a friend of the United States. . . . . .

It is erroneous, so far as foreign nations are concerned, to suppose that any war exists in the United States. Certainly, there cannot be two belligerent powers where there is no war. There is here, as there has always been, one political power, namely, the United States of America, competent to make war and peace, and. conduct commerce and alliances with all foreign nations. There is none other, either in fact, or recognized by foreign nations. There is, indeed, an armed sedition seeking to overthrow the Government, and the Government is employing military and naval forces to repress it. But these facts do not constitute a war presenting two belligerent powers, and modifying the national character, rights, and responsibilities, or the characters, rights, and responsibilities of foreign nations. It is true that insurrection may ripen into revolution, and that revolution, thus ripened, may extinguish a previously existing State, or divide it into one or more independent States, and that, if such States continue their strife after such division, then there exists a state of war affecting the characters, rights, and duties of all parties concerned. But this only happens when the revolution has run its successful course. . . . .

The United States will maintain and defend their sovereignty throughout the bounds of the Republic, and they deem all other nations bound to respect that sovereignty until, if ever, Providence shall consent that it shall be successfully overthrown. Any system of public law or national morality that conflicts with this, would resolve society, first in this hemisphere, and then in the other, into anarchy and chaos. . . . . .

The case, as it now stands, is the simple, ordinary one that has happened at all times and in all countries. A discontented domestic faction seeks foreign intervention to overthrow the Constitution and the liberties of its own country. Such intervention, if yielded, is ultimately disastrous to the cause it is designed to aid.

Down deep in the heart of the American people—deeper than the love of trade, or of freedom—deeper than the attachment to any local or sectional interest, or partisan pride, or individual ambition—deeper than any other sentiment, is that one out of which the Constitution of this Union arose, namely, American independence—independence of all foreign control, alliance, or influence. Next above it lies the conviction that neither peace, nor safety, nor public liberty, nor prosperity, nor greatness, nor empire, can be attained here with the sacrifice of the unity of the people of North America.

WILLIAM L. DAYTON, Esq., &c., &c.

[*Papers relating to Foreign Affairs*, p. 208.]

NOTE SECOND.

[*See Part First, Chap. III.*]

IS SLAVERY REALLY IN QUESTION?

[*Mr. Black (Sec. of State) to all the Ministers of the United States.*]

CIRCULAR.

DEPARTMENT OF STATE,
WASHINGTON, February 28, 1861.

SIR: You are, of course, aware that the election of last November resulted in the choice of Mr. Abraham Lincoln; that he was the candidate of the republican or anti-slavery party; that the preceding discussion had been confined almost entirely to topics connected, directly or indirectly, with the subject of negro slavery; that every Northern State cast its whole electoral vote (except three in New Jersey) for Mr. Lincoln, while in the whole South the popular sentiment against him was almost absolutely universal.

[*Papers relating to Foreign Affairs*, p. 15.]

NOTE THIRD.

[*See Part Third, Chap. V.*]

FACTS EXPLAINING THE SUPERIORITY POSSESSED AT THE FIRST MOMENT BY THE SOUTH.

[*Mr. Seward to Mr. Adams.*]

DEPARTMENT OF STATE,
WASHINGTON, April 10, 1861.

One needs to be as conversant with our federative system as perhaps only American publicists can be to understand how effectually, in the first instance, such a revolutionary movement must demoralize the General Government. We are not only a nation, but we are States also. All public officers, as well as all citizens, owe not only allegiance to the Union, but allegiance also to the States in which they reside. In the more discontented

States the local magistrates and other officers cast off at once their Federal allegiance, and conventions were held which assumed to absolve their citizens from the same obligations. Even Federal judges, marshals, clerks, and revenue officers resigned their trusts. Intimidation deterred loyal persons from accepting the offices thus rendered vacant. So the most important faculties of the Federal Government in those States abruptly ceased.

The most popular motive in these discontents was an apprehension of designs on the part of the incoming Federal administration hostile to the institution of domestic slavery in the States where it is tolerated by the local constitutions and laws. That institution and the class which especially cherishes it are not confined to the States which have seceded, but they exist in the eight other so-called slave States, and these, for that reason, sympathize profoundly with the revolutionary movement. Sympathies and apprehensions of this kind have, for an indefinite period, entered into the basis of political parties throughout the whole country, and thus considerable masses of persons whose ultimate loyalty could not be doubted, were found, even in the free States, either justifying, excusing, or palliating the movement toward disunion in the seceding States. The party which was dominant in the Federal Government during the period of the last administration embraced, practically, and held in unreserved communion, all disunionists and sympathizers. It held the Executive administration. The Secretaries of the Treasury, War, and the Interior were disunionists. The same party held a large majority of the Senate, and nearly equally divided the House of Representatives. Disaffection lurked, if it did not openly avow itself, in every department and in every bureau, in every regiment and in every ship-of-war; in the post-office and in the custom-house, and in every legation and consulate, from London to Calcutta. Of four thousand four hundred and seventy officers in the public service, civil and military, two thousand one hundred and fifty-four were representatives of States where the revolutionary movement was openly advocated and urged, even if not actually organized. Our system being so completely federative and representative, no provision had ever been made, perhaps none ever could have been made, to anticipate this strange and unprecedented disturbance. The people were shocked by successive and astounding developments of what the statute book distinctly pronounced to be sedition and treason, but the magistracy was demoralized and the laws were powerless. By degrees, however, a better sentiment revealed itself. The Executive administration hesitatingly, in part, reformed itself. The capital was garrisoned; the new President came in unresisted, and soon constituted a new and purely loyal administration. They found the disunionists perseveringly engaged in raising armies and laying sieges around national fortifications, situate within the territory of the disaffected States. The Federal marine seemed to have been scattered everywhere except where its presence was necessary, and such of the military forces as were not in the remote States or Territories were held back from activity by vague and mysterious armistices, which had been informally contracted by the late President, or under his authority, with a view to postpone conflict until impracticable concessions to disunion should be made by Congress, or, at least, until the waning term of his administration should reach its appointed end. Commissioners, who had been sent by the new Confederacy, were already at the capital, demanding recognition of its sovereignty and a partition of the national property and domain. The treasury, depleted by robbery and peculation, was exhausted, and the public credit was prostrate.

It being assumed that peaceful separation is in harmony with the Constitution, it was urged, as a consequence, that coercion would, therefore, be unlawful and tyrannical; and this principle was even pushed so far as to make the defensive retaining by the Federal Government of its position within the limits of the seceding States, or where it might seem to overawe or intimidate them, an act of such forbidden coercion. Thus it happened that, for a long time, and in very extensive districts even, fidelity to the Union manifested itself by demanding a surrender of its powers and possessions, and compromises with or immunity toward those who were engaged in overthrowing it by armed force.

[*Papers relating to Foreign Affairs*, p. 55.]

NOTE FOURTH.

[*See Part Fourth, Chap. IV.*]

THE PART OF SPAIN IN THE MEXICAN EXPEDITION.

The *Blue Book* published by the English Government on the negotiations which preceded the Mexican Expedition, contains a despatch from Sir John Crampton, which thus sets forth the disposition (at that time) of the Spanish Government:

"The Government of Her Catholic Majesty is of the opinion that it would be well for the combined forces to seek to profit by the impression which cannot fail to be produced among the Mexican people, to exercise a moral influence over the contending parties, to bring them to lay down their arms and come to an understanding, in such a manner as to form a Government which may offer to the allies some guarantee of the accomplishment of the engagements contracted toward them, and of the more faithful observation, in the future, of international obligations—a Government which may give some hope, at least, of seeing an end put to the miseries to which this unfortunate country has been exposed."

This language forms an evident contrast to that of England proclaiming the absolute determination to exercise no influence whatever over the internal affairs of Mexico and the form of its Government.

We will add that Spain, which had just effected a first colonial restoration in St. Domingo, was at this moment taking all the initiative measures against Mexico; first, negotiation; then, active operations. It will be remembered that the despatch of its quota to Vera Cruz preceded that of France and England.

www.ingramcontent.com/pod-product-compliance
Lightning Source LLC
Chambersburg PA
CBHW032300280326
41932CB00009B/642